Millennial Edition

Divine Metaphysics of Human Anatomy

by

Rev. Joseph Adam Pearson, Ph.D.

Copyright

Illustrations by Kathleen Foss

Copyright 2022 by Rev. Joseph Adam Pearson, Ph.D.

This work is a revision of earlier versions copyrighted by The United States Copyright Office:

Copyright 2022 (TX-009-069-991)
Copyright 2018 (TX-008-577-762)
Copyright 2015 (TX-008-174-780)
Copyright 2012 (TXU-001-814-536)
Copyright 2011 (TXU-001-788-674)
by Joseph Adam Pearson

All rights reserved.

Paperback Identifier:
ISBN-13: 9780985772819

Library of Congress Control Number: 2012943662

Published by
Christ Evangelical Bible Institute
(SAN: 920-3753)
Dayton, Tennessee

Last edited on August 27, 2022

A Note to the Readers

Do not be conformed to this world but be transformed by the renewing of your mind to demonstrate what the Will of God is, which is good, acceptable, and perfect.

ROMANS 12:2 KJV (PARAPHRASE*)

* To ensure their accuracy throughout this book, all paraphrases of the public domain King James Version of the Holy Bible were finalized only after first checking: (1) the Masoretic Hebrew text of the Tanakh (the Jewish Bible) for passages from the Old Testament and (2) the earliest existing Greek text for passages from the New Testament.

Transliterated Hebrew and Greek words referenced within the text of this book are noted by their respective numbers in brackets with a preceding "H" for Hebrew or "G" for Greek from the *Dictionary of the Hebrew Bible* and the *Dictionary of the Greek Bible* found in *Strong's Exhaustive Concordance of the Bible* by James Strong (Copyright 1890), Crusade Bible Publishers, Inc., Nashville. The original Hebrew and Greek words indicated by numbers in brackets are provided in the Appendix to this book.

As used in this book, the word *God* only refers to the God of the Holy Bible. (And, for the sake of clarity, the Holy Bible is the one true and only real Scripture.)

Although God the Father (i.e., the *Lord God Almighty*) and God the Son (i.e., the *Lord Jesus Christ*) are consubstantially united in the Godhead along with God the Holy Spirit, in order to distinguish *God the Father* from *God the Son,* the present author uses an upper case "H" for personal pronouns specifically referring to *God the Father (He, His,* and *Him)* and a lower case "h" for personal pronouns specifically referring to *God the Son (he, his,* and *him)*.

For the sake of clarity, when the author of this book uses the phrase *the present author* in this book, he is referring to himself.

Table of Contents

Copyright.. 2

A Note to the Readers 3

Foreword: *An Introduction to the Author* 7

Chapter One: *An Introduction to Divine Metaphysics*.......................... 15

Chapter Two: *Divine Metaphysics of the Integument and Skeletal Muscle*.. 47

Chapter Three: *Divine Metaphysics of the Skeletal System* 79

Chapter Four: *Divine Metaphysics of the Nervous System* 109

Chapter Five: *Divine Metaphysics of the Cardiovascular System*...... 191

Chapter Six: *Divine Metaphysics of the Lymphatic System and Immunity* 223

Chapter Seven: *Divine Metaphysics of the Urinary System* 255

Chapter Eight: *Divine Metaphysics of the Digestive System* 279

Chapter Nine: *Divine Metaphysics of the Respiratory System*......... 311

Chapter Ten: *Divine Metaphysics of the Endocrine System*............. 329

Chapter Eleven: *Divine Metaphysics of the Reproductive System*..... 343

Afterword 367

Appendix 369

Bibliography 371

Books by the Author 377

Foreword
An Introduction to the Author

This book is a sequel to my works entitled *As I See It: The Nature of Reality by God* and *God, Our Universal Self: A Primer for Future Christian Metaphysics*.[1] The two prequels lay the foundation for understanding corporeality (i.e., physicality) and spirituality from the standpoint of the metaphysical truths contained within the Holy Bible — which truths are often overlooked, misinterpreted, and misunderstood. This current work is intended to be a spiritual *next step* in understanding who we are, what we are, and why we are on Earth as well as what we can expect to become in God's spiritual universe in contrast to who and what we seem to be in the material universe (i.e., the physically observable universe).

My interests, desires, nurturance, education, training, experiences, teaching responsibilities, aptitude, and sensitivity have brought me to the place in my life where I am finally able to articulate what I have experienced in — and understand of — spiritual, supernatural, and metaphysical realms in a way that is relatable to corporeal existence.

It seems to me that I have lived my entire life believing that thoughts are things and that things are thoughts. *For example,* I remember a recurring dilemma throughout most of my childhood concerning the meaning of "exit" and "entrance" signs. Most times, I had to pause at a door with such signage and think: "Am I exiting the store to enter the world or am I exiting the world to

---

1 *As I See It: The Nature of Reality by God,* Copyright 2015, ISBN 978-0615590615. *God, Our Universal Self: A Primer for Future Christian Metaphysics,* Copyright 2020, ISBN 978-0985772857.

enter the store?" I often needed to look at the direction in which the doors would swing open to solve the problem. This was a regular thing. As I saw it, life was *only* filled with conceptual puzzles that needed to be figured out. Now, as a senior adult, signage on restroom doors continue to pose the following questions that I ask myself, and must answer correctly, before I proceed: "Do I belong to the group of people known as *men?* Or do I belong to the group known as *women?*"

As a child, I usually laughed when I fell and hurt myself. I thought it funny that the cumbersome body in which I found myself could be so clumsy and unaware of its surroundings or that its nervous system could be so incapable of making right decisions relative to the direction of its movements. I still laugh for similar reasons when I am in physical pain regardless of cause. I always felt and still feel like a stranger in a strange land. I always felt and still feel that physicality is alien to me and that I am an alien in it. Throughout my whole life, I have always made a distinction between physical existence and *spiritual being.*

Throughout my life, words, phrases, and statements have come to me from out of nowhere. *For example,* I remember walking home one day in 1966 and inwardly hearing: "Time is a sequence of related events." Everything that I received I would ponder and reflect on, often for many years. Even the topic for the book that you are currently reading was given to me in a dream. It was a dream that prompted me to focus in detail on divine metaphysics of human anatomy. Dreams and supernatural thoughts and ideas that I received helped me to know about what next to work on throughout the course of writing each chapter and section of this book.

I am very grateful for my mentoring as a young person by an aunt who had a substantial understanding of Christian metaphysics. She posed just the right questions to me about who I thought I was and who I really *am.* As a preteen, I remember her telling me to look at myself in her wall mirror. She asked me if the image in the mirror represented who I really *am.* I remember her telling me that it did not and why it did not. We then met regularly to explore together who and what I was, and *am,* in God. During her tutelage, I became very comfortable with the concepts and language of Christian metaphysics, comparing and contrasting such concepts as: *corporeality versus spirituality, absolute truth versus relative truth,* and *statements of existence versus declarations of being.*

As a young person, I loved traditional children's Sunday School. And I was a Vacation Bible School (VBS) junkie: During the summers, I would attend the Baptist VBS, Lutheran VBS, Methodist VBS, and Presbyterian VBS for two weeks each to study the Bible, memorize Bible verses, and work on Bible-related crafts. I also attended Bible Camp during the summers. I loved — and still love — reading, studying, and comprehending the Holy Bible and using the metaphysical truths that it contains as a filter through which to view the world, its reality, and its unreality.

I remember deciding as a sophomore in high school what I wanted to do with my life: I wanted to become a biology teacher, a pastor, and an author.

Although I majored in biology as a college student, I took various elective courses in world religions, Aristotelian logic and ethics, and metaphysics. My metaphysics professor hated my written compositions because I always tried to link metaphysics to Christianity. I inferred that he thought the two were forever distinct and different. However, I now understand that he believed in an invisible reality that was intellectual and not spiritual in nature. I enjoyed reading obscure books directly and indirectly related to metaphysics, like Immanuel Kant's *Prolegomena to any Future Metaphysics* (1783) and Walter Haushalter's *Mrs. Eddy Purloins from Hegel* (1936). (The former addresses the fabric, or essence, of reality and the reality of the latter is that the major premise articulated in its title is a complete fabrication.) Today, I still read such works. *For example,* I have recently finished reading Friedrich Nietzsche's *Also sprach Zarathustra* (1885). I read the German original side-by-side with an English translation *(Thus Spoke Zarathustra)* to see if they were the same book. Because the two languages do not possess the same nuances of word meaning, I concluded that they really are not *exactly* the same.

After majoring in biology as a college student and earning my

Bachelor of Science degree in biology at Loyola University (Chicago),[2] I remained at Loyola for an additional two years to earn a Master of Science in biology with an emphasis in cell biology. Serving as a graduate teaching assistant in the Department of Biology at Loyola permitted me to finance my graduate studies: I especially enjoyed teaching human histology laboratory sections while I was there. During my Junior and Senior years as well as during my graduate years at Loyola, I also worked as an electron microscopist in the Department of Oral Histology at the University of Illinois Dental School.

After receiving my M.S. degree in 1971, I became a high school biology teacher at a prestigious, all-boys college preparatory school where I taught for two years. I then served for two years on the faculty as a Research Associate in the Department of Ophthalmology at the University of Illinois Medical Center, where I first-authored and co-authored many scientific papers in reputable, refereed (i.e., peer-reviewed) journals under my birth name of Joseph Vlchek (J.K. Vlchek). During this time, I entered a doctoral program as a graduate student in the Department of Anatomy at the University of Illinois Medical Center. While in that program, I took advanced human anatomy, advanced human physiology, and advanced human histology. During that time, I began to teach "Structure and Function of the Human Body" and "Genetics, Evolution, and Development" as an adjunct faculty member in the Department of Natural Science at Loyola University (Lewis Towers).

Although I continued adjunct teaching at Loyola for a number of years, I left the University of Illinois Medical Center to take a full time teaching position with the City Colleges of Chicago, where I taught human anatomy and physiology for eight years to students of medical education (primarily nursing students). Because the Department of Anatomy at the University of Illinois permitted only full time status for its doctoral students at the time, I matriculated

---

2   As an undergraduate student, my favorite science courses included comparative embryology of vertebrates, comparative anatomy of vertebrates, physiology, histology, genetics, physics, and organic chemistry.

into a doctoral program at the University of Chicago in its Department of Biology with the endorsement of the distinguished cell biologist, Dr. Hewson Swift, in whose laboratory I had conducted research for my Master's thesis while at Loyola. At the University of Chicago, I took courses in biochemistry,[3] lipoproteins and enzyme kinetics, and cell biology.

Eventually, I decided that I knew all that I needed to know for future independent learning in the content area of human anatomy and physiology. I became more intrigued and challenged by the presentation of information to enhance its assimilation and accommodation by learners. So, in 1981, I left everything in Illinois to move to Arizona to enter a doctoral program in education at Arizona State University with an emphasis in teacher education, language, literacy, linguistics, and textual analysis[4] as well as to teach for the Maricopa County Community College District, where I served full time as: (1) biology and chemistry faculty at South Mountain Community College for five years; (2) lead professor in human anatomy and physiology (as well as Biology Department Chairperson) at Scottsdale Community College for ten years; and (3) founding instructional dean at the Red Mountain Campus of Mesa Community College (MCC) and director of MCC's Extended Campus for a total of ten years. Altogether, I worked in the Maricopa County Community College District for twenty-five years. During that time, I earned my Doctor of Philosophy (Ph.D.) from Arizona State University in 1988 with a dissertation entitled *Testing the Ecological Validity of Student-Generated versus*

---

3 This biochemistry course at the University of Chicago was the most difficult course I have ever taken. We covered the 1,000-page eighth edition of *Principles of Biochemistry* by Albert L. Lehninger in nine weeks and students were responsible for remembering all formulas, equations, and molecular structures in the book.

4 In one of my semesters at Arizona State University, I remember that I was one of only four students that entire academic year who took Advanced Multivariate Analysis (EDP 722). Although it was not required for my approved doctoral program of studies, I found the course both challenging and interesting. (I also took graduate level independent study through the Department of Chemistry during my doctoral program.)

Teacher-Provided Postquestions in Reading College Science Text (1988). I am pleased that my research findings were accepted for publication in the highly respected *Journal of Research in Science Teaching* (1991).[5]

Throughout my life, I have always multi-tasked and led double professional lives. *For example,* during the last ten years of the time that I worked for the Maricopa Community College District, I also served as Senior Pastor for Healing Waters Ministries in Tempe, Arizona. Additionally, for the past thirty years (1992-2022), I have served as International President and Chief Executive Officer of Christ Evangelical Bible Institute (CEBI), which has thriving branch campuses in India, Pakistan, and Tanzania (East Africa). In that capacity, I have been responsible for developing, designing, and deploying Bible curriculum as well as for in-servicing the various branch campus administrators, ministerial students, and local pastors. At the time of this edition (2022), I am still serving as International President and CEO of CEBI as well as teaching online Bible courses.

When I was three years of age, I remember someone from Heaven telling me during an afternoon nap what my specific purpose for being on Earth is. I was then told that when I awoke I would not remember the specific purpose but that I would remember that I had been told. When I awoke from that nap, it was and is so: I did not remember my specific purpose, but I did remember that I had been told. I suspect that the writing of this book — as well as other books that I have completed — is part of why I am here.

After I began writing this book, I was puzzled why I was writing it. I felt certain that few people would be interested in the information and perspective that it contains and that even fewer people would ever read it. However, in June of 2011, I received this heavenly message of encouragement:

---

5   Pearson, J. A. (1991), *Testing the ecological validity of teacher-provided versus student-generated postquestions in reading college science text.* J. Res. Sci. Teach., 28: 485–504. (2006) doi: 10.1002/tea.3660280604 <http://onlinelibrary.wiley.com/doi/10.1002/tea.3660280604/abstract>.

> Joseph, do not become discouraged about your work and studies in the divine metaphysics of human anatomy. Even though it may, at times, appear to be a stationary vehicle, after your time on Earth is over it will prove to be a new Eldorado,[6] providing transportation to higher levels of consciousness for many of your brothers and sisters yet to come.

I took great comfort from that message. My continuing prayer in response to it has been:

> Dear Heavenly Father, Help me to live up to Your expectations concerning my work and studies as I seek to help others on Your behalf to bless Your Holy Name. Cause, enable, and permit me to dedicate the remainder of my life to Your noble cause, challenge, and desire for us all. I pray this prayer in the Name of Your only-begotten Son, my Lord and Savior, Jesus Christ.

With this book, I have only scratched the surface of divine metaphysics concerning human anatomy. I hope that it gives you food for further thought on the subject. I am trusting God that it will.

---

[6] In this context, *Eldorado* means "gilded, golden, or blessed vehicle."

Chapter One
An Introduction to Divine Metaphysics

For those whom God foreknew, God also predestined to become conformed to the image of His Son in order that His Son would be the firstborn of many.

ROMANS 8:29 KJV (PARAPHRASE)

Metaphysical Paleoanthropology

I have recently discovered the remains of the original and unfallen creation of God known as the Adamic Race. Surprisingly, the fossil evidence for this original and unfallen race is found in all of the cells, tissues, organs, and organ systems of our current human anatomy.

For the sake of clarity, the word *fossil* is defined in this book as "*any* remains, impressions, or traces of a living thing from a former age." Thus, for the purpose of this book, contemporary human beings will be considered "living fossils" and their current functioning cells, tissues, organs, and organ systems will be considered representations, vestiges, remnants, and "fossilized impressions" of what originally existed before the Adamic Fall. To be sure, what existed before the Adamic Fall was in a much earlier time period, in a different age, and in a much different world.

The fossil evidence of the original and unfallen creation of God includes structural and functional elements of our current human organ systems: integumentary (skin and associated structures), muscular, skeletal, nervous, cardiovascular, lymphatic, urinary, digestive, respiratory, endocrine (hormone-producing glandular), and reproductive systems.

Indeed, some schools of thought exist that utilize the concept of energy centers and pathways associated with human organs and organ systems. But such schools of thought have never elaborated or utilized a paradigm that these energy centers and pathways exist because they are remnants of (1) divine energy centers and (2) pathways originally found in the created, immortal bodies of the Adamic Race before the Adamic Fall.

Some popular therapeutic methods and practices that incorporate concepts of energy centers and pathways include: acupuncture, acupressure, reflexology, diathermy, chakra therapy, yoga, Pranayama, Shiatsu, Tai Chi, Chi Kung, aromatherapy, mantra therapy, Reiki, hands-on healing, distance healing, radionics, sound therapy (harmonics), electromagnetic therapy, light therapy, color therapy, crystal therapy, and metal therapy. (This acknowledgement does not constitute an endorsement of any of these methods or practices.)

Conceptually closest to the theme of this book is the speculation that there is an esoteric anatomy and physiology in an etheric body double (i.e., electromagnetic body or subtle body) for every human being. In other words, there is an individual spiritual reality that transcends human form and function. However, this speculation falls short in providing us with a full understanding of who we once were — or what we became and now are — because it does not explain that human anatomy and physiology have their origins in, as well as their causality from, invisible structures and invisible functions in God's original creation. Here, "invisible" does not refer to the submicroscopic, biochemical, atomic, or subatomic levels of organization of matter. Rather, "invisible" refers to a spiritual, supernatural, and metaphysical state of *being*.

In the Holy Bible, an individual electromagnetic body is

referred to as a *spirit*,[7] *ghost*, or *spiritual body* (or, in the word order of the original Greek, *body spiritual*) in contrast to a flesh body, corporeal body, or physical body:

> *But when the Apostles saw Jesus walking upon the sea, they supposed it had been a* spirit *[or ghost], and cried out...*
>
> MARK 6:49 KJV (PARAPHRASE)

> *And when Jesus had cried out with a loud voice, he said: "Father, into Your hands I commend my* spirit.*" Then, having said this, he gave up the ghost.*
>
> LUKE 23:46 KJV (PARAPHRASE)

> *{36} As the Apostles spoke, Jesus himself stood in the midst of them, and said to them: "Peace to you." {37} But they were terrified and afraid, and supposed that they had seen a spirit.*
>
> LUKE 24:36-37 KJV (PARAPHRASE)

> *[In the world of the visible] each person has a natural body [or body natural]. [In the world of the invisible] each person has a spiritual body [or body spiritual]. There is a natural body, and there is a spiritual body.*
>
> 1 CORINTHIANS 15:44 KJV (PARAPHRASE)

Jesus himself acknowledged the existence of a *spirit* or *ghost* (or using the vocabulary in this book, an *electromagnetic body)* when he appeared to his disciples after his death:

---

7   To be sure, because the Greek word from which "spirit" has been translated has multiple meanings, the specific meaning of the word must be determined from its context.

"Behold my hands and my feet, that it is I myself: touch me, and see; for a spirit [or ghost] does not have flesh and bones, as you see me have."

LUKE 24:39 KJV (PARAPHRASE)

Before the Adamic Fall, the electromagnetic body, or spirit, for each person was emanated flawless and untarnished from God Himself. At the time of the Adamic Fall, the electromagnetic body became a distortion of the original. At the time of one's salvation, the electromagnetic body is restored to its original flawless and untarnished condition of being. Of course, the electromagnetic body or *body spiritual* is only visible to the spiritual eye and not to the naked eye. Regardless of one's salvation and the condition of one's electromagnetic body (or *electromagnetic body double),* the human body remains corruptible and still subject to disease, deterioration, death, and decay.

As a side note, souls who openly and unashamedly reject Jesus Christ as their personal Savior while on Earth have only a tarnished and distorted electromagnetic body double in which to dwell after their life on Earth is over; in this way, they become unclean *spirits* or *ghosts* — which is to say, they each retain only a *ghosted* image. (This ghosted image has a brownish or muddy cast when seen with the spiritual eye.)

I first made my discovery in 2010 after completing an earlier book, entitled *As I See It: The Nature of Reality by God,*[8] which is a prequel to this book. My "metaphysical paleoanthropological" discovery was a spiritual *next step* in understanding our fleshly existence, or corporeality, vis-à-vis its current anatomy and physiology in contradistinction to our original somatic condition of being. I coined the phrase *astral gelatinous*™ to describe our original somatic condition of being since no comparable, suitable terminology already existed to describe the highest standard for such created and unfallen living substance.[9] (For the sake of clarity, *immortality* and *mortality* are states of being and *incorporeality* and

---

8   See Footnote 1.
9   The phrase *astral gelatinous*™ is further explained in Footnote 15.

corporeality are conditions of being. From a human standpoint, an *astral gelatinous*™ somatic identity is *incorporeal* and, therefore, a *condition* of being.)

I am a *metaphysical paleoanthropologist*. Understanding what constitutes "metaphysical paleoanthropology" requires understanding what is encompassed in this book by the words *metaphysics* and *paleoanthropology*.

To some secular philosophers, a study of metaphysics would not be complete without understanding the works — as well as historical relevance — of authors like Aristotle (384-322 B.C.), David Hume (1711-1776), Immanuel Kant (1724-1804), Georg Wilhelm Friedrich Hegel (1770-1831), and Jean Paul Sartre (1905-1980). To some Christian theologians, a study of metaphysics would not be complete without understanding the works — as well as historical relevance — of such authors as Mary Baker Eddy (1821-1910) and Pierre Teilhard de Chardin (1881-1955). Certainly, the works of all of the authors just mentioned (as well as other secular and religious authors not mentioned) have merit, depending on each author's degree of insight and ability to articulate that insight in a clear, concise, and cogent manner.

As used in this book, *divine metaphysics* has its underpinnings in the truths that were discerned and described by Mary Baker Eddy as "Christian Science." At the time of this writing, the organized religion known as "Christian Science" is almost extinct because it never established clear-cut connections with mainstream Christian theology. For that reason, with the death of its leader, organizational Christian Science not only lost its founder but its most effective proponent, best apologist, and greatest spokesperson.

Because the overwhelming majority of earliest converts to Christian Science were already Christian, most of them were knowledgeable about the efficacy of the shed blood of God's only-begotten Son, Jesus Christ. Consequently, for them, Christian Science was their *next step* in understanding God and practicing the application of God's truth in daily living. In the later years of my lifetime, however, virtually no Christian Scientist recognizes or acknowledges the underpinnings of their faith in the shed blood of

Jesus Christ. The truth be told (and it is being told here), the few Christian Scientists that exist at the time of this writing would find God's requirement for an atoning blood sacrifice astonishingly barbaric.[10] Therefore, without acknowledging the full power of the shed blood of Jesus Christ to appease God's wrath as well as to invoke God's presence, Christian Science lost its greatest power to heal. As I have stated in *As I See It: The Nature of Reality by God* (pages 9-10), "without the shed blood of Jesus Christ, all spiritual truths are of null effect within our personal lives. To be sure, the truths are not untrue and are not of null effect within the spiritual universe; they are just "untrue" in our personal lives — that is, there is no efficacy to their application within our day-to-day experience."

Never mistake that I am an advocate of the institutional bureaucracy known as "Christian Science" (also known as the "Church of Christ, Scientist"). Although I believe that some aspects of the doctrines it represents are beneficial, this organized religion has neither grown with the times nor matured into what it might have become had it not backed itself into a theological corner as a self-proclaimed complete, perfect, and intact systematic theology with a "forever leader." Personally, I believe that Christian Science would have fared much better had it functioned in perpetuity as (1) an evolving interdenominational Christian society, (2) an international Christian metaphysics publishing company, and (3) a world class Christian college of metaphysics.

Regardless, because the name *Christian Science* is relevant to my discussion of the meaning of *metaphysics,* I will explain a few benefits from some of its most-often used nomenclature.

In the 1611 King James Version of the Holy Bible,[11] the words *Christian* and *science* are each used only twice, and then only separately. Yet those two words were combined by Mary Baker Eddy as the ensign for an entire movement of religious thought. To

---

10 Mary Baker Eddy attempted to answer the question "Is There No Sacrificial Atonement?" in her work entitled *No and Yes,* published by the Christian Science Board of Directors. Boston, 1908, pages 33-38.

11 The public domain King James Version of the Holy Bible is referenced throughout this book by the initials "KJV."

those who are familiar with her literary works, it is clear that Mary Baker Eddy did not choose her words lightly. What caused her to use these two words in combination to describe her systematic theology?

Some insights are provided when one looks up the word *science* in the 1828 edition of Noah Webster's *An American Dictionary of the English Language*. There, the primary purport of *science* is given as "knowledge, or certain knowledge; the comprehension or understanding of truth or facts by the mind."[12] Then, using that sense in example, Webster declares: "The *science* of God must be perfect!" Further on, Webster states that the term *science* may be applied to subjects "founded on generally acknowledged truths, as *metaphysics*." These are first keys to understanding Mary Baker Eddy's use of the word "Science" almost forty years later. (When capitalized, "Science" generally represents an order of abstract reality that is higher than that found in natural science, physical science, or applied science.)

Let us now compare Webster's 1828 etymology of the word *science* with the Hebrew and Greek words from which "science" has been translated in the 1611 King James Version (KJV) of the Holy Bible. Webster traced the English word back to the Latin noun *scientia* — which comes from *scio/scire*, originally meaning "to discern or distinguish," only later taking on the sense "to know." Fortunately, for the Hebrew and Greek etymologist, the word *science* is used once in the Old Testament (Daniel 1:4 KJV) and once in the New Testament (1 Timothy 6:20 KJV). The Hebrew word from which *science* has been rendered is *mad-da'* [H4093 in Appendix Table A], meaning "intelligence" or "consciousness." Stepping to the side and examining that Hebrew word's closely related heteronym *ma-du'-ah* [H4069 in Appendix Table A], primitive particle *ma* [H4100 in Appendix Table A], and probable root word *ya-dah'* [H3045 in Appendix Table A], we may extrapolate the truer sense of the word *science* in its earliest usage

---

12 Noah Webster's *First Edition of An American Dictionary of the English Language*, republished in facsimile edition by the Foundation for American Christian Education. Anaheim, California, 1967.

in the English language as "the discovering, discerning, and comprehending of the what, when, why, and how of *being*."

Looking to the Greek New Testament, we find that the word *science* has been translated from *gno'-ses* [G1108 in Appendix Table B], a word that has the connotation of "inner knowledge," "knowledge not derived from the physical senses," or "knowledge derived from spiritual cognition." So, again, as with the Hebrew so with the Greek are we brought to an understanding of *science* as "the spiritual sense, or awareness, of *being*."

As a side note, John Wycliffe (d. 1384), the first complete translator of the New Testament into English from St. Jerome's Latin Vulgate, chose the phrase "science of health" (contemporary English spelling is used here) instead of "knowledge of salvation" as found in the King James Version. Thus, Wycliffe rendered the prophecy of the priest Zacharias concerning the Messiah, Christ Jesus, as "he shall bring [the] science of health to his people" (Luke 1:77 Wycliffe, brackets mine).

What we are to make of this is that the word *science* did not always mean the systematized knowledge of physicality nor imply a multi-step process for investigation — which is now called "natural science" and commonly thought of in terms of the scientific method that is used today in biology, chemistry, and physics or their convergent disciplines as well as their extensions in various applied areas. In its earliest usage, the word *science* had a different meaning.

Paradoxically, there are many Christian foundationalists[13] today who would object to the use of the word "Science" with "Christ" or "Christian" at the same time that they would feel entirely comfortable in using the phrase "Creation Science" to describe their posited alternative to the theory of evolution. Moreover, those who object to the nomenclature "Christian Science" might use the words *theology* and *Christology* with ease and frequency. This is

---

13   Because of the many negative connotations associated with the phrases "Christian fundamentalism" and "Christian fundamentalists," the present author prefers to use the phrases "Christian foundationalism" and "Christian foundationalists." The meanings are essentially the same without carrying the baggage of a political right and wrong.

especially ironic since the suffix *–ology* means "study, or science, of" and that, thus understood, *theology* may be defined as "the Science of God" and *Christology* as "the Science of Christ."

Throughout her writings, Mary Baker Eddy uses these terms and phrases almost interchangeably: "Christian Science," "absolute Science," "All Science," "Divine Science," "Spiritual Science," "Mind-science," "the Science of being," "the Science of Life," "the Science of Mind," "the Science of Soul," "the Science of Spirit," "the Science of God," "the Science of man," "the Science of Truth," "metaphysical Science," and "divine metaphysics."

To me, the most practical definition of *metaphysics* given by Mary Baker Eddy is in terms of what metaphysics does. In her primary work, *Science and Health with Key to the Scriptures*,[14] she states that "Metaphysics resolves *things into thoughts*" (page 269, lines 14-15, italics mine). For the sake of clarity, I would like to add that metaphysics also resolves *thoughts into things,* which "things" are discernible not only to spiritual sense but also are capable of being apprehended by the intellect of human beings when that intellect has been properly nurtured physically, emotionally, mentally, and spiritually.

For the purpose of this book, *metaphysics* is defined as "the nature of reality, consisting of: (1) *ontology* (i.e., the study of being and existence); (2) *natural theology* (i.e., the study of God and how God relates to this world and the things in this world); and (3) *universal science* (i.e., the study of ultimate principles and how they impact on our understanding of causality and on our understanding of the levels of organization of matter and their interactions as well as their finitude)." By extension, *divine metaphysics* is defined as "the *nature* of supernatural reality" (i.e., the *essence* of spiritual reality). To be sure, divine metaphysics has no physical bounds except in its description.

Thus, *divine metaphysics* is beyond explanation based on natural law. To be sure, there is a science to divine metaphysics but

---

14 *Science and Health with Key to the Scriptures* by Mary Baker Eddy, published by the Christian Science Board of Directors. Boston, Massachusetts, 1906.

it is, by definition, *beyond* the physical sciences because it transcends natural science, material phenomena, and physical observation. Divine metaphysics can only be understood when we use a *cultivated* spiritual, supernatural, and Christian metaphysical sense.

For the purpose of this book, *metaphysical paleoanthropology* combines paleontology and physical anthropology not to study ancient hominids/hominins related to humankind but to study modern human beings as living fossil evidence of the original and unfallen creation made in God's complete image and perfect likeness.

Regardless of whether you "believe in" (which is to say, "accept") the theory of evolution, the major strength of neo-Darwinism is found in the unifying concept that it presents to the human mind for understanding the interrelationship of all life forms on Earth (and, perhaps, throughout the material universe). Similarly, regardless of whether you "believe in" (which is to say, "accept") Creationism, the major strength of Creation Science is found in the unifying concept that it presents to the human mind for understanding the origin of all life forms on Earth (and anywhere else they may exist, for that matter).

The theme of this book is that current human anatomy and physiology represent fossilized physical impressions and biochemical expressions of what was once primarily spiritual in nature but is now *fallen*. The strength of this theme is in the construct that it presents for the unification of: (1) various and diverse theories and philosophies of reality; (2) various and diverse religious and spiritual paradigms of human origins; and (3) various and diverse therapeutic approaches that are today often considered part of "alternative medical practices" and "nontraditional healing arts."

Tools common to the conventional paleoanthropologist include shovels, chisels, picks, brushes, drills, microscopes, and various chemical reagents as well as clearing agents. Tools common to the metaphysical paleoanthropologist include literature from various religious, philosophic, and healing arts perspectives as well as supernatural impressions of spiritual reality.

Because many people might not understand all that is meant to be conveyed by the word *hypothesis* when used in an investigatory or research sense, I have used the word *premise* to represent each of the three statements foundational to this written work:

Premise One
The unfallen creation that originally reflected God's complete image and perfect likeness was *astral gelatinous*™ [15] in nature.

Premise Two
As a result of the Adamic Fall, the *astral gelatinous*™ substance of immortal beings — originally created in the complete image and perfect likeness of God — manifested as living physical substance (i.e., protoplasm) and the various cells, tissues, organs, and organ systems of the modern human appeared, becoming mere representations, vestiges, remnants, and "fossilized impressions" of what they used to be.

---

15 *Astral gelatinous*™ is coined here to describe a substance that predominantly has spiritual qualities like the created substance of unfallen angels, which substance may also take on physical qualities depending on the dimensionality in which it is found. *For example*, when some angels enter the physical realm (i.e., *push* themselves into our relative time and space), they voluntarily take on human form and appear to be human even though they have not originated from a biological life form. (This is exemplified by the two angels who first visited Abraham and, later, Lot in the city of Sodom — which visitations are recorded in Chapters Eighteen and Nineteen of the Book of Genesis.) At one time, certain angels even stepped into physicality to mate with human beings. (This interaction is recorded in Genesis 6:1-4 as having taken place between "the sons of God" and "the daughters of men.") The giant "nephilim" (or "fallen ones") are believed to have been the offspring of these unnatural sexual liaisons. The sexual liaisons were *unnatural* because they took place between immortals and mortals. The Holy Bible is clear that the angels who mated with human beings are now in the "Pit" of Hades awaiting God's Final Judgment for their unholy activity (see the Epistle of Jude, verse 6).

Premise Three
Upon Christ's return, those who are joint heirs with him will receive new bodies that not only resemble his body[16] but are also returned to the original *astral gelatinous*™ form and substance immortal beings once had in God before the Adamic Fall.

Distortion, Corruption, Restoration, and Resurrection

After the Adamic Fall, human beings would not only have a distorted view of who God is, they would also have a distorted view of who and what they were originally created to be relative to their true spiritual nature as well as their original somatic identity in an unfallen and immortal body.

Before the Adamic Fall, people were made in the complete image of God and, thus, had their individual spiritual identities *absolutely* in Him. Additionally, their somatic identities were perfect reflections of His likeness as well:

> *Then God said: "Let us make humankind in our image, in our likeness [or similitude]..." So God created humanity in His own image; in the image of God humanity was created male and female.*[17]

With its Fall, the Adamic Race not only lost its spiritual identity, or "image" in God, but also its somatic identity, or bodily "likeness" to Him. The Adamic Race fell through its disobedience to the command of God. For that reason, after the Adamic Fall, God Himself was no longer woven into the spiritual fabric of Adam and Eve. Hence, their spiritual identities were altered. Concomitantly, the living substance of their bodies no longer

---

16   1 John 3:2
17   Genesis 1:26-27, King James Version (Paraphrase)

reflected the highest standard of God's goodness. In other words, their somatic identities became corrupted because of their fallen spiritual nature. Their somatic identities were no longer *astral gelatinous*™. They had become *protoplasmic.*

At the time of the Fall of Adam and Eve, their bodies were changed from incorruptible bodies to corruptible bodies. Thus, their bodies became subject to deterioration, disease, death, and decay. Having fallen, Adam and Eve were no longer made in the complete image of God. In other words, their spiritual identities had become distorted through the Adamic Fall. Concomitantly, their somatic identities were no longer perfectly like God's appearance; their somatic identities had become corrupted and corruptible. This is why the Bible records that, although Adam was originally made in the image and likeness of God (Genesis 1:26), Adam's son Seth was made in the image and likeness of Adam after Adam's Fall and not in the image and likeness of God:

> *This is the written account of Adam's generations. When God created humankind, He made them in His own likeness. He created them male and female and blessed them. And He named them "Adam" when they were created. When Adam had lived 130 years, he had a son in his own [corrupted] likeness, in his own [fallen] image; and he named him Seth.*[18]

Because Adam and Eve were no longer made in the complete image and perfect likeness of God, their spiritual identities were distorted and their somatic identities were corrupted. Their very beings had been altered! It is not that Adam and Eve did not resemble their Creator at all, it is that they no longer reflected their Creator completely and perfectly. Adam and Eve had become perverted versions of God's original creation; they became fallen versions of what God had originally intended for them to be. They no longer reflected their Creator without wrinkle and without

---

18   Genesis 5:1-3, King James Version (Paraphrase)

spot.[19]

However, regardless of the Adamic Fall, today's Good News, or Gospel of Salvation, includes that, once a person accepts Jesus Christ as his or her own Savior, that person is remade, recast, and reborn a new creature in Christ and his or her own spiritual identity (in contrast to one's somatic identity) is immediately restored to the complete image of God. That is why God sees saved people as already whole and holy: God is looking at their spiritual identities through the shed blood of Jesus Christ. Unfortunately, most saved people still view themselves as having unrestored, or distorted, spiritual identities. Why? They misinterpret that their old carnal nature and its related somatic identity — which is fleshly or corporeal — accurately represent their spiritual nature and its related somatic identity when they do not.

Most saved people misunderstand and, consequently, undervalue the expiation of their sins through the shed blood of Jesus Christ. The word *expiation* means not only that our past sins have been remitted and removed far from us but also that our current and future sins have been remitted and removed far from us as well. It is not that saved people do not continue to sin; it is that even our future sins are already atoned for and remitted. God never stops viewing saved people through the shed blood of Jesus Christ even when, and *as,* we sin. God understands when saved people sin that it is their old carnal natures, or old selves, that are sinning and not their new or divine natures (i.e., their new or reborn selves). As the Apostle Paul states: "Nothing can separate [saved people] from the love of Christ."[20] And "there is now no condemnation for those who are saved through Christ Jesus."[21] Saved people need to understand that their spiritual identities have already been completely remade, recast, and reborn through the shed blood of Jesus Christ. Although this is a mystery to people ignorant of the meaning of salvation, this is not a mystery to God nor should it be a mystery to those who belong to God.

---

19 This language of pristine and holy beauty is taken from the King James Version of Ephesians 5:27.
20 Romans 8:35, King James Version (Paraphrase)
21 Romans 8:1, King James Version (Paraphrase)

Mirrors may reflect physical reality, but they do not reflect spiritual, supernatural, and metaphysical reality. Consequently, in order for us to see ourselves spiritually, supernaturally, and metaphysically, we must view ourselves and each other through the shed blood of Jesus Christ — just like God views us! When saved people hold their own sins against themselves or the sins of others against them, they fail to see themselves and others as God sees them. In other words, we are not to accept guilt ourselves nor try to impose guilt upon any other saved person. God does not impose guilt upon us. Why, then, should we impose guilt upon ourselves or other saved people?

If we were to view our current physical likenesses in a carnival or "funhouse" mirror (i.e., a mirror whose surface is randomly convex and concave), views of our natural selves would be imperfect. In other words, our various views of ourselves would be distorted, unreal, and untrue even though our actual physical beings remain unaltered. In such cases, our views would not be representative of our true physical reality. If we were to accept these distorted reflections as representative of who and what we are, then our activities and the results of our activities would be ineffectual or at least not as effectual as they could be. We would neither relate to ourselves nor to others accurately.

Similarly, if we are not viewing our true image, or spiritual identity, as restored through the shed blood of Jesus Christ, then we are not able to declare, affirm, and lay claim most effectively to the truth of who and what we *really* are because we are placing too much stock, or belief, in our old carnal nature and its related somatic identity as constituting the only reality (rather than in who and what we are in God through Christ Jesus). Remember, God sees each saved person as satisfying His complete image because God sees that person through the shed blood of Jesus Christ. Therefore, if we are saved, we need to view ourselves and other saved people through the shed blood of Jesus Christ, too.[22]

---

22   The more we look at reality through the shed blood of Jesus Christ, the more that reality becomes crystal clear for us. Concomitantly, the longer we look at life through the shed blood of Jesus Christ, the more clearly individual metaphysical truths crystallize for us as well.

For people who like to make their physical appearances more attractive, it is easier for them to change appearances as they view their physical reflections using pocket, hand, or wall mirrors. The same principle is also true metaphysically for those who are seeking to apply spiritual truths to correct, or heal, physical, mental, and emotional disabilities, disorders, and diseases. It is easier to change these appearances, or manifestations, if one is, first and foremost, treating them by visualizing one's spiritual identity as already whole and holy in God through Christ Jesus despite one's current somatic identity or physical appearance. In other words, we should treat physical, mental, and emotional disequilibria by recognizing and proclaiming the true spiritual reality of who and what we are in Christ as unblemished individual reflections of God's complete image. This is the essence, or nature, of using divine metaphysics to treat unhealthy conditions.

To be sure, we need to view our reflections using a metaphysical mirror image of ourselves enveloped in God's goodness rather than a physical mirror image of our old carnal selves and their lingering somatic likenesses (that is, the physical appearances we still "carry" around). Because each one of us is remade, recast, and reborn through the shed blood of Jesus Christ, we need to view ourselves and every other saved person as individuals completely whole and holy. We need to stop holding sins against ourselves individually; and we need to stop holding the sins of others against them — which includes their sins against us, their sins against themselves, and their sins against God. We should stop feeling guilty for our own sins and we should stop wanting other saved people to feel guilty about their sins as well. Just as expressed anguish or grief is not a measure of how much we loved a person who has died, so, too, is guilt not a measure of how penitent or repentant we are concerning our past sins. Rather, the cessation of sinning is a measure of how penitent or repentant we are. Living in contrition, and not dying of shame, is the only payment necessary for God's expiation of our sins.

Here, it is important to acknowledge that not holding sins against ourselves or each other in active forgiveness is the first measure of our love for God and for us all. Educating others about

God's love for "us all" through Christ Jesus is the second measure. The third measure is living our lives in the name of Jesus Christ for the benefit of others.

Although saved people are an "us all," we are not fragments of a whole: We are individually, collectively, and corporately complete members of the body of Christ. God not only sees us altogether as a composite reflection of Himself but as compound reflections of Himself as well. The eyesight of a typical vertebrate is a useful analogy for understanding a "composite," or whole, image of the entire body of Christ; and the eyesight of a typical arthropod is a useful analogy for understanding "compound" images of individuals that make up the body of Christ (i.e., multiple images all seen at the same time). God sees us as parts of a whole in His composite view, but God also sees us as individually-complete images of Him in His compound view. Each one of us is interdependent on all others but each one of us has been created as a complete individual with his or her own free will. Thus, saved people have both an interlocking group identity and their own individual identities as fully functioning "cells" (i.e., members) in the body of Christ.

If we employ a spiritual view of ourselves as the new creatures in Christ that we are, God will raise our somatic identities to a *higher* standard for living substance — minimally, through heightened joy and diminished anxiety and, maximally, through complete emotional, mental, and physical well-being. As a side note here, God will raise, or translate, the somatic bodies of all who are saved in Christ to the *highest* standard for living substance at the time of Christ's return. In the Holy Bible, this is referred to as the *redemption of our bodies.*[23] (The redemption of our bodies is in contrast to the salvation of our souls.) In other words, our bodies will one day be raised to an incorruptible condition and restored to an *astral gelatinous*™ form.

Viewing ourselves as whole and holy does not abrogate the responsibility for each saved person to discover, acknowledge, and confess sin in his or her own life. Every saved person must still be

---

23　Romans 8:23, King James Version

on guard against self-deception. Although each saved person is made righteous in Jesus Christ, he or she must still live up to that image by yielding to God's Will not only daily but also moment by moment, especially if one seeks change in the physical world of appearances.

Physicians treat maladies physically, psychologists treat maladies psychologically, and metaphysicians treat maladies metaphysically — not only for themselves but also for others who are entrusted to their care.

Summarizing this section: *Metaphysics* is "the nature, or essence, of invisible reality." *Divine metaphysics* is "the nature, or essence, of supernatural reality." *Distortion* is "the alteration of our original spiritual identities, or individually complete images in God." *Corruption* is "the alteration of our originally incorruptible somatic identities — which is to say, the change of those unfallen bodies made exactly in God's perfect likeness — to those that are now subject to deterioration, disease, death, and decay." *Restoration* is "the rebirth of our spiritual identities — or the salvation of our individual souls — through the shed blood of Jesus Christ." And *resurrection* is "the redemption of our somatic identities — that is, the restoration of our substantive bodies (i.e., somatic identities) — to perfect reflections of God's likeness or appearance."

Distortion of our spiritual identities and corruption of our somatic identities happened in our primordial past. Restoration of our spiritual identities occurs now, albeit at a different time for each saved person (i.e., at the time of their individual salvation). And resurrection of our somatic identities (i.e., restoration of our somatic identities or redemption of our bodies) occurs in the future. (There is a first resurrection *en masse* for all people saved by the beginning of Christ's millennial rule on Earth; and there is a second resurrection *en masse* at the end of Christ's millennial rule for all people saved during that rule.)

Regardless of what type of somatic identity one currently has or does not have, or what type one will have in the future, every created being with free will has a spiritual reality that transcends both human form and function. Based on their rejection or acceptance of the Lord Jesus Christ as personal Savior, the spiritual identity of individual human beings either remains "distorted" from the original or becomes "restored" to the original. To be sure, "distorted" and "restored" spiritual images are seen using metaphysical insight and not physical sight. Change in the mental, emotional, and physical is effected metaphysically only when truth is applied correctly and in good measure through the shed blood of Christ Jesus. Change never occurs through human will or by affirming or dictating to God what we want. Change can only occur through the Will of God and what God wants for us individually, collectively, and corporately. That is why we should make the Will of God our own by submitting to it daily as well as moment by moment in contrition and in gratitude for the expiation of our sins. And that is why we should make a conscious effort to join with others who are in a similar pursuit to make God's Will their own.

Cytology and Morphogenesis

Cytology is "the study of cells" and *morphogenesis* is "structural development." Morphogenesis includes embryogenesis, histogenesis, and organogenesis. "Embryogenesis" refers to the development of the embryo; "histogenesis" refers to the development of the embryo's primary germ layers into tissues; and "organogenesis" refers to the development of the embryo's organs and organ systems. Obviously, embryogenesis, histogenesis, and organogenesis are inseparable except for the purpose of discussion because one cannot exist without the other. *Embryogenesis* is the overarching process; *histogenesis* and *organogenesis* are subsumed within embryogenesis and continued during fetal development.

Modern day cellular structure with its protoplasm and various organelles and inclusions is merely a remnant of the *astral gelatinous*™ material of which original, unfallen mankind was made. As such, modern day cellular structure provides fossil evidence of the highest standard of living substance that reflected and transmitted God's glory. Although protoplasm is translucent, it certainly *does not* reflect or transmit the light, or spiritual brightness, of God. The *astral gelatinous*™ material of which original mankind was made did reflect and transmit that light. The bioluminescence that occurs in some creatures on Earth is from the oxidation of luciferin. In contrast, astral luminescence is from reflecting the glory of God.

The various organelles of modern-day cellular structure represent the compartmentalized energy centers within the smallest components of which original, unfallen mankind was made. The nucleus of each cell represents its control center as well as its original creative connection to God. The inclusions within modern day cells represent the precious *astral gelatinous*™ substances that imparted unique characteristics to the original living substance, including its dynamic spectral hues, electromagnetic fields, and harmonic vibrations. The DNA of modern-day cells is a vestige of the original, living, and inherited substance of God that was altered, bent, or refracted from the primordial and glorious substance of which original, unfallen mankind was made before the Adamic Fall. (From x-ray crystallography, we know from our physical senses that DNA is twisted. From a spiritually-enlightened understanding of the Adamic Fall, we know metaphysically that DNA represents an altered, or bent, spiritual state.)

Metaphysically speaking, we know that the substance we inherited from God was altered from its original condition at the time of the Adamic Fall. Our original condition was *astral gelatinous*™ and, therefore, completely capable of reflecting the glory, or luminosity, of God. Our current condition is corporeal and, therefore, completely incapable of reflecting the glory, or luminosity, of God.

Although contemporary biological science would lead us to believe that cellular differentiation, tissue formation, and organogenesis occur strictly based on the interactions between and among cells and various products produced by those cells within the developing embryo, these processes actually occur as the embryo "grows into" the *preformed electromagnetic field of its etheric body double.*[24]

All cells, tissues, organs, and organ systems grow into a preformed electromagnetic mold for each individual. Every preformed human electromagnetic mold is predetermined by a set of spiritual records as well as the spiritual growth requirements for each individual. The records and requirements dictate each mold's pattern based on each individual's experiential needs as well as the experiential needs of each individual's future "nearest neighbors."[25] (Remember, we are not only individuals but an "us all," collectively and corporately.)

The German biologist Ernst Haeckel (1834-1919) is sometimes derided by modern biologists for his theory that "ontogeny recapitulates phylogeny." The signification of his theory includes that the embryogenesis of an individual provides a summary of the ancestral species that preceded it from an evolutionary standpoint. Of course, ontogeny *does not* precisely recapitulate an organism's phylogeny, but ontogeny does generally provide a panoramic review of successive stages of development within various species that are distant, earlier relatives of the organism (and "lower" on the phylogenetic tree of biological life).

All biological life is related because all living substance was created by God. All created life "fell" (i.e., was altered) when Adam and Eve fell. The disobedience of Adam and Eve brought God's curse upon all living things, the world, the Earth's solar system,

---

24 The *preformed etheric body double* for each developing human embryo may also be described as a "subtle body" or "electromagnetic *bas relief.*"

25 *For example*, an individual's future companions and yet-to-be-born children would be among that individual's future "nearest neighbors." Because every person has his or her own unique experiential needs, they are taken into consideration by God while the experiential needs of every other person are taken into consideration. There is one Master Plan that includes us all individually, collectively, and corporately. God is not limited. God does not love one person to the exclusion of another. Therefore, God does not meet the needs of one person without establishing a comprehensive plan for meeting the needs of all others at the same time even if some components of the plan are deployed at a future time. (This does not mean that all people are eventually saved.)

and what we know as (or think is) the universe. This curse changed all living substance, which was originally *astral gelatinous*™, into its *protoplasmic* equivalent that currently exists. In other words, what we see today is not what God originally created. What took place over eons in the physically observable universe took place in an instant from the perspective of the spiritually observable universe.

Although earlier I stated that the major strength of neo-Darwinism is found in the unifying concept that it presents to the human mind for understanding the interrelationship of all life forms on Earth, I am not advocating that the readers of the present author's written work accept the theory of evolution as fact. Rather, I am advocating that the readers of this written work accept that there is continuity between and among all biological life forms on Earth: All living things are related to one another by the living substance of which they are composed. Life on Earth, as we know it, is all fallen from God's original creation. Although pantheism[26] is not true for the physical world in which we live, a metaphysical pantheism is true for the spiritual world from which we are fallen and to which saved people will eventually be returned.

All living things on Earth are but parables, figures, types, or allegories of things that already exist in Heaven.[27] Metaphysically speaking, all flowers in Heaven are like continuously discharging mini-fireworks that individually and collectively "sing" through their harmonic vibrations. All trees in Heaven are well-springs of joy whose "trunks" and "branches" are conceptually similar to fountainary spouts, jets, and sprays. Remember, "eye has not seen nor ear heard what God has prepared for those who love Him and patiently wait for Him."[28] We cannot now know what God has prepared for us in Heaven, but we can imagine.

Although earlier I stated that the major strength of Creation

---

26 Pantheism is the belief that God is found *in* all living things rather than just reflected *by* all living things in their intelligent design.

27 "Heaven" is the spiritual universe — in other words, the space and place where God resides.

28 Paraphrased from the King James Version of Isaiah 64:4 and 1 Corinthians 2:9

Science is found in the unifying concept that it presents to the human mind for understanding the origin of all life forms on Earth, I am not advocating that the readers of the present author's written work accept that each day of creation was a twenty-hour period of time. Rather, I am advocating that the readers of this written work accept that there is a sequence of related events that we have come to understand as the Genesis account of creation. Indeed, since the Biblical account of creation indicates that the sun, moon, and stars were not created until the fourth "day,"[29] solar time, lunar time, and sidereal (or stellar) time did not exist to measure time for the first three so-called days of creation.

The eisegesis[30] of conservative theologians would argue that the Hebrew word *yom* [H3117 in Appendix Table A] always means a twenty-four-hour period of time throughout the entire Holy Bible. They fail to take into consideration that "one day with the Lord is as a thousand years, and a thousand years as one day"[31] and that the planet Earth during its formation had days that were much shorter than they are now. The rotation of the planet Earth about its axis has slowed considerably since its formation, and it continues to slow. (The Earth's earliest days were closer to six hours in duration.)

Conservative theologians would also argue that the use of the words "morning" and "evening" for the first three days — recorded in Genesis 1:5, 1:8, and 1:13 — reinforces that the days in the Genesis account were exactly as they are now. However, without solar, lunar, and stellar light during the first three days of creation, there could be no morning and evening as we understand them today. Therefore, either "morning" and "evening" are referring to different referents or they are included simply for the purpose of literary parallelism for each of the recorded seven "days" of creation, much like the parallelism found in the repeating fourteen generations in the genealogy of Jesus Christ that is recorded in Chapter One of the Gospel of Matthew. (That some generations

---

29   Genesis 1:14-19
30   *Eisegesis* is defined here as "interpretation with personal, or subjective, bias."
31   2 Peter 3:8, King James Version (see also Psalm 90:4)

have been omitted by Matthew is acknowledged by many Bible scholars.) Regardless of what one believes concerning the days of the Genesis account of creation, it should not be a fellowship-breaker. In contradistinction, disbelieving the saving power of the shed blood of Jesus Christ *is* a fellowship-breaker.

All living forms on Earth are connected and interrelated and, therefore, can be studied based on their comparative anatomy and physiology. But all living things on Earth today are mere representations, vestiges, remnants, and "fossilized impressions" of what originally existed before the Adamic Fall. As such, all living things on Earth represent metaphysical realities that exist in the invisible world of God, which realities *cannot* be experienced (i.e., "known") through the physical senses.

To be sure, all life forms on Earth today grow into the electromagnetic patterns that are mere shadow images (imploded *bas relief* impressions) of what they once were before the Adamic Fall. Our souls are frozen in a warp of relative space-time because of that Fall, and our somatic identities are bent, distorted, and perverted holographic images[32] of what originally existed in an unfallen spiritual, supernatural, and metaphysical reality.

The Vocabulary of Divine Metaphysics

Metaphysics (noun): the nature, or essence, of invisible reality. Generally speaking, the invisible reality of metaphysics may be intellectual, spiritual, or a combination of intellectual and spiritual.

Divine metaphysics (noun phrase): (a) the nature, or essence, of spiritual, or supernatural, reality;[33] (b) that which is beyond

---

32 The use of the phrase "holographic images" is metaphorical and not meant by extension to endorse Gnosticism or Docetism.

33 Here, the words *nature* and *supernatural* are not mutually exclusive, opposing, or contradictory terms because *nature*, as used here, does not mean "biology" (i.e., biological nature) or "physics" (i.e., physical nature) but "inherent character," "basic constitution," or "essence."

explanation based on natural science or the laws of physics, chemistry, and biology; (c) that which resolves things into thoughts, concepts, ideas, and principles as well as that which resolves thoughts, concepts, ideas, and principles into things — based on spiritual or supernatural reality and sight (i.e., spiritual insight, hindsight, and foresight). When all of the chapters of this book are taken together, they provide a composite view of divine metaphysics, its practice, its practicality, and its relevance to Christianity.

Metaphysical (adjective): (a) of, or related to, metaphysics; (b) from a view beyond or higher than physical or material reality, comprehension, and explanation; (c) spiritual; (d) supernatural; (e) essential (i.e., essence-based).

Examples of use:

> Certain characteristics of living things on Earth represent the *metaphysical* realities of living things in the spiritual universe.

> Certain parts, aspects, and ideas associated with the anatomy and physiology of fallen man[34] represent *metaphysical* parts, aspects, and ideas associated with original Man.[35]

Metaphysically (adverb): (a) of, or pertaining to, metaphysics; (b) from a metaphysical standpoint; (c) as seen, or understood, from a view beyond or higher than that which can be seen from a physical or material standpoint; (d) spiritually; (e) supernaturally; (f) essentially (i.e., concerning that which is essence-based).

Examples of use:

---

34 Throughout this book, the phrase "fallen man" is used synonymously with "*Homo sapiens,*" "human beings," "mortal man," "corporeal man," and "humankind."

35 Throughout this book, the phrase "original Man" is used synonymously with "unfallen man," "immortal man," "Man," and "original, unfallen man."

Certain parts, aspects, and ideas associated with original Man are represented *metaphysically* by certain parts, aspects, and ideas associated with the anatomy and physiology of fallen man.

The phrase "metaphysically speaking" also means: (a) spiritually speaking; (b) supernaturally speaking; (c) speaking from a metaphysical standpoint; (d) speaking from a supernatural standpoint; (e) speaking from a spiritual standpoint.

Metaphysician: (a) a professional person who is educated and trained to apply spiritual principles to physical, emotional, mental, spiritual, and/or social problems that manifest in an individual or in a collective human condition; (b) a philosopher-theologian (or theologian-philosopher) who seeks to resolve things into thoughts and thoughts into things by focusing on their spiritual essence, supernatural meaning, and metaphysical import.

Metapractitioner: (a) a professional person, both educated and trained, who seeks to apply the highest levels of medical, psychological, and spiritual knowledge and understanding to diagnose and treat physical, emotional, mental, spiritual, and social problems that manifest in an individual or in a collective human condition; (b) a person who calls upon, as well as helps to coordinate[36] the activities of, other specialists in medicine, psychology, and divine metaphysics in order for them to work together — either in unison or in sequence — to treat physical, mental, emotional, spiritual, and social problems that manifest in

---

36 It is important to emphasize that, although the metapractitioner coordinates treatment between and among the areas of medicine, psychology, and divine metaphysics, the metapractitioner is a specialist in one of the three areas and has additional education and training in the other two areas as well as in coordinating a systematic approach to treating physical, mental, emotional, spiritual, and social problems that manifest in an individual or in a collective human condition. In other words, the role of the metapractitioner is well beyond the role of a case manager.

an individual or in a collective human condition.

Example of use:

> Dr. Chan (a fictitious person) is not only an ophthalmologist but also a *metapractitioner*. She regularly consults with specialists in the fields of psychology and divine metaphysics as she treats her patients. She herself understands and appreciates that true sight is spiritual and not physical. She works with her patients and other specialists in order for her patients to learn, understand, and appreciate not only the physical basis for their diagnosis and treatment but also the psychological and metaphysical principles that have implications for her patients' personal well-being. To be sure, as a medical specialist, Dr. Chan also fully understands the role of proper nutrition in maximizing vision for her patients. Consequently, she regularly advises her patients concerning what to eat and what not to eat as well as what dietary supplements to take, especially as diet and nutrition relate to human vision. Although Dr. Chan understands that true sight is spiritual and not physical, she also understands the need for a comprehensive treatment plan to correct physical disorders and diseases when they occur.

The Following Chapters

As a metaphysical paleoanthropologist, it is incumbent on me to identify "missing links" between modern human anatomy and the *astral gelatinous*™ form of immortal beings from before the Adamic Fall for the purpose of conceptually understanding: (1) form and function in God's original, unfallen creation; (2) how to better apply metaphysical principles for the treatment of physical, mental, emotional, and spiritual disequilibria in our current human condition; and (3) what structures and functions each saved person will possess when our individual somatic identities are restored (vis-à-vis somatic resurrection/bodily redemption) to an incorruptible state.

In this chapter, I have indicated that the past, present, and future sins of saved human beings are expiated because of the shed blood of God's only-begotten Son, Jesus Christ. And, because our sins are expiated, our spiritual identities have been restored to what they once were before the Adamic Fall even though our souls are still in corruptible bodies. Despite the spiritual restoration of saved people, that we are still in human bodies presents unique challenges because saved people may, at times, revert to past carnal behaviors and old sinful addictions. Fortunately, because our Lord Jesus Christ was tempted like us in all points,[37] our God understands and forgives us for reverting and relapsing to behaviors associated with our old carnal selves. Our Creator understands why saved human beings struggle with flesh and that they will continue to struggle with flesh until they are released from its mortal coil at the time that their lives on Earth are over. Please do not confuse the Lord God Almighty's understanding of why we revert to carnal behaviors with permission to revert to them. Regardless of our continuous struggles, God desires for us to become victors over — not victims of — temptation from our old carnal thinking. For this reason, our God executes plans for us to overcome and to become increasingly resilient by providing us with opportunities for overcoming!

In the following chapters, I will consider an understanding of various cells, tissues, organs, and organ systems of human anatomy as they relate to their original counterparts in order to better image and affirm the healing, restoration, and recovery of diseased and/or disabled human beings through the more accurate understanding of: (1) their originally-unfettered form and function; (2) their current metaphysical reality in God; and (3) their future somatic state.

As a foundational principle throughout this book, metaphysical treatment through imaging — as well as affirming, declaring, and proclaiming — mean absolutely nothing without our acceding to

---

37 Hebrews 4:15

God's covenant with us through the shed blood of His only-begotten Son, Jesus Christ, and without our acknowledging that all healing virtue proceeds and processes solely from the throne of God through Jesus Christ.

Chapter Questions

This section is intended to facilitate learning by providing relevant activities, exercises, and experiences to aid students of divine metaphysics in their quest for grasping spiritual concepts, integrating them into their own belief systems, holding them more assuredly, and making them more practical in daily life.

The following questions should be answered after reading each titled section. To answer a few of the questions, students may need to consult outside resources or external references. Students are also encouraged to answer these questions with others during group discussions.

Metaphysical Paleoanthropology

1. According to the author, where can one find fossil evidence for the original, unfallen Adamic Race?

2. (a) How does the author define the word *fossil*? (b) Is the author's definition out of step with contemporary dictionary definitions of the word *fossil*? Please explain. (c) How is the author's definition different from a traditional understanding of what a *fossil* is?

3. Using outside resources, briefly describe how popular healing arts practices incorporate concepts of energy centers and pathways. (For the purpose of this question and others that follow, "briefly describe" usually intends that one to two paragraphs be written.)

4. (a) Provide a complete dictionary definition for the word *metaphysics*. (b) Provide a complete dictionary definition for the word *paleoanthropology*.

5. What is the intended significance of capitalizing the word *Science*?

6. Provide a complete dictionary definition for the word *etymology*.

7. In its earliest usage, briefly describe the meaning of the word *science*.

8. (a) According to Mary Baker Eddy, what does metaphysics resolve? (b) According to the author of this book, what else does metaphysics resolve? (c) What general areas are subsumed within an Aristotelian study of *metaphysics*?

9. (a) Give a practical definition for *divine metaphysics*. (b) Briefly describe how divine metaphysics relates to natural law.

10. (a) What is the major strength of neo-Darwinism? (b) What is the major strength of Creation Science (i.e., Creationism)?

11. State the three major premises (i.e., hypotheses) of *Divine Metaphysics of Human Anatomy*.

12. (a) Give a two-sentence definition of the phrase *astral gelatinous*™. (b) Briefly explain how *astral gelatinous*™ substance relates to protoplasm. (c) How is *astral gelatinous*™ luminescence different from bioluminescence?

Distortion, Corruption, Restoration, and Resurrection

13. Explain the meaning of the phrase *somatic identity*.

14. (a) How were Adam and Eve's spiritual identities changed because of the Adamic Fall? (b) How were Adam and Eve's somatic identities changed because of the Adamic Fall?

15. How is our fallen spiritual identity restored to the complete image of God?

16. In what way is *expiation* a part of *atonement* and/or *remission*?

17. What is the essence of using divine metaphysics to treat unhealthy conditions and disease?

18. According to the present author, what are the three measures of our love for God?

19. In what way or ways does God see saved people?

20. How is the salvation of our souls different from the redemption of our bodies?

21. (a) Compare and contrast the terms *distortion, corruption, restoration,* and *resurrection.* (b) Compare and contrast spiritual restoration and somatic restoration using the following words: soul, spirit, body, salvation, saved, rebirth, born again, re-creation, resurrection, and redemption. (c) Compare and contrast the redemption of our souls with the redemption of our bodies.

Cytology and Morphogenesis

22. Provide simple definitions for the terms *cytology, morphogenesis, embryogenesis, histogenesis,* and *organogenesis.*

23. In what ways was *astral gelatinous*™ substance impacted by the Adamic Fall?

24. Metaphysically speaking, what determines the future shape of a fertilized human egg (i.e., zygote)?

25. Consult an embryology textbook and share its explanation for Ernst Haeckel's theory that "ontogeny recapitulates phylogeny." (Be sure to include publication information for the cited textbook.)

26. What does the present author advocate relative to the theory of evolution?

27. What is the difference between *solar time, lunar time,* and *sidereal time?*

28. What is the difference between *exegesis* and *eisegesis?*

The Vocabulary of Divine Metaphysics

29. What are the differences between a metaphysician and a metapractitioner?

Chapter Two
Divine Metaphysics of the Integument and Skeletal Muscle

You have clothed me with skin and flesh, and have fenced me with bones and sinews.[38]

JOB 10:11 KJV (PARAPHRASE)

---

[38] *Sinews* include ligaments (bone to bone attachments), tendons (bone to muscle attachments), and aponeuroses (muscle to muscle attachments). Although large nerve trunks might be included in a definition of "sinews" (because they are tough and, therefore, difficult to break in dissection), the most obvious reference of "sinews" is to the "cords" that help bind the body together. (The singular form of "aponeuroses" is "aponeurosis.")

Part One: The Integument

The Delineation of Form

The characteristics of living things on Earth represent the metaphysical realities of living things in the spiritual universe. However, there is often not a simple one-to-one relationship between the individual characteristics and properties of biological life forms and the individual characteristics and properties of spiritual life forms, especially those that possess creative consciousness[39] in addition to *astral gelatinous*™ somatic identities.

Living things on Earth, and throughout the physical universe, are characterized as "living" because they: (1) require a food source or nutrient supply, (2) ingest, (3) metabolize, (4) grow, (5) respire, (6) excrete, (7) reproduce, and (8) die. Conceptually speaking, one might argue that fire is a living thing because: (1) fire survives (or *continues to continue)* as long as it has an available fuel supply (i.e., food source) — such as the organic molecules in wood, oil, or methane; (2) fire ingests by consuming (or burning) its fuel/food; (3) fire metabolizes by breaking down its fuel/food in the presence of an oxidizing agent *(for example,* oxygen); (4) fire grows by increasing in size if it has sufficient fuel/food; (5) fire excretes unusable products — such as ash and carbon dioxide as byproducts from its metabolism/respiration; (6) fire reproduces or *makes others like* itself *(for example,* one fire can become two, and two fires can become four, etc.); and (7) fire dies, or ceases to exist, when there are no longer sufficient quantities of fuel/food for it to survive.

Obviously, fire is *not* a living thing because it lacks three characteristics that distinguish it from things that are genuinely

---

[39] Creative consciousness includes both the ability to analyze and think logically (i.e., structured consciousness) as well as the ability to discern, make choices, and use one's free will (i.e., unstructured consciousness).

living: (1) fire is not self-controlled; (2) fire is not self-organized; and (3) fire is not self-contained. Fire has no hereditary substance and no enzymes to direct its activities. And fire is not delineated by having a border or boundary that provides for its definition (i.e., size and shape). Even if fire is compared to the parasitic submicroscopic particles known as viruses (whose status of living versus non-living has long been debated by philosopher-biologists), fire still lacks the three major characteristics of living things: self-control, self-organization, and self-containment. Of course, these three major characteristics are associated with cells, which are the fundamental units of biological life.

At the cellular level, cell membranes provide for our self-containment. Because of cell membranes, our living protoplasm does not "spill out" until the time of cellular death. At the organismic (organismal) level, our integument (i.e., skin) encases us, delineates us, and separates us individually from everything else. Regardless of the descriptors we might use personally to define ourselves, human beings individually think of themselves on the basis of what is "me" and "not me" (i.e., *self* and *nonself*) as well as what is "like me" and "not like me" (i.e., *like myself* and *not like myself*). It is from such thinking that human beings develop characteristics not only associated with individual identities but also associated with individual group identities. And it is from such thinking that human beings develop feelings about other human beings relative to whether they are: (1) similar and, therefore, familiar; or (2) dissimilar and, therefore, unfamiliar. Both hospitality and hostility toward others are dependent on such conclusions.

Although individuals imbued with creative consciousness each have a soul, spirit, and somatic identity, no one in the world of Spirit is really separate from one another. There is metaphysical unity in the world of Spirit because: (1) all saved souls have the Mind of Christ; (2) all are members of the Body of Christ; (3) all are indwelt by, and immersed in, the Spirit of God; (4) everyone is in the Presence of the Creator; (5) everything that is done is done within the framework of the Will of God to bless His Holy Name; and (6) everyone has the highest love and utmost respect for their

Creator and for one another. In the world of Spirit, people understand that there is an "us all" rather than just a "you and me" because all have their individual, collective, and corporate identities in Christ Jesus. Although all people in the world of Spirit know that we are all parts of an "us all," most people on Earth have not matured sufficiently to recognize "us all" as a fundamental truth.

No matter where they are, all living beings with souls have creative consciousness. Creative consciousness always includes free will or volition to make choices as well as to exercise self-control. In the world of Spirit, the only thing that delineates one person from another is the love they have for God and for each other. Love forms their *spiritual skin,* so to speak, because it maintains their integrity and, hence, their identity. On Earth, our individual love for others is demonstrated through: (1) forgiveness, (2) nurturing one another in the name of Jesus Christ, and (3) laying down our lives for one another in lifelong, daily sacrifice and/or the sacrifice of our own physical life to help protect or save another. Although this spiritually delineates people on Earth, such delineation is only fully observable from the world of Spirit.

Among highly intelligent, well-educated, and academically gifted people, there has always been a large contingent who question the need for the crucifixion of Jesus Christ. These well-intentioned people often embrace the idea that Jesus Christ did not come to die for the sins of humankind or to save us from our sins. They have a very difficult time grasping the concept of the substitutionary atonement for — and propitiation[40] of — our sins through the shed blood of Jesus Christ. One of the reasons that they do not grasp the concept is because they do not comprehend with a childlike simplicity the gospel message of salvation. Also, because they do not grasp the concept of God's Wrath (i.e., they believe God has *no* wrath because "God is Love"), they do not understand the meaning and importance of end-time prophecies

---

40   *Propitiation* means "appeasing the perfect justice of a holy and righteous God." Together, "propitiation" and "expiation" constitute *atonement*. (The definition of *expiation* is given in Chapter One of this book.)

within the Old and New Testaments — which understanding, admittedly, requires more than the mind of a child. *For example,* they might think that the Book of Revelation in the Bible is not important or can only be understood figuratively and/or metaphysically, mainly because they do not understand the current signification and future actuality of prophesied end-time events. They do not trust (because they do not understand) that "the spirit of prophecy is the testimony of Jesus Christ."[41] To them, Jesus only came to show us a better way. To them, Jesus did not need to come to save humankind because we were never really separated from the Creator in the first place. These fail to recognize the heinous nature of our iniquity and sin and how it originally separated us from God at the time of the Adamic Fall. Consequently, they fall short of acknowledging the evil within themselves. And, as long as they walk in such darkness, they can never be genuinely penitent because they see no need for repentance or for penitent holy living. They have fooled themselves and are, therefore, foolish.

Yes, it is true that we are not really separate from God or from each other, but this is only true for those who acknowledge that Jesus Christ is the only-begotten Son of God and who accept his shed blood as the only sacrifice acceptable to God the Father for their sins; and it is true that we are made whole individually, collectively, and corporately as well as made one with God and each other, but this is only true through the atonement of Jesus Christ on the cross by the shedding of his blood for our iniquity and sin. Paradoxically, it is often poorly-educated believers who understand and accept without question the substitutionary atonement of Jesus Christ. This is most unfortunate, both for themselves and for their highly-educated Christian siblings. It is most unfortunate for their highly-educated siblings because the highly-educated often feel a huge disconnect with poorly-educated believers and, therefore, fail to appreciate the profound nature of simple faith. And it is most unfortunate for the poorly-educated believers because, without the necessary tools of analytical thinking derived from higher education, they often fall prey to warped and

---

41   Revelation 19:10, King James Version

twisted so-called Christian doctrines, especially those with great emotional appeal. (Make no mistake, one can be gifted enough to discern and apprehend spiritual truth without being highly educated, but that is the exception rather than the rule.)

In the previous paragraph, I used the expression "made one with God." The Biblical concept of being made one with God is best expressed by this prayer of Jesus Christ:

> *{11} "And now I am no more in the world, but these are in the world, and I come to You. Holy Father, keep through Your Own Name those whom You have given me, that they may be one, as we are one. {20} Neither pray I for these alone, but for them also which shall believe on me through their word;[42] {21} That they all may be one; as You, Father, are in me, and I in You, that they also may be one in us: that the world may believe that You have sent me. {22} And the glory which You gave me I have given them; that they may be one, even as we are one: {23} I in them, and You in me, that they may be made perfect in one; and that the world may know that You have sent me, and have loved them, as You have loved me."*
>
> JOHN 17:11, 20-23 KJV (PARAPHRASE)

All life is from the one true and only real God, consisting of Father, Son, and Holy Spirit. We are only made one with God the Father and each other through our demonstrated belief in God the Son (i.e., through our confession and profession of Jesus). To begin to understand this, one needs to begin to understand the concept of spiritual purity at the highest level, which is achieved only through accepting the shed blood of Jesus Christ. One also needs to understand that only what is holy can be spiritually pure. In

---

42 If we truly believe Jesus Christ to be our personal Savior, then we must not be ashamed to share that truth with others through spoken confession and profession of our faith in him.

contrast, what is unholy is spiritually impure. In metaphysical reality, there is no such thing as *pure* evil. To be sure, evil exists, but it is never pure. (What people are trying to say in using the expression "pure evil" is actually "unmitigated evil.")

The shape and size of cells are greatly dependent on the physical characteristics of surface area, volume, and viscosity as they relate to diffusion rates. The rates of diffusion of nutrients into cells — and of excretory products out of cells — greatly depend on the surface area to volume ratio of the individual cells (i.e., how much surface is available in proportion to their size) as well as the viscosity (i.e., the density or thickness) of the protoplasm within them.

The greater the surface area to volume ratio of an individual cell, the faster the rate of diffusion of nutrients into and throughout the cell and, concomitantly, the faster the rate of diffusion of excretory products out of the cell. And the greater the viscosity of each cell's protoplasm, the slower the rate of diffusion of nutrients into and throughout the cell and, concomitantly, the slower the rate of diffusion of excretory products out of the cell. Rates of diffusion help to determine cellular efficiency. Both a smaller surface area to volume ratio and a greater viscosity of protoplasm diminish cellular efficiency.

Thus, surface area, volume, viscosity, and diffusion rates all serve as limiting factors for the sizes and shapes of cells and, therefore, indirectly for the sizes and shapes of entire organisms. To be sure, there are some cells within the human body that are quite long (i.e., certain neurons are up to one meter in length and some skeletal muscle cells are up to 0.3 meter in length), but their thickness is minuscule. For multicellular organisms, contributing to the limitation for both size and shape of the entire organism is the efficiency of the various organ systems that: (1) assimilate through the digestive and respiratory systems nutrients destined for all of the cells of the body; (2) carry those nutrients to the cells of the body through the cardiovascular and lymphatic systems; and (3) dispose of waste products from the various cells of the body through the cardiovascular, digestive, and urinary systems.

Because there are no such constraints in the world of Spirit, the shapes and sizes of living things, whose substance is *astral gelatinous*™, cannot be measured in terms of three, four or five dimensions.[43] To be sure, when *astral gelatinous*™ life forms "step into" physicality,[44] they exhibit the properties and characteristics of the biological life forms common to where they enter. However, because such an entrance is extremely rare, the majority of life forms that remain *astral gelatinous*™ in nature[45] always retain the characteristics and properties associated with spiritual, and not biological, life forms. Hence, they are not constrained by surface area, volume, viscosity, or diffusion rates. Nor are they constrained by the dimensions of (1) length, (2) width, (3) depth, (4) time, or (5) unified spatial force (i.e., the five major dimensions in the physical universe).

Thus, although spiritual life forms have a "skin," or outer covering, their skin is unlike the integument of human beings. Instead, their skin is an electromagnetic force field that reflects as well as emanates the spiritual light, or glory, of their Creator. (Please be assured that there is only one Creator.) And, although such reflected spiritual light vibrates and pulses, it is not at a rate associated with natural light, which has a velocity of 186,282 miles per second.[46] The velocity of spiritual light is immeasurable. And, although the qualities of spiritual light may be described, its quantities are indescribable. In its native state, spiritual light is neither quantum-based nor wavelength-based nor a combination of both. To be sure, the equation $E=mc^2$ is true for physicality (i.e., the physical universe) but not for spirituality (i.e., the spiritual

---

[43] The first four dimensions of the physical universe are commonly called length, width, depth (or height), and time. Because it is still debatable what to call the fifth dimension, the present author calls it "unified spatial force." (To the present author, "unified spatial force" includes quantum mechanics, wave theory, electromagnetism, and gravity.)

[44] See comments for Footnote 15.

[45] The word *nature* here means "essence."

[46] Velocities measured above 186,282 miles per second involve subatomic particles bouncing through unknown dimensions.

universe). In their native state, spiritual beings "wear white,"[47] or are "images in white," because they channel and reflect God's spiritual light. The Creator is not only the source of all life but also the source of all spiritual light, which is His "heavenly glory" or the "brightness" of His Supreme Being.

Emitting, emanating, and radiating spiritual light is characteristic of being holy. Because the Creator is holiness-in-itself, the Creator is holy without measure. Therefore, the Creator's purity is without measure and the degree and amount of spiritual light that the Creator emits, emanates, and radiates is also without measure. With some exceptions, human beings do not see the Creator's spiritual light because they live in physicality and are, therefore, corporeal beings. Corporeal beings cannot see the fullness of God's glory without being consumed by the brightness of His Supreme and Sovereign Being.

A Metaphysical Understanding of Skin

Metaphysically speaking, our true integument, or skin, is the delineation or outline of our spiritual somatic identity. In the world of Spirit, such delineation does not separate us from God or from each other. Like our corporeal skin, our spiritual skin is in a state of constant renewal. Unlike our corporeal skin, however, our spiritual skin does not age, wither, or die. Before the Adamic Fall, we were each covered by God's glory. This glory constituted our original covering as well as constitutes the covering to which the saved of Christ will be restored at the time of Christ's return. As human beings, we are covered by sin's thin skin because of the Adamic Fall.

Immediately after the Fall, both Adam and Eve realized that they were naked (Genesis 3:7, 10-11). At the same moment that they sinned against God by breaking His commandment not to eat from the Tree of Knowledge of Good and Evil, they were instantly

---

47 Revelation 1:1; 3:4-5 & 18; 4:4; 6:11; 7:9 & 13-14; 15:6; 19:8,14; 20:11 (King James Version)

denuded of the glory that they had had in God. They no longer reflected God's spiritual light because of the synchronous (1) coalescing of their spiritual energy and (2) concretioning of their fundamental substance: At the time of the Adamic Fall, their energy and substance changed from being free, unbound, and *astral gelatinous*™ to becoming constrained, bound, and *protoplasmic*. This occurred at the precise moment of the Adamic Fall. They were now human beings as we understand and know *Homo sapiens* today. They were no longer immortal and unfallen. They were now mortal and fallen. They no longer reflected God's glory because they no longer were continually bathed in the holiness of God's Presence.

The change in their outer covering from God's glory to human integument is figuratively referenced by the following Bible verse:

> *Unto Adam also and to his wife did the LORD God make coats of skins, and clothed them.*
>
> GENESIS 3:21 KJV

God's curse for their having transgressed His commandment included changing their outer "garment," "covering," or "skin" from spiritual substance to physical fabric. However, the so-called "coats of skins" that God provided to them at the time of their Fall were not woven out of cotton or linen but out of living cells and organic fibers. It is at the precise moment of their Fall that Adam and Eve were "clothed" by an integument of epidermis, dermis, and hypodermis.[48] They no longer had a spiritual outer covering. In fact, their entire somatic identity was changed from a spiritual body to a natural body (i.e., from a supernatural life form to a biological life form). Their souls were now trapped in physical and corruptible bodies subject to disease, deterioration, death, and decay!

After Moses spoke with the Lord God Almighty on Mount Sinai,

---

[48] The *hypodermis* is also known as the "subcutaneous layer." The hypodermis is usually continuous with superficial fascia and other connective tissue elements that underlie the dermis.

the exposed skin of his face reflected God's glory from having been in His Presence. The Bible records that Moses' face radiated:

> *{29} And it came to pass, when Moses came down from Mount Sinai with the two tablets of testimony in his hand, Moses did not know that the skin of his face shone while he talked with the LORD. {30} And when Aaron and all the children of Israel saw Moses, the skin of his face shone; and they were afraid to come near him.*
>
> EXODUS 34:29-30 KJV (PARAPHRASE)

Although Moses' body was made of unholy and impure *fallen substance,* it could not help but reflect God's glory, even if only to a limited extent. Moses' face did not radiate because it had a healthy glow from good circulation and heightened pigmentation; Moses' face radiated because it retained the reflected glory of God.

When the Prophet Daniel saw a heavenly messenger in a vision (possibly the Angel Gabriel[49]), he described his appearance as follows:

> *His body also was like beryl [or chrysolite], and his face as the appearance of lightning, and his eyes as lamps of fire, and his arms and his feet like in color to polished brass, and the voice of his words like the voice of a multitude.* [brackets mine]
>
> DANIEL 10:6 KJV

The heavenly appearance of an angel is relevant to this discussion because Jesus told us that, after we die, we would be "as [or like] the angels of God in heaven" (Matthew 22:30 KJV, brackets mine). In other words, in Heaven we will no longer have bodies composed of unholy and impure substance (i.e., fleshly

---

49   See Daniel 8:16.

bodies that are *protoplasmic)*. Instead, we will have bodies made of holy and pure substance (i.e., heavenly bodies that are *astral gelatinous*™). We will then emit, emanate, and radiate the reflected glory of God in the same way that Adam and Eve did before their Fall.

When we are in Heaven, perhaps we will reflect God's glory to the degree that we honored Him while we were on Earth. To be sure, the souls of all saved people are *justified* (that is, "made the same" in righteousness) by the shed blood of Jesus Christ, but our individual motives, intentions, and desires while on Earth may determine our degree of reflectance of God — which is to say, how bright we are — when we are in Heaven. *For example,* although cut gemstones made of pure diamond are all the same (i.e., they are each made of pure diamond), they differ from one another in type of cut and number of facets that collectively determine the degree of their reflectance of natural light. Similarly, brilliance in Heaven may be determined by the number and kinds of spiritual facets cut here on Earth based on our responses to suffering and adversity. Thus, the more facets we have in Heaven, the greater will be the degree of our reflectance of God's spiritual light and, thus, the more brilliant we are in His Glory.

Cut diamonds with their many facets serve as an excellent metaphor for the living stars of God. Although diamonds are not the source of light, they reflect natural light brilliantly. Likewise, although the living stars of God are not the source of God's brightness, they reflect God's glory radiantly. (See Figure One.)

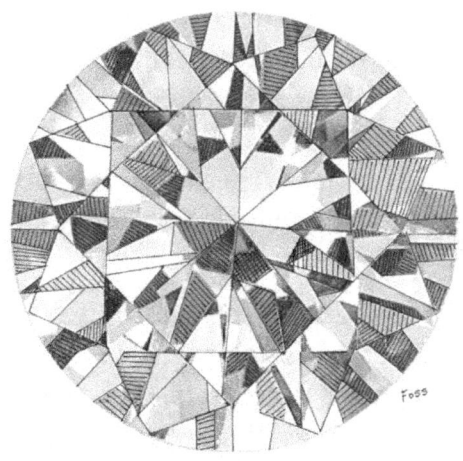

Cut Diamond with Multiple Facets
Figure One

When Jesus was transfigured on the mountain and Moses and Elijah appeared with him, all three of them literally stood in the Presence of God. Although Jesus was in physical form, that form underwent a metamorphosis (i.e., transfiguration), or "change in structure and appearance" (from the Greek *me-ta-mor-fo'-o* [G3339 in Appendix Table B]):

> *{1} And after six days Jesus took Peter, James, and John his brother, and brought them up into a high mountain, {2} And he was transfigured before them: and his face did shine as the sun, and his clothing was white as the light. {3} And, behold, there appeared unto them Moses and Elijah talking with him.*
>
> MATTHEW 17:1-3 KJV (PARAPHRASE)

Unlike Moses, who retained only a small degree of God's holiness in his radiant face after he received the Ten Commandments, Jesus was completely bathed in spiritual light because Jesus was pure and holy despite his presence in physicality. And both Moses and Elijah were completely bathed in spiritual light at the time of the transfiguration of Jesus because they no longer were in physicality. (Moses had died a natural death and Elijah had been carried directly to Heaven by a *chariot of fire*.[50])

Many years later, when the Apostle John saw the post-incarnate Christ, he described his appearance as follows:

> *{14} His head and his hairs were white like wool, as white as snow; and his eyes were as a flame of fire; {15} And his feet like unto fine brass, as if they burned in a furnace; and his voice as the sound of many waters.*
>
> REVELATION 1:14-15 KJV

(1) That Moses' earthly face shone, (2) that the Prophet Daniel saw the lightning-like appearance of a heavenly messenger, (3) that we will one day be like the angels in Heaven, (4) that Jesus was transfigured on the mountain, (5) that the departed Moses and Elijah appeared in the glory of God, and (6) that the Apostle John saw the glorified Christ: all provide us with a glimpse of — or insight into — how we shall appear when the somatic identities of saved people are fully restored to the glory of God at the Second Coming of His Christ:

> *In a moment, in the twinkling of an eye, at the last trump: for the trumpet shall sound, and the dead shall be raised incorruptible, and we [i.e., those still living on Earth] shall be changed.* [brackets mine]
>
> 1 CORINTHIANS 15:52 KJV

> *{2} Beloved, now are we the heirs of God, and it does not yet appear what we shall look like: but we know that, when Christ shall appear, we shall look like him; for we shall see him as he is. {3} And every person that*

---

50   2 Kings 2:11

has this hope in Christ purifies himself, even as Christ is pure.

1 JOHN 3:2-3 KJV (PARAPHRASE)

While he was still on Earth, Christ Jesus taught us that new wine should not be poured into old skins.[51] Germane to the discussion here, the expression "new wine" also represents our spiritually-restored identities and the expression "old skins" represents our current physical forms. To be sure, the changes that will take place at the Second Coming of Christ not only impact our integument but also our individual bodies.

Relative to our human integument, individuality is partly determined by concentration and type of skin pigmentation, skin texture, and elasticity as well as the presence or absence of whorls, ridges, lines, and furrows *(for example,* in fingerprints, palm prints, and footprints). In contrast, our spiritual identity is determined by the degree of reflectance of God's glory and the roles He has assigned to us to bless His Holy Name and the degree to which we carried them out while on Earth. Therefore, the questions that we should each be asking ourselves while on Earth include: (1) "Are we fulfilling God's destiny for us individually, collectively, and corporately?" And (2) "Are we reflecting God in all that we do?"

Treating Contagious Diseases and Malignancies of the Skin

The present author recommends that the following comments on skin-related disorders be generalized to include all infectious and contagious diseases regardless of organ system:

If skin-related disorders are infectious and contagious, they must be treated medically. To be sure, one may treat the condition medically in combination with other types of treatments. However,

---

51   Matthew 9:17 and Mark 2:22 — especially as rendered in Young's Literal Translation and the Darby Bible Translation.

in the interest of public health, the primary treatment must be medical. If patients are unwilling to be treated medically for a diagnosed contagious condition, they should be quarantined at a sliding scale cost to them and attended by practitioners and helpers who are willing to be placed at risk during their association with the infected person or persons, provided that the practitioners and helpers themselves are not serving as carriers or vectors of the disease for any other segment of the general population.

Adult patients have the right to decline any medical treatment for any reason. However, they do not have the right to put others at risk. If they put others at risk, especially those who are unwilling to be placed at risk, then they should lose their right to decline medical treatment for a condition that is diagnosed as infectious or contagious.

If judicious and circumspect provisions have been made for quarantine, then individuals may choose to decline the medical treatment of an infectious or contagious disease but only for themselves and not for anyone else — even for someone who is legally entrusted to their care. Why? No one has the right to limit care for someone else with an infectious or contagious disease. It is unfair to the patient and it is unfair to the public.

The present author supports the spiritual treatment of any and all disorders, diseases, ailments, illnesses, and syndromes with one stipulation, which is that no one else should be placed at medical risk because a patient opts out of medical treatment for an infectious or contagious disease. In addition, no legal custodian or guardian has the right to opt out of medical treatment for a ward with an infectious or contagious disease, including wards who are statutory minors. Addressing these issues helps to lay the foundation for a sensible and practical approach to spiritual healing that includes both intercessory prayer and metaphysical treatment.

The present author also recommends another sensible and practical approach for the majority of diagnosed malignancies that are localized. Cancerous lesions and tumors (as well as damaging benign growths) should be removed in accordance with the expert recommendation and skill of board-certified medical practitioners.

This issue is addressed here because many people who choose spiritual healing for physical disorders would view any medical intervention as a defeat when, in fact, it should not be viewed as such for malignant lesions and damaging benign growths. Just as spiritual malignancy should be identified and removed spiritually *(for example*, through exorcism), so should physical malignancy be diagnosed and removed physically *(for example*, through excision). This does not preclude spiritual treatment prior to, during, and/or after the removal.

It is important to have infectious and contagious diseases, as well as malignancies, credibly diagnosed by board-certified medical practitioners. The issue of diagnosis is addressed here because many people who choose spiritual healing would view naming a disease or malignancy as lending credibility (or "granting power") to the disorder when, in fact, naming a disease or malignancy does not remove power from the spiritual intercessor, prayer partner, or metaphysical practitioner: The name of Jesus Christ is still "above every name,"[52] including the name of every contagious disease and malignancy. All power in Heaven and on Earth has been irrevocably given to Jesus Christ.[53] Paradoxically, fleeing from the name of a diagnosable condition is often based on fear, ignorance, and superstition and is not representative of true spiritual power in Christ. Such flight represents dysfunctionality, ignorance, a desire for control, and/or arrogance. True spiritual power includes knowing exactly what you are up against and remaining steadfast in the Lord Jesus Christ despite the spiritual whores and hordes (i.e., lies and evil forces) against you.

No one who has a physical ailment should be embarrassed by its existence. Rather, a physical ailment should be viewed as a problem to be solved and a challenge to be resolved medically, psychologically, and spiritually. Embarrassment is an issue because many people of faith believe that they have insufficient, weak, or compromised faith because they have — or admit to having — an ailment, deformity, or disease. Such embarrassment is

---

52 Philippians 2:9, King James Version (see also Ephesians 1:21)
53 Matthew 28:19

unnecessary and a waste of time, effort, and energy; it can even hinder treatment. Embarrassment is a sign of fear that one is not in complete control when one thinks he or she should be in complete control. (Only God is in complete control.)

Skin ailments serve as a good example for the need to investigate the etiology, or cause, of each unhealthy condition. *For example,* just because someone's skin is jaundiced does not mean that a skin condition is the cause of the problem. Rather than a problem caused in or by the integument, the jaundice is more likely linked to a problem of the liver and/or the kidneys. *Similarly,* although persistent psoriasis is a horribly difficult skin rash to treat, its presence does not automatically mean that the origin of the problem can be traced back to the skin itself. Rather than a problem caused by the skin, psoriasis can be linked to rheumatoid arthritis, which is an autoimmune disorder associated with tissue much deeper than the skin. To be sure, not all physical ailments need to have a specific cause sought in order for them to be effectively treated medically, psychologically, and spiritually. However, knowing the cause can sometimes help to decide on the best method, best combination of methods, or the best sequence of methods for treatment.

Treating Malignancies Metaphysically

This section gives the present author an opportunity to discuss the metaphysical treatment of a human organ system (i.e., the integumentary system) that is relatively straightforward and easy to understand for beginning students of human anatomy and physiology who might also like to apply metaphysical principles in correcting disabilities, diseases, and disorders. Please know that the object of this book is not to get the reader to think exactly like its author but to help the reader to learn *how* to think metaphysically and intelligently (i.e., judiciously and circumspectly) at the same time: Thinking metaphysically and intelligently should not be mutually exclusive processes.

A great disadvantage for most practitioners of divine metaphysics is that they have not received an academic education in human anatomy and physiology. Due to this lack of education, they have a tendency to think about the human body in mysterious ways, often with magical thinking, misconclusions, and sweeping generalizations. In such ignorance, practitioners of divine metaphysics might conclude that ignoring an unhealthy physical condition will help to dispel its existence and — as a result of ignoring the condition — unwittingly and unnecessarily complicate (i.e., make worse) their lives or the lives of the people they are treating metaphysically.

For example, basal cell carcinoma is an easily understood non-melanoma cancer of the skin. One can't really ignore basal cell carcinoma in order for it to go away. In fact, ignoring basal cell carcinoma only permits it to spread to adjacent areas and deeper tissues. For that reason, basal cell carcinoma should be diagnosed and then medically treated as soon as possible because it can continue to spread to nearby areas if left untreated. Because it is such an easy disease to treat medically at its early stages, it is better to excise[54] basal cell carcinoma earlier than later, when more skin and underlying tissues might need to be removed. This is not to say that the condition of basal cell carcinoma can't be handled prayerfully and metaphysically at the same time that it is treated medically. Rather, it is to say that, once the disease has been diagnosed accurately by a medical practitioner, the condition should receive prompt medical treatment at the same time that the patient is receiving spiritual treatment. (The same is true for many other diseases.)

What are the benefits of prayer and metaphysical treatment if the disease is already being handled medically? Certainly, prayer helps us to be at peace with — or not be afraid of — unhealthy physical conditions by reminding us that we belong to God, the Source of all peace. And metaphysical treatment helps us to be at

---

54 Excision is not the only way to treat basal cell carcinoma medically. Other medical treatments include: (1) cryosurgery, (2) curettage and electro-dessication, (3) radiation, and (4) carcinoma-specific skin creams.

peace with an unhealthy physical condition by reminding us of who we really are in God and that our true identity is in Him. In prayer, we ask God that an unhealthy physical condition be removed from us and not recur. In metaphysical treatment, we declare (1) that we are already complete and perfect in God through the shed blood of Jesus Christ and (2) that God does not visit sickness upon those who belong to Him and abide by His Will. Simultaneously, we proclaim our gratitude to God for our already-existing wholeness in Him. Prayer invites God's active participation in our healing. Metaphysical treatment uses the tools that God has given to us for our return to a healthy equilibrium and equipoise. Prayer asks God for supernatural intervention (i.e., a miracle). Like prayer, divine metaphysics includes faith and trust in God, but divine metaphysics also includes realization and direct application of God's truth through affirmation, declaration, and proclamation of His goodness. To be sure, prayer and divine metaphysics go hand in hand when responding to unhealthy conditions.

Just as evil should be purged from our lives and this entire world, so should basal cell carcinoma be removed from the human body. If evil is attacking you, then you need to ask for deliverance from it by God and God will either remove the source of the evil from you or He will remove you from its source. In removing the source of the evil from you, God may give you the knowledge and strength to combat the evil yourself through Him. Or, in removing you from its source, God may actually have you remove yourself, not by fleeing in terror from evil but by recognizing that it may hurt or harm you emotionally, mentally, physically, and spiritually if you remain in its presence; then, God may have you cautiously remove yourself from its presence. Similarly, if basal cell carcinoma is encroaching upon your physical territory, then you need to ask for deliverance from it by God and God will either remove you from the basal cell carcinoma or He will remove the basal cell carcinoma from you. In removing it from you, God may actually have you remove the basal cell carcinoma from yourself by having it treated medically at the same time that you pray and trust God for its complete disappearance as well as non-recurrence.

Aren't you a traitor to divine metaphysics if you seek a medical remedy for an unhealthy physical condition? No, as students of divine metaphysics, you are still learning what applies where and when and how best to apply it. You are still learning how to depend on God as your sole source of life and well-being and how to apply that dependence to solve challenges practically. God does not judge or condemn any of us for using all of the resources He has made available, some of which have been made available through medical education and training. Every ailment should be carefully considered, and all options for treating an ailment should be considered. Treatment plans need to be comprehensive.

Never be embarrassed by a physical, mental, emotional, or spiritual problem. Ironically, pretending that it does not exist grants power to it. Divine metaphysics is not built on pretense but on knowledge, intelligence, and commitment.

Part Two: Skeletal Muscle

Categories of Muscle

Muscle is categorized based on its histologic (i.e., microscopic) appearance and type of control. Skeletal muscle is voluntary and striated. Skeletal muscle is: (1) "voluntary" because its contractions are consciously controlled; and (2) "striated" because its stripes, or striations, can easily be seen microscopically. Cardiac muscle is also striated but involuntary (i.e., not consciously controlled). Smooth muscle is involuntary and called "smooth" because it lacks a banding pattern when viewed with a light microscope. Cardiac muscle will be discussed in the chapter on divine metaphysics of the cardiovascular system. And smooth muscle will be discussed in the chapters on divine metaphysics of the cardiovascular, digestive, respiratory, and urinary systems. A discussion of skeletal muscle is reserved for this chapter.

The Meat of Skeletal Muscle

Regardless of Bible translation or version, the word *muscle* is rarely used in the Holy Bible even though skeletal muscle is often referred to by other words, such as "flesh" and "meat." However, even the words "flesh" and "meat" do not always refer to skeletal muscle. Depending on its use in context, the word *flesh* in the Bible can mean: (1) all of humankind; (2) the entire human body; (3) individuals related genetically (i.e., "by blood" or through shared ancestry); (4) individuals united by a covenant ratified via an exchange of material goods, vows, and/or bodily fluids; (5) corporeal substance that is corruptible and, therefore, temporal; (6) carnal desires; (7) genitals; (8) all tissues of the body except blood; (9) soft tissues of the body; (10) the integument alone; (11) the integument plus underlying connective tissue and muscle; or (12) skeletal muscle alone.[55] Similarly, *meat* has multiple meanings in the Holy Bible, including: (1) substance, (2) food, (3) nourishment, (4) fuel, (5) prey, and (6) animal skeletal muscle.

The skeletal system provides basic anatomic structure and shape to the human body (and will be discussed in the next chapter), but the muscular system helps provide form and physique to the human body. To be sure, accomplished portrait artists who draw or paint human nudes know much about bones, bone markings, and the relationship of those markings to skeletal muscle size, geometry, and action, but it is the skeletal muscles themselves — captured on paper, canvas, or digital screen — that produce the aesthetic by suggesting motion, mood, and affect, all of which especially evoke emotional responses from individual viewers. Skeletal muscles: (1) add beauty to the boney[56] frame of the body; (2) display character and attitude through carriage, gait, and gesticulation; and (3) help define the human form in a way unlike any other organ system.

---

55 Regardless of its macroscopic appearance (i.e., gross anatomic structure), the microscopic appearance (i.e., histologic structure) of muscle reveals that connective tissue is always in association with muscle.
56 The adjective *boney* can also be spelled *bony*.

Metaphysically speaking, skeletal muscle represents strength and movement. Skeletal muscle represents strength because the more exercised a body portion or part is, the more clearly defined are its muscles and the greater capability the muscles have for exerting and withstanding force. Skeletal muscle represents movement because it is not only responsible for mobility (i.e., "locomotion" or external body movement) but also for some motility (internal body movement).[57]

Although strength and movement exist in the world of Spirit, strength and movement are not dependent on muscles there. Indeed, skeletal muscles — as we know and understand them — do not exist in the Kingdom of God. Although we are not disjointed in the world of Spirit, we have no body joints to exert force upon and, hence, skeletal muscles are unnecessary. Scripture states that "flesh and blood cannot inherit [or enter into] the Kingdom of God"[58] because flesh and blood are not needed there and because physical systems cannot exist in a spiritual state. (As members of the Body of Christ, saved human beings articulate with one another but only in a metaphysical sense.)

To be sure, souls wedded to God will each possess a somatic identity in the world of Spirit but their form will be of an *astral gelatinous*™ composition. The living substance of an *astral gelatinous*™ body moves but does not need to counteract gravity or other opposing physical forces. Thus, not only do the souls of saved people "live and move and have their being"[59] in Jesus Christ while they are on Earth, their redeemed bodies "live and move and have their being" in Jesus Christ as well.[60] (Remember, saved souls

---

57   To be sure, not all contractions of skeletal muscle produce movement. Some partial states of sustained contraction contribute to posture and conscious immobility (i.e., purposely remaining in a particular position for a prolonged period of time).

58   1 Corinthians 15:50, King James Version [brackets mine]

59   Acts 17:28, King James Version (Paraphrase)

60   Although some souls are "saved" during their sojourn on Earth, their bodies are not "redeemed," "resurrected," or "restored" until the Second Coming of Jesus Christ. See the King James Version of 1 John 3:2-3, 1 Corinthians 15:52, and Romans 8:23.

do not receive their redeemed, resurrected, or restored bodies until the Second Coming of Jesus Christ.[61]) Concerning mobility in the world of Spirit, thinking makes it so. In other words, as we desire to be somewhere in the world of Spirit, we are there immediately! And, concerning strength in the world of Spirit, all power rests in God through Jesus Christ. In other words, no one possesses power without Jesus Christ, who is the source of all power. Regardless of place or state of being, true power is never derived from musculature.

That we have been created with an imagination permits us to understand movement in the world of Spirit. Nothing constrains our imaginations except the constructs and beliefs we have been taught and have accepted as true. Imagination should be free to wander, provided that it neither reigns over us nor focuses on carnal desires. When we are awake, our imagination permits us to move effortlessly. And, when we are asleep, our imagination has even greater freedom of movement in dreams. In the world of Spirit, our imagination is an extension of our volition or free will and self-control. After we have returned to be with God, we will dwell only within Him and never outside of Him. Thus returned, when we "imagine" ourselves to be somewhere within the Kingdom of God, it is because we want to be there and, consequently, are there *instantly!*

Of course, it is true that there is no spot in Heaven where God is not. On Earth, however, there are plenty of spots where God is not, even though He is aware of everything and knows all because He is omniscient. In Heaven, there are no places off limits to those who

---

61   For the sake of clarification, all souls saved before the Second Coming of Jesus Christ receive their redeemed, resurrected, or restored bodies upon his Return. All souls saved during *the Millennium* of Peace (when Jesus Christ rules from Earth after his Return) will receive their redeemed, resurrected, or restored bodies at the Great White Throne Judgment, which is presented in Chapter Twenty of The Book of Revelation in the Holy Bible. The Great White Throne Judgment is at the end of World War IV (known in *Revelation* as the Battle of Gog and Magog). That battle follows *the Millennium* of Peace and precedes the creation of "a new heaven and a new earth" (Revelation 21:1 KJV).

live there. For the sake of clarification, souls in Heaven are not permitted to communicate with — or appear to — souls in dust (i.e., human beings) unless it is within God's Will for them to do so. Souls in dust live in a quarantine zone and must learn to depend on God and not on souls in Heaven or on angels. That is why communications and appearances from souls in Heaven or from angels are rare for us on Earth. Moreover, hearing our prayers is not the business of angels or souls in Heaven (i.e., saints) nor is it their desire to be worshiped. Although angels and souls in Heaven are *of God,* they are *not God.* They know and understand this much better than we.

Energy, Opposing Forces, and Muscle Fatigue

The most efficient muscle contractions require not only calcium ions and glucose but also oxygen and stored energy in the form of adenosine triphosphate (ATP). Without sufficient quantities of any one of these, muscle contractions either will not take place at all, or they will not take place at their greatest strength or for the longest duration possible. However, even with sufficient quantities of those requirements, muscle cells lose tension because of muscle fatigue during sustained contractions as well as rapid contractions in succession, which fatigue is partly due to oxygen debt and the excess accumulation of lactic acid. In other words, regardless of their exercised condition and tone, muscles are still organic and, therefore, subject to the physiologic constraints unique to them. Skeletal muscles fatigue in sustained and/or rapidly repeated contractions depending on opposing forces. The strength of opposing forces is determined by: (1) the mass of the object or body part to be held stationary and/or moved; (2) the direction in which it is to be moved; (3) the distance it is to be moved; and (4) the velocity at which it is to be moved. Muscles that act antagonistically to an action also provide resistance (similar to a carried load) when they are contracted.

Actions in the world of Spirit require energy but not the energy associated with human physiologic processes. Within the cells of living organisms on Earth, energy is released when certain chemical bonds are broken[62] and exchanged or stored when chemical bonds are formed. In contrast, living and moving beings in the world of Spirit are supernaturally abiological.[63] They live and move and have their being in God without constraint. To be sure, their spirits and souls are energy-based, but the energy used in the world of Spirit does not consist of quanta (i.e., discrete bundles) nor does it travel in wavelengths. Although spiritual energy might occasionally be observed and measured with physical instrumentation during the recording of some paranormal events, it does not mean that the source of such energy is physical in nature.

Because spiritual warfare is not yet over (complete and perfect peace does not reign eternally until "a new heaven and a new earth"[64] are created circa 3000 A.D.), opposing spiritual forces still exist within an invisible realm associated with the current earth plane of consciousness. In contrast, opposing forces no longer exist within Heaven. In fact, after the ascension of Jesus Christ to rule from Heaven,[65] Satan and the angels who followed Satan were permanently thrown out of Heaven:

> *{7} And there was war in heaven: Michael and his angels fought against the dragon; and the dragon fought and his angels, {8} And they prevailed not; neither was their place found any more in heaven. {9} And the great dragon was cast out, that old serpent, called the Devil, and Satan, who deceives the whole world: he was cast out into the Earth, and his angels were cast out with him. {12} Therefore, rejoice you heavens and you that dwell in them. Woe to the*

---

62 Not all energy released is usable chemical energy.
63 Although the word *abiological* commonly refers to inanimate objects, the word here is meant to convey "without the substance of biological life (i.e., without protoplasm)." For the purposes of this book, "spiritually extrabiological" and "abiological" are synonymous.
64 Revelation 21:1, King James Version
65 Revelation 12:5

inhabitants of the earth and of the sea, for the Devil has come down to you, having great wrath because he knows that he has but a short time.

REVELATION 12:7-9 & 12 KJV (PARAPHRASE)

Energy is expended by angels and souls in Heaven who minister to souls in dust, especially when they help us fight demonic forces now in operation throughout this world of appearances. However, although they expend energy in such activity, their energy is not dissipated. Instead, in the long term, their energy increases exponentially by favorably impacting the people of God who are still on Earth.

Because all flesh is temporal, all flesh goes the way of grass — meaning, it withers and dies:

For all flesh is as grass, and all the glory of human beings as the flower of grass. The grass withers, and its flowers fall away.

1 PETER 1:24 KJV (PARAPHRASE)

In Heaven, we will no longer be clothed by an outer garment of human skin and an undergarment of skeletal muscle and associated connective tissue. Rather, we will be clothed *by, with,* and *in* Christ — "because all of us who have been baptized into Christ are now wearing Christ."[66]

While we are still on Earth, let us make sure that our spiritual power does not atrophy through disuse. Let us exercise our faith by putting it to work for the Lord God Almighty in prayer and in praise through service to Him and to others in His Name. Indeed, we can become strong in these ways.

---

66 Galatians 3:27, King James Version (Paraphrase)

Metaphysical Treatment of Disability, Disorder, and Disease

The metaphysical treatment of disabilities, disorders, and diseases should be affirmational and not refutational. In other words, we should not say that there is no pain when pain exists. And we should not say that we do not have cancer when it has been diagnosed in us. Rather, we should proclaim in the face of pain: "God still provides for our every need!" And, regardless of a diagnosed cancer, we should affirm: "We are already whole in the reality of Christ!" Refutational statements that ascertain we don't have something when we do represent dysfunctionality and arrogantly imply that we are ready to take on the world alone through our own strength and power when, in the reality of God, we are only overcomers to the degree that we depend on Him and His power.

As stated earlier, all healing power proceeds and processes from the throne of God; and it courses through our human bodies only in accordance with the goodness of His Will. Rather than refuting the existence of disabilities, disorders, and diseases, we need to proclaim who we really are in God through Christ Jesus. We need to acknowledge that God's spiritual reality supersedes any and all physical reality. Affirming the truth of God is far more efficacious for treating disabilities, disorders, and diseases than refuting or ignoring their existence and pretending that they do not exist.

Rather than pretending that a condition does not exist or refuting its existence, mature authentic Christians can also use spiritual falconry in addition to prayer and affirmation. Spiritual falconry employs metaphysically-trained, self-disciplined thinking to target and hunt down unclean thoughts and unholy feelings within oneself much like a trained falcon soars after and captures targeted quarry when released in the wild. Spiritual falconry is very much a part of "bringing into captivity every thought [and feeling] to the obedience of Christ" (2 Corinthians 10:5 KJV, brackets mine). Even demons flee when they become aware of the presence of a spiritual falconer who trusts fully in the Lord Jesus Christ.

Refutation is largely an ineffective, passive process; in contrast, affirmation and spiritual falconry are effective, active processes when metaphysically treating oneself or others.

Chapter Questions

This section is intended to facilitate learning by providing relevant activities, exercises, and experiences to aid students of divine metaphysics in their quest for grasping spiritual concepts, integrating them into their own belief systems, holding them more assuredly, and making them more practical in daily life.

The following questions should be answered after reading each titled section. To answer a few of the questions, students may need to consult outside resources or external references. Students are also encouraged to answer these questions with others during group discussions.

The Delineation of Form

1. Explain how the characteristics of living things on Earth represent the metaphysical realities of living things in the spiritual universe.

2. Which characteristics does fire share with biological life forms?

3. Which characteristics of biological life forms does fire not possess?

4. (a) Using external resources, briefly discuss why viruses might be considered non-living by a philosopher-biologist (biologist-philosopher). (b) Explain what it means to be *submicroscopic, parasitic,* and *acellular.*

5. How is our integument related to how we perceive ourselves individually?

6. Discuss "me," "not me," "you and me," and "us all" as they relate to physical identity and spiritual identity.

7. (a) Based on this textbook, what do all living beings with souls have in common with each other? (b) Name a few common characteristics not mentioned in this textbook.

8. What spiritually delineates and distinguishes human beings from one another?

9. Review your answer to question number 16 from Chapter One and explain how both *expiation* and *propitiation* are complementary.

10. (a) Is it necessary to become highly educated academically to discern and apprehend spiritual truth? (b) Briefly explain your answer.

11. How are we made one with God and each other?

12. What is *diffusion* and how does it relate to the maximum volume of a cell?

13. What is *viscosity* and how does it relate to diffusion and the maximum volume of a cell?

14. The efficiency of which organ systems helps to determine the size of a multicellular organism?

15. Name the ways in which the skin of spiritual beings is unlike the skin of human beings?

16. Briefly discuss spiritual light in relationship to purity.

A Metaphysical Understanding of Skin

17. How were Adam and Eve "naked" after the Adamic Fall?

18. What happened to Adam and Eve's somatic identity (i.e., *astral gelatinous*™ body) at the precise moment of the Adamic Fall?

19. How might our appearance in Heaven be like a multifaceted cut diamond on Earth?

20. Discuss passages from the Holy Bible that imply we will be wearing the glory of God when we are in Heaven.

Treating Contagious Diseases and Malignancies of the Skin

21. Briefly discuss patient rights as they relate to skin infections and contagious diseases.

22. Briefly discuss primary causes as they relate to secondary conditions.

Treating Malignancies Metaphysically

23. When treating them metaphysically, should unhealthy physical conditions ever be ignored?

24. In what way is treating basal cell carcinoma a good model for treating many other diseases of the integumentary system as well as other organ systems?

25. (a) How do prayer and divine metaphysics differ from one another in the treatment of an unhealthy physical condition? (b) Are prayer and divine metaphysics complementary or contradictory to one another? (c) In what ways are intercessory prayer and metaphysical treatment similar?

26. Are you a traitor to divine metaphysics or your faith in God if you seek a physical or medical remedy for an unhealthy condition? Why or why not?

Categories of Muscle

27. What distinguishes skeletal muscle from cardiac muscle and smooth muscle?

The Meat of Skeletal Muscle

28. *Most words in the English language have multiple meanings and, therefore, must each be assigned a meaning based on its use in context.* How does this italicized statement pertain to the words "flesh" and "meat" in the King James Version of the Bible?

29. Provide dictionary definitions of *mobility* and *motility* as they relate to human structure and function.

30. Why are skeletal muscles unnecessary in the world of Spirit?

31. What does our imagination help us to understand relative to movement in Heaven (i.e., the world of Spirit)?

Energy, Opposing Forces, and Muscle Fatigue

32. Consult external resources to explain "oxygen debt" and "lactic acid" as they relate to muscle fatigue.

33. What opposing forces limit muscle contraction?

34. How is physical energy different from spiritual energy?

35. When were Satan and the angels who followed him thrown out of Heaven?

36. Does God's energy dissipate? Why or why not?

Metaphysical Treatment of Disability, Disorder, and Disease

37. Why is it more efficacious for metaphysical statements to be affirmational rather than refutational?

Chapter Three
Divine Metaphysics of the Skeletal System

This is what the LORD God says to these bones: I WILL MAKE BREATH[67] ENTER INTO YOU, AND YOU SHALL COME TO LIFE.

EZEKIEL 37:5 KJV (PARAPHRASE)

Introduction to the Skeletal System

Original, unfallen man (also referred to as "Man," "immortal man," "original mankind," "original man," and "unfallen man" by the present author) did not need a skeletal system (as we know it today) because original, unfallen man was weightless and, therefore, not subject to gravitation. Bones in fallen, corporeal man (that is, "*Homo sapiens*," "human beings," "humankind," "mortal man," and "corporeal man") are necessary because fallen, corporeal man is subject to gravitation.

---

67 The Hebrew word *ru'-wach* [H7307 in Appendix Table A], translated here as "breath," also means "spirit" or "life force."

Resistance to gravity by attached muscles contributes to the normal development and maintenance of the skeletal system. *For example:* (1) Because of the loss of skeletal muscle use in their appendages, quadriplegic children experience diminished linear bone growth, significant osteoporosis, and misshapen limbs; and (2) because of their weightlessness when in space, astronauts must perform special exercises to ensure that their bones do not lose density.

Bones help to hold up the human body against gravity by serving as anchors, levers, and fulcrums (i.e., *fulcra*) for skeletal muscles, whose contractions provide for both conscious movements and reflex movements as well as for normal muscle tone. Normal muscle tone is seen in the so-called "relaxed" anatomical position (that is, standing erect with face and palms forward, as shown in Figure Two).

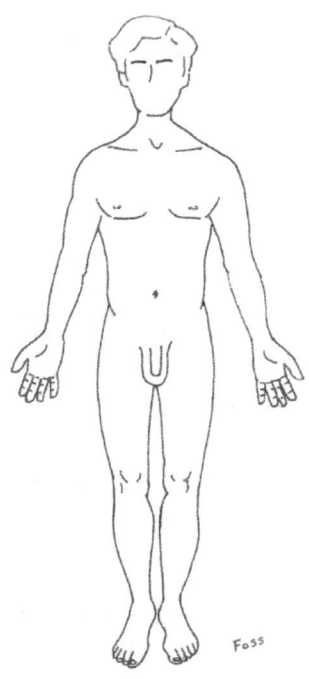

Anatomical (Anatomic) Position
Figure Two

In addition to mobility and posture, skeletal elements also help to protect various soft tissues found throughout the human body. In unfallen man, such protection was not necessary because the substance of our original creation was *astral gelatinous*™ and, therefore, incorruptible as well as incapable of being damaged, hurt, or harmed.

Connective Tissue

Histologically, the skeletal system of mortal man is composed of various connective tissues: (1) connective tissue proper, including loose connective tissue, elastic connective tissue, reticular connective tissue, dense (or fibrous) connective tissue, and adipose (or fat); (2) cartilage, including elastic cartilage, fibrous cartilage (or fibrocartilage), and hyaline cartilage; (3) bone (or osseous tissue), including spongy bone and dense bone; and (4) hematopoietic tissue (i.e., myeloid tissue or red bone marrow), which produces the formed elements in blood (i.e., blood cells as well as cellular fragments known as thrombocytes or platelets).

Relative to hematopoietic tissue, contemplating the Genesis account of the creation from a purely biological standpoint, one might conclude that Eve was simply a clone of Adam. Indeed, since God had already created Adam, there was no need for Him to create again. All God needed to do was to clone Eve from a primordial stem cell in Adam's red bone marrow — *for example,* from one of his ribs. To be sure, as physical descendants of Adam and Eve, we are all hybridized clones of Adam and Eve many generations far removed. Scripture teaches that all human beings were biologically in the "loins" of Adam at the time that Adam lived.[68] (Concerning hematopoietic tissue, read the chapter entitled *Divine Metaphysics of the Lymphatic System and Immunity.*)

Although they are part of the respiratory system, it could be argued that the larynx, trachea, and bronchi should be included in the skeletal system since their shapes are maintained and their

---

[68] This concept is acknowledged in Acts 2:29-30 and Hebrews 7:5-10.

passageways are kept open by cartilage. To be sure, I am not advocating such an inclusion. I merely mention this to emphasize that the general role of connective tissue is to provide support and protection as well as prevent collapse.

As indicated in Chapter One of this book, immediately after its conception the human body begins growing into its invisible electromagnetic body double through embryogenesis, histogenesis, and organogenesis. Areas that are eventually going to be bone are first laid down as connective tissue proper and cartilage, which are eventually replaced by true bone tissue in the case of dense bone (in contradistinction to calcified cartilage).

Bone is a special form of mineralized connective tissue. In other words, minerals impregnate connective tissue fibers — specifically, collagenous fibers — destined to become part of bone. Although the minerals may seem to be laid down in a rather haphazard pattern, deposition of calcium-containing compounds and molecules is highly organized. Organization is based on (1) polarity of the compounds and molecules and (2) the alignment of those compounds and molecules on invisible electromagnetic lines associated with the organic matrices that were first laid down before ossification.[69] Understanding the deposition of a boney matrix and its various compounds and molecules along electromagnetic lines, and in relationship to gravitation, requires an understanding of the rudiments of metallurgy and metallography as they relate to calcium's properties and its relative abundance on the planet Earth. At this point, students of divine metaphysics using this textbook are encouraged to research the properties of (1) the alkaline Earth metal *calcium* as well as (2) *calcium's* nearest neighbors on the periodic table.

---

69 Although the word *ossification* may be used interchangeably with *osteogenesis,* it can also refer more specifically to the deposition of bony matrix in developing bone tissue.

The Stellate Nature of Original Man

Leonardo da Vinci's famous depiction of mortal man in Figure Three provides visual clues to the original six-pointed, stellate nature of original, unfallen man:

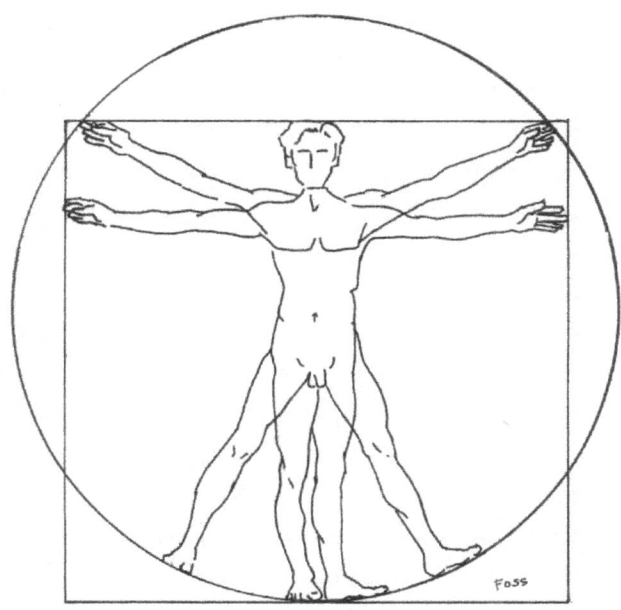

Representation of Sketch by
Leonardo da Vinci
Figure Three

The six-pointed, stellate nature of immortal man is retained in mortal man's four appendages (i.e., two arms and two legs) as well as two generative areas, one area found in between the arms (i.e., the head) and the other area in between the legs (i.e., the genitals). In immortal man, "arms" and "legs" are exactly the same size and shape. In mortal man, arms and legs are different from each other based on their different embryonic development patterns as well as their different functions and uses. Differences between the form and function of human arms and human legs are also based on how they are used in relation to gravitational pull from the mass of the planet Earth. Thus, appendages of extraterrestrial biological life forms elsewhere in the physical universe are different in appearance from forms on Earth based not only on the availability and properties of such elements as carbon and calcium (or similar elements, such as silicon and strontium) but also based on the different gravitational pulls of the individual planets on which extraterrestrial biological life forms develop. In other words, human morphogenesis is different from alien morphogenesis but they are both based on somewhat similar processes with slightly different results. Although the gross morphological differences between human beings and extraterrestrial biological life forms may seem to be significantly different, they are not. (The ability to simultaneously picture human and alien biological life forms requires superimposing multiverses of thought on one another in one's imagination.)

Despite the differences in their form and function, the skeletal pattern of a human arm is virtually the same as a human leg: the human arm has fourteen phalanges, five metacarpals, eight carpals, two lower arm bones (radius and ulna), and one upper arm bone (or humerus); and the human leg has fourteen phalanges, five metatarsals, seven tarsals, two lower leg bones (fibula and tibia), one patella and one upper leg bone (or femur).

The total number of bones in the human arm is thirty and the total number of bones in the human leg is thirty. One difference between the two types of appendages is in the number of carpals (eight) in the wrist of the hand and the number of tarsals (seven) in the ankle of the foot; however, that difference is negligible since the carpal bone in the foot known as the talus is probably a fusion of multiple bones. The only other major difference in bone numbers is due to the patella in the leg; however, this difference can be easily understood since the patella and the olecranon process (elbow), attached to the proximal[70] end of the ulna, fit the same general pattern for form and function.[71] There are significant similarities in

---

70   In this case, *proximal* means "closest to the midline of the body."

71   It is important to note that other anatomists might take issue with the present author's comparison of the patella and the olecranon process of the ulna because of differences in their histology and development. The patella is a sesamoid bone, but the olecranon is not. (The present author

the shoulder and the hip. When studying the appendages and their respective girdles, students of human anatomy should look for, and identify, these similarities.

The six-pointed, stellate nature of immortal man is also represented by the Star of David, which is composed of two triangles, as shown in Figure Four:

Interlocking Triangles of the Star of David
Figure Four

One triangle in the Star of David represents the tripartite nature of the Supreme Being as *God the Father, God the Son,* and *God the Holy Spirit.*[72] The other triangle represents the tripartite nature of immortal man as body (one's somatic identity), soul, and spirit.[73]

---

would respond that, although the patella and olecranon process of the ulna are not perfectly homologous or perfectly analogous, he is simply generalizing about similarities in their forms and functions.)

72 Matthew 28:19
73 1 Thessalonians 5:23, King James Version

The Star of David is designed to show many things, including that the Creator and His created are complementary to each other and that each created being is an interlocking mirror image, or inverted image, of the Creator.

The Creator and His created are not really complete without each other only because the Creator has designed, determined, and deigned it to be so and not because we are, or ever will be, equal to the Creator. Although we collectively and corporately constitute the Creator's companion, or *bride,* we are not now, and never will be, the Creator. Although the saved of Christ are individually, collectively, and corporately indwelt by God through His Holy Spirit, we are not now, and never will be, the Creator. And, although one day we individually, collectively, and corporately will be infused by the Creator at the time of the end, when God the Son presents us to God the Father (at which time there will also be "a new heaven and a new earth"),[74] we are not now, and never will be, the Creator. We are only "co-creators" with God in the very loosest sense because the Creator can choose to create *through* us. Human beings are not supreme beings nor destined to become supreme beings. It was thinking that we could become supreme beings that got us into trouble in the first place.[75] To be sure, in that we were originally created in the complete image and perfect likeness of the Creator, each one of us has a creative consciousness, but that does not make us supreme beings, destined to be supreme beings, or equal to the Lord God Almighty. If the word *gods* is defined as "immortal beings" *(for example,* from *elohim* in the Hebrew of Psalm 82:6), then saved souls are destined to become *gods* but only in that sense.

The spirit and soul of a person are basically amorphous (that is, without shape). The somatic identity of original, unfallen man had shape, just as the somatic identity of fallen, corporeal man has shape. The somatic identity of fallen, corporeal man is the human body, which is corrupt and corruptible. The human body is a corrupted version of original, unfallen man. Fallen man is subject

---

74 1 Corinthians 15:28 and Revelation 21:1
75 Genesis 3:5

to deterioration, disease, death, and decay. Unfallen man was not subject to such changes or events.

For the sake of clarification, the words "spirit" and "soul" are often used interchangeably in the Holy Bible. That is because they are really *indivisible* from one another even though they are *distinguishable* from one another. Pure[76] sugar water provides a good physical analogy for "spirit" and "soul." Under normal circumstances and conditions, one cannot separate sugar that has been added to water to make pure sugar water. Of course, one could heat the sugar water until all water evaporates and the sugar remains; or one could supersaturate the water by continuously adding more sugar until the sugar separates out by recrystallizing. Similarly (that is, under normal circumstances and conditions), one can't separate the soul from its spirit or life force even though one can discuss each of them separately and, in that sense, distinguish them.

Based on the two Greek words used in the New Testament for "spirit" and "soul," *pneu'-ma* [G4151 in Appendix Table B] (spirit, life force, or breath) and *psu-khay'* [G5590 in Appendix Table B] (soul), one might define *spirit* as "the invisible essence of a being characterized by its unique personality" and *soul* as "the seat of an immortal and moral being's thoughts and feelings that impart its unique personality." (These definitions have been extrapolated by the present author from a variety of sources.)

Highly educated philosophers, theologians, historians, and linguists might spend their entire academic lives trying to elucidate and clarify the differences between the "spirit" and the "soul" of an immortal and moral being. So, we will leave that debate to them. Suffice it to say at this point, the "spirit" and "soul" of an immortal and moral being are like pure sugar water. They are indivisible from one another under normal circumstances and conditions. However, together, one's "spirit" and "soul" are not only distinguishable but also divisible from one's somatic identity even though the spirit and soul influence one's outward form, likeness, and appearance.

---

76   Here, the word *pure* means "without impurities."

Although God the Holy Spirit is amorphous, God the Father and God the Son both have somatic identities. (Indeed, to be a son, one must look like one's father.) Unfortunately, many people resist the notion that God the Father has a somatic identity: (1) partly because of the fiery appearance of the Lord God Almighty presented in the Old Testament; (2) partly because of the fantastic descriptions of the Lord God Almighty in Ezekiel, Isaiah, and Revelation; and (3) partly because of people's resistance to the literal anthropomorphization of Deity.

For the sake of clarity, "literal anthropomorphization of Deity" occurs whenever we assign human qualities to God. The literal anthropomorphization of Deity makes God too small (that is, with weaknesses, vulnerabilities, and infirmities), just as the figurative (or symbolic) representation of Deity as only a supernatural force makes God too big (that is, impersonal and inaccessible). So, we need to be careful not to anthropomorphize God the Father as well as not to amorphize Him (i.e., conceptualize Him as a *being* without form or shape).

If God the Father were amorphous, (1) He would not have been able to walk in the Garden of Eden in the cool of the day (Genesis 3:8); (2) He would not have been able to fight physically with Jacob at Peniel (Genesis 32:24-32); (3) He would not have been able to show Moses the "hinterparts" (i.e., back parts) of His Form (Exodus 33:18-23); (4) the Prophet Isaiah would not have been able to see the appearance of the LORD of Hosts (Isaiah 6:1-9); (5) the Prophet Ezekiel would not have been able to see "the appearance of the likeness of the glory of the LORD" upon His throne (Ezekiel 1:26-28); and (6) the Prophet Daniel would not have been able to describe the appearance of "the Ancient of Days" (Daniel 7:9-10).

Although we can describe Deity in terms of original, unfallen man (because original man was made in the complete image and perfect likeness of God), we are not able to as easily work backwards (i.e., regress) from the somatic identity of fallen, corporeal man to the somatic identity of God the Father because of the extra inserted step — which step is "the Adamic Fall." Nevertheless, we can elucidate God the Father's appearance by gaining insight from the Holy Bible.

That our somatic identity resembles God the Father's somatic identity is supported by the reference to "the Ancient of Days" in Chapter Seven of the Book of Daniel:

> *{9} I beheld until the thrones [or earthly powers] were cast down, and the Ancient of Days did sit, whose garment was white as snow, and the hair of His head like pure wool: His throne was like the fiery flame, and His wheels [or energy vortices] as burning fire. {10} A fiery stream issued and came forth from before Him: millions ministered unto Him, and tens of millions stood before Him: the judgment was set, and the books were opened.*[77]
>
> DANIEL 7:9-10 KJV (PARAPHRASE)

Although you might think, or have been taught, that verses 9 and 10 are describing the appearance of the Lord Jesus Christ, the "Ancient of Days" refers to *God the Father* because "the Son of Man" from verses 13 and 14 of the same chapter of Daniel clearly refers to *God the Son* (who is, of course, Jesus Christ):

> *{13} I saw in the night visions, and behold, one like the Son of Man [God the Son] came with the clouds of heaven, and came to the Ancient of Days [God the Father], and they brought him before Him [brought God the Son before God the Father]. {14} And there was given him [God the Son] dominion, and glory, and a kingdom that all people, nations, and languages should serve him [God the Son]: his [the Son's] dominion is an everlasting dominion, which shall not pass away, and his [the Son's] kingdom shall not be destroyed.*[78]
>
> DANIEL 7:13-14 (PARAPHRASE)

---

[77] This judgment is the "Great White Throne" Judgment described in Revelation 20:11-15.

[78] Compare with Matthew 28:18.

Although God is Spirit,[79] whose totality of Being cannot be seen by human beings without their physical annihilation,[80] God the Father has a somatic identity that can step into physicality on occasion. *For example,* Jacob fought with God at Peniel when God chose to step into corporeality (Genesis 32:22-32). This, of course, presupposes an appearance at Peniel by God the Father rather than a theophany[81] by God the Son. (It is obvious that God would have had to *throw the fight* [82] at Peniel for Jacob to win.)

The somatic identity of unfallen man had a shape, just as the somatic identity of fallen man has a shape. The former is supernatural and spiritual and understood metaphysically; the latter is natural and corporeal and understood physically. Indeed, the two shapes are different. The shape of fallen man is merely a shadow and corruption (i.e., holographic distortion) of the perfect likeness of God that original, unfallen man possessed. The shape of fallen man is three dimensional in a physical universe; the shape of original, unfallen man was dimensionless in a spiritual universe.

Concerning God the Father's somatic identity, we must seek to understand it metaphysically, not physically. If you focus on God the Father conceptually, then you, too, will begin to see His Form take shape in the fabric of His spiritual universe. Neither phantasm nor phantom, God the Father is every bit *phenomenon* as He is *noumenon* (or causality). Today, God the Father shows Himself to all whom He will through His only-begotten Son, Jesus Christ. To be sure, conceptualizing God the Father's somatic identity is as difficult as conceptualizing His intellect.

---

79 John 4:24
80 Exodus 33:20
81 "Theophany" generally refers to an appearance by the pre-incarnate Christ during Old Testament times.
82 "Throw the fight" is an English idiom that means "lose on purpose."

The Head and the Skull

Both physically and metaphysically, the head of anything is always the most important part. Indeed, the head represents the most important part of the spiritual universe as the tripartite "Godhead,"[83] the totality of whose Being infuses the entire spiritual universe and whose Spirit resides within all saved people both in Heaven and on Earth. The head also represents Jesus Christ, who reigns over the entire Church — which is to say, his Body — as its Lord and Sovereign Savior.[84]

The human head represents: (1) all self-volition; (2) all thinking and feeling associated with personal free will; and (3) the main control center over involuntary reflexes for each human body. As such, the human head is the center of all senses, sensibilities, communications, conclusions, and actions that serve as parables, figures, types, and allegories of the Creator's intimate relationship with His created.[85] This last statement is not designed to take away from the function of the divine Logos as Creator[86] but to affirm the unity[87] of the Godhead and the relationship that the Godhead has to all created beings as their sole source of life.

Biblically speaking, the top surface of the human head represents the site of God's blessing and anointing. This is exemplified by the "laying on of hands" with oil that is often mentioned in the Holy Bible. The human head also represents the site of the body upon which God metes out His divine justice to recalcitrant and recidivist human beings who repeatedly reject His only-begotten Son as Lord and Savior. To be sure, God's Wrath upon those who consciously and continuously reject Christ Jesus as

---

83 The word *Godhead* is used in the King James Version of Acts 17:29, Romans 1:20, and Colossians 2:9.
84 See the King James Version of Ephesians 5:23 and Colossians 1:18.
85 Hebrews 8:5
86 *Word* in Greek is *lo'-gos* [G3056 in Appendix Table B] and often refers to "God the Son" in the Holy Bible, especially in the works of the Apostle John. See John 1:1-5 and Revelation 19:13 in the King James Version.
87 Deuteronomy 6:4

only-begotten Son of God and only Savior of the world is their just recompense.

The human head also represents the place where communion with God takes place. That is why "bowing the head" by bending the neck signals humility and reverence when worshiping God and praying to Him. And the human head carries the burdens of the human heart. That is why ashes and dirt are sometimes placed upon the head as a sign of grief, sorrow, and mourning.

The forehead is an important site metaphysically for people of different religious backgrounds. For Jews, the forehead is one of the two sites where they are to bind the tefillin (singular *tefilah*), or phylacteries, which contain at least the following two verses from the Bible:

> *{4} Hear, O Israel: the LORD our God, the LORD is one. {5} And you shall love the LORD your God with all your heart, and with all your soul, and with all your might.*
>
> DEUTERONOMY 6:4-5 KJV

Head Tefilah or Shel-Rosh
Figure Five

For Christians, the forehead is the site where the *Name of God the Father,* the *Name of the City of New Jerusalem,* and the *New Name of Jesus Christ* will be written.[88] The forehead is also the site where the saved of God on Earth are sealed for protection against the Wrath of God while they are still in fleshly bodies.[89] In these ways, the forehead especially represents connection to God for Christians and Jews, both of whom are the chosen people of God.

To be sure, the human head rules over the passions and lusts of the human body but only when the Lord God Almighty sits fully enthroned within it through His Holy Spirit. (Remember, Satan is always trying to unseat the Lord from our consciousness by getting us to exalt ourselves above the one true and only real God.)

The Cranial Cavity and the Mercy Seat of God

The Mercy Seat of God is part of God's throne. Yes, all of Heaven is God's throne,[90] the place where God's Presence resides or is "seated." And, to be sure, God's Presence has been seen visibly on Earth as His Shekinah, or cloud of "heavenly glory." But the Mercy Seat was that specific place from which God communed with His created — that is, the place from which God spoke to original Man as well as the place where He spoke to the Old Testament people of God.

In Mosaic Law, God's Mercy Seat is described in Chapter Twenty-Five of the Book of Exodus as the cover or lid of the Ark of the Covenant. Upon the lid were found two cherubs (or *cherubim*), who face each other with their wings outstretched. It is upon (and in front of) this Mercy Seat that Aaron — and each successive high priest after Aaron — would sprinkle the blood of bullocks and the blood of goats to make atonement for the sins of the people of

---

88   Revelation 3:12; 14:1; 22:4
89   Revelation 7:3; 9:4
90   Isaiah 66:1; Matthew 5:34; Matthew 23:22; Acts 7:49

Israel.[91]

Ark of the Covenant in the Holy of Holies
Figure Six

In the New Testament dispensation of God's grace through the sacrificial offering of His only-begotten Son, God's Mercy Seat is now located — metaphorically and metaphysically[92] — within the temple of the Holy Spirit. This temple not only includes the physical body but also the etheric and electromagnetic body double (i.e., the subtle body) of each authentic Christian believer.[93] Today, Christ Jesus sits enthroned within the soul of every authentic Christian believer and serves as God's High Priest, or only Mediator, between God the Father and each believer. Indeed, the shed blood of Jesus the Messiah, Y'shua H'Moshiach, has been eternally sprinkled on the Mercy Seat — once and for all[94] — for

---

91 Leviticus 16:14-15
92 Hebrews 9:24
93 1 Corinthians 6:19
94 Hebrews 10:10

every soul restored to God. Consequently, God communes directly with each Christian believer through His Holy Spirit, or Soul.

Although the individual soul of every authentic Christian believer is eternally saved and fully restored, the human body remains in a fallen, or corrupted, state. However, despite that body's corrupted state, we find a vestige of the original Mercy Seat once located in each unfallen created being. The vestige of this Mercy Seat in our fallen, or corruptible, bodies is found in the sphenoid bone of the cranial floor. The sella turcica (or "Turkish saddle") shown in Figure Seven is part of the sphenoid bone:

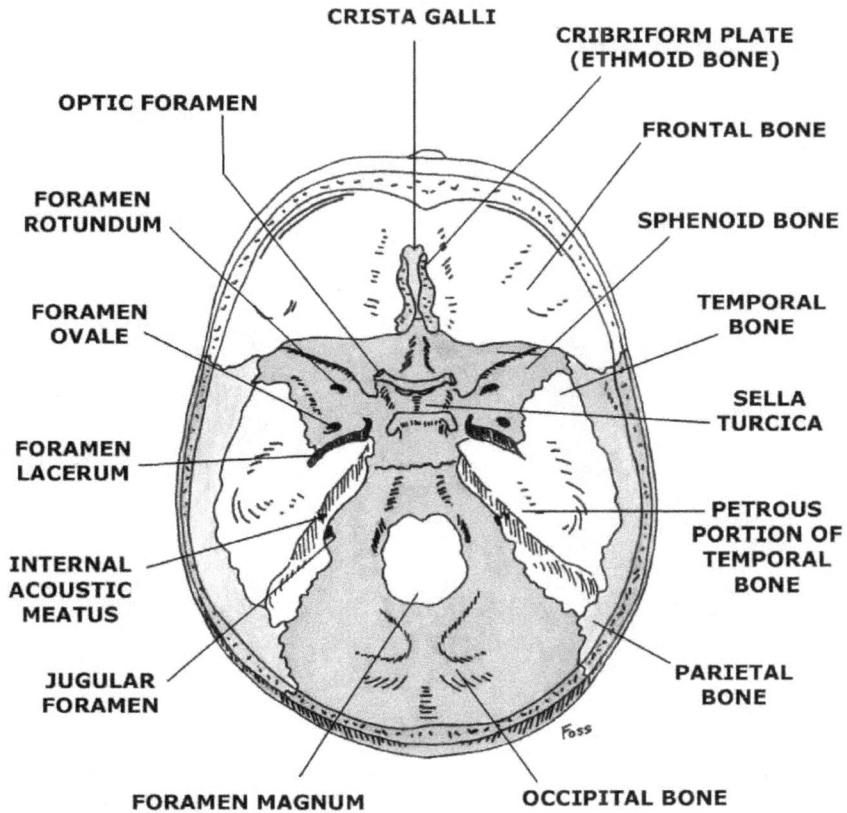

Floor of the Cranial Cavity
Figure Seven

A specific area of the sella turcica, known as the *hypophyseal fossa,* is labeled in Figure Eight. "Hypophyseal fossa" refers to the slightly curved depression into which the hypophysis, or pituitary gland, fits. The hypophyseal fossa is the vestige of the original Mercy Seat that was in each created being before the Adamic Fall. The hypophyseal fossa represents the place where God's Spirit communed with original Man. Remember, original Man was made in the complete image and perfect likeness of God. (As a reminder, "Man" is capitalized here to keep God's original, unfallen creation distinct from the fallen beings we now call *Homo sapiens* or "human beings.") The greater wings and lesser wings of the sphenoid bone are also labeled in Figure Eight. They represent the pairs of outstretched wings of the cherubs described in Exodus 25:20 and 37:9 and illustrated in Figure Six:

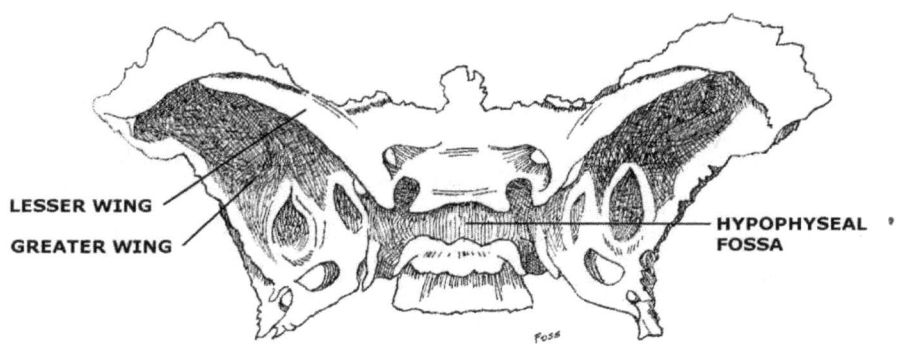

Superior View of the Sphenoid Bone
Figure Eight

Together, the two sinuses located within the body of the sphenoid bone represent the storage space within the Ark of the Covenant. It is the Ark of the Covenant into which the Testimony (or tablets of the Ten Commandments given to Moses) and Aaron's rod were placed. (Number 1 in Figure Nine is pointing to one of these two sinuses.) The tablets and rod represented God's Superior Lordship over — and Supreme Leadership of — those who belong to Him. Metaphysically speaking, the downward pterygoid processes of the sphenoid bone (Numbers 3 and 4 in Figure Nine), which serve as anchors for muscles that move the mandible, represent the stability and constancy of God's communication *to,* as well as *through,* each authentic Christian believer by His Holy Spirit. God's Spirit originally hovered above the Mercy Seat in unfallen man. In Figure Nine, God's Mercy Seat is represented by Number 2, pointing to the hypophyseal fossa that is seen from a different angle (i.e., a superior view) in Figures Seven and Eight.

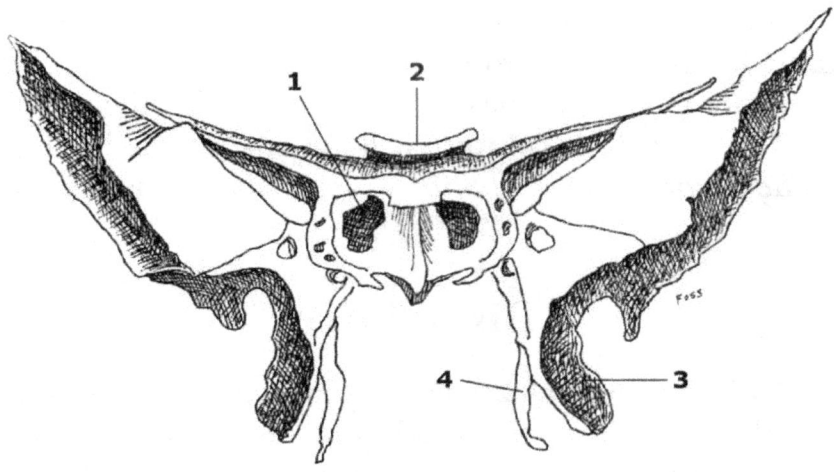

Sphenoid Bone
Figure Nine

The communion that authentic Christian believers have with God is not only represented by the vestige of the Mercy Seat known as the hypophyseal fossa, their communion with God is also represented by the olfactory foramina (i.e., passageways) within the cribriform plate of the ethmoid bone shown in Figure Seven. In human anatomy, olfactory receptors responsible for the sense of smell pass through these olfactory foramina to the olfactory bulbs at the base of the brain. As vestiges of anatomy in the Adamic Race before the Fall, the olfactory foramina represent the pathways which channeled spoken adoration (exhaltative communication) from the original and unfallen created beings to their Creator as a "sweet savor" or "sweet incense."[95] This incense or savor is called "sweet" because praise (and prayer is a form of praise) stimulates pleasure within the Supraconsciousness of God. The Creator desires to be acknowledged in both praise and prayer from His created beings.

The Vertebral Column

Together, the skull and the vertebral column comprise the axial skeleton, which is distinct from the shoulder and pelvic girdles and their associated appendages that comprise the appendicular skeleton. The vertebral column will be discussed in the section entitled *The Spinal Cord and Spinal Nerves* in the next chapter.

Disclaimer

It is important to emphasize as well as regularly reiterate to the readers of this book that the modern human anatomic structures are themselves no longer what they represent metaphysically. *For example,* the hypophyseal fossa is *no longer* the Mercy Seat of God and communion with God no longer takes place there or through the olfactory foramina. All human structures simply represent a supernatural reality that existed within original Man as well as exists within the etheric body double of every restored soul (i.e., each saved human being).

The invisible and etheric body double for each saved person is a shadow or type of electromagnetic impression — more specifically, a spiritual *alto relief* (or high definition image) — of immortal man's original somatic identity. (This is in contrast to the spiritual *bas relief*— or low definition image — found in unsaved persons.)

Just as the photograph of a person only *represents* the person, so do modern human anatomic structures merely represent higher spiritual verities. Just as the photograph of a person is not the

---

95   Luke 1:9-10; Revelation 8:3-4

actual person, so are modern human anatomic structures *not* the verities-in-themselves.

Articulations

Articulations, or joints, are categorized based on (1) movability, (2) specific types of associated movements, and (3) structural elements that connect two or more bones together. Articulations may be immovable, partially movable, or freely movable. Freely movable articulations (or *diarthroses*) are associated with one or more of a variety of movements — *for example:* flexion, extension, hyperextension, abduction, adduction, rotation, and circumduction. And each freely movable articulation (or *diarthrosis*) has: (1) a synovial joint cavity associated with synovial membranes on opposing cartilages, (2) synovial fluid, (3) ligaments (i.e., bone to bone connections), and (4) tendons (i.e., bone to muscle attachments).

More than all other areas and regions in the body, articulations best demonstrate the mechanical nature of the human body. Freely movable joints demonstrate *work* — as defined in physics — based on the nature of force acting upon an object to change its kinetic energy and expressed in the following equation:

$$W = \Delta E_k = E_{k2} - E_{k1} = \tfrac{1}{2}m(v_2^2 - v_1^2) = F \cdot d \cos \Theta$$

W = Work
Δ = delta (change)
E_k = kinetic energy
m = mass
v = velocity
F = Force
d = distance
Θ = angle of movement
$\cos$ = cosine = $\dfrac{\text{length of adjacent side}}{\text{length of hypotenuse}}$

Diarthroses are like simple machines that contain a lubricating fluid along with various levers, hinges, fulcrums *(fulcra),* pulleys (i.e., drums or sheaves), axles (or shafts), flanges, grooves, and anchors in association with various ropes, cables, belts, and chains. Like moving mechanical parts anywhere in the physical universe, joints wear out and may tear, depending on degree of friction from use, overuse, and misuse. In the case of diarthroses, friction from constant use as well as use over many decades can cause irritation, inflammation, and deterioration. In other words, all human beings should expect changes in their joints as they age; these changes are independent of the positive attitudes and optimism they may have about life. This should come as no surprise.

My major point in discussing the physics and mechanics of movement in relationship to joints is to help bring guilt over, and condemnation toward, joint-related disorders to the null value (i.e., zero). This is explained further in the section immediately following.

Medical or Metaphysical Treatment?

In the section entitled *Treating Contagious Diseases and Malignancies of the Skin* in Chapter Two, I mentioned that no one with a physical ailment should be embarrassed by its existence. Here, I add that people of faith should not feel guilty or embarrassed because they are not healed instantly or in what they think is a timely manner.

Many people of faith — especially those who steadfastly trust in the power of prayer and radically rely on metaphysical healing — remember these two passages from the Holy Bible:

> *And the Apostle Peter took the lame man by the right hand and lifted him up: and immediately his feet and ankle bones received strength.*
>
> ACTS 3:7 KJV (PARAPHRASE)

> *Truly, truly, I [Jesus Christ] say to you: "Those who believe on me and the works that I do, they also shall do such works; and greater works than these shall they*

do because I go to my Father."

JOHN 14:12 KJV (PARAPHRASE)

People of faith remember that the Apostle Peter said to the man who was lame since birth: "In the name of Jesus Christ of Nazareth rise up and walk."[96] They remember that the healing response was immediate, or instantaneous. And they also remember that Jesus Christ promised his followers that they would be able to accomplish works greater than the miracles he performed. Even if one interprets "greater" to refer to quantity and not quality, people of faith often feel guilty and/or embarrassed if they remain unhealed, or if they are not healed immediately or within a short period of time, after they prayerfully call out to God for healing or metaphysically proclaim healing and wholeness in the name of Jesus Christ.

People of faith are forgetting two things if they feel guilty about not being healed immediately. First, they are forgetting that Jesus Christ died that they no longer should feel guilty about anything because they no longer stand condemned for their iniquity and sins. And, second, they are forgetting that God is omniscient. In being omniscient, God knows if and when people are ready for their healings. Some people are not yet ready for their healings because they have not yet learned important lessons from their disabilities, disorders, and diseases. And some people of faith are not yet ready for their healings until the time of their death — when all permanent, perfect, and complete healing takes place.

God sometimes permits chronic pain to help people learn that they do not get everything they want and that they do not always get what they want when they want it. Consequently, chronic pain can be especially useful for teaching people who are stubborn or who swindle God by withholding their pain, suffering, and adversity from Him. This is one reason why some chronic pain is unyielding to intercessory prayer and/or metaphysical treatment.

In 1 Peter 4:1-2, the Apostle Peter teaches us that suffering can

---

96 Acts 3:6b, King James Version (Paraphrase)

also be useful in other ways. Many Christian monastics, ascetics, and hermits knew the value of suffering. Many cloistered medieval Christians understood its value as well. Even some modern-day Christians understand (but most modern Christians are unwilling to understand) that, for some of us, pain is allowed by God as a gift to us. When a Christian is in gifted pain, he or she will not entertain, indulge, or act on sinful thinking. Thus, when in pain, Christians are less easily ensnared by Satan's temptations to desire what we ought not to desire.

God is omniscient. We are not omniscient. Because we do not know everything, we don't know how disability, disorder, and disease fit into God's plan: (1) for us individually, (2) for those who currently surround us, or (3) for those with whom we will be coming into contact decades from now. But God knows. Remember, God does not look at physical healing as the most important healing. God looks at the salvation and sanctification of our souls as the most important healing. And God sees in what ways our physical disabilities, disorders, and diseases might positively impact and influence that most important healing — *for example,* by softening hearts and enabling others to learn how to care for someone other than themselves as well as to dedicate their daily activities to higher purposes other than self-gratification, self-satisfaction, self-absorption, and self-indulgence.

Healings take place at the specific intersection of: (1) our faith in Jesus Christ; (2) the Will of God for us individually, collectively, and corporately; and (3) His perfect timing. Sometimes a "breakthrough" in spiritual recognition or understanding is necessary before there can be change and healing for a particular condition.

It is important for people of faith to study human anatomy and physiology so that they can also be people of knowledge and understanding. Yes, people of faith need to know and understand the mechanisms that God has put into place for natural healing as well as for supernatural healing.

Understanding the natural physiologic mechanisms in place for the healing of a bone fracture or for the healing of trauma to a joint is important. Yes, pray for the healing of a bone fracture. Yes, declare, affirm, and proclaim God's goodness concerning a ripped rotator cuff muscle in the shoulder or a detached cruciate ligament in the knee. But have the fractured bone set and wrapped by medical practitioners who know what they are doing. And have the ripped tendon or detached ligament surgically reattached by the appropriate medical specialist. When your bicycle chain comes off its sprocket, you think nothing of mechanically reattaching it so that you can get on with your journey. Do no less for the mechanical parts of your human body. We should submit to common sense even at the same time we are praying for spiritual healing and receiving metaphysical treatment. We must also commit to memory that it makes good sense to treat mechanical injuries mechanically (i.e., by surgical intervention).

Have you sprained a joint or strained a muscle? Then, be patient with the pain and swelling since they will gradually diminish during the natural healing process. Patience is especially in order since some pain and swelling are actually helpful: The pain will remind you not to put too much weight on the injured area and not to pick up more than you should be carrying to avoid further damage and injury; and the swelling can help to stabilize the area and aid the natural healing process. To be sure, too much pain and too much swelling can cause complications and, therefore, necessitate additional medical observation and diagnosis — *for example,* to ensure that a blood clot is not causing such pain and edema (i.e., swelling).

Learning, knowing, and understanding natural physiologic processes will help correct inaccurate assumptions about the structures and functions involved. They will help elevate intercessory prayer and metaphysical treatment to higher levels. Why higher? They will be higher because expectations will no longer be skewed by ignorance, superstition, mysticism, and magical thinking.

Although many people of faith would deny that they become self-loathing or condemning of others when they themselves or others have not been supernaturally healed through intercessory prayer or metaphysical treatment, such feelings may exist — if not consciously, then unconsciously (i.e., subconsciously). However, the suffering Christ carrying his cross on the Via Dolorosa[97] serves as the perfect illustration for people who might be disappointed with themselves or others because of the absence of supernatural strength and healing. Would you chide Jesus during that historic walk for the inability of his joints and muscles to withstand such a burden? Would you chastise Jesus for not living up to his faith? Would you deride Jesus for not proclaiming his wholeness in God? Would you be disappointed with Jesus for not demonstrating an immediate healing result?

Just as it is legitimate to not have medical treatment supersede metaphysical treatment, so is it legitimate (1) to not exclude medical treatment and (2) to ally medical treatment to metaphysical treatment. It is also legitimate to take into consideration wear and tear of body parts based on one's earthly life and the fact that the human body is not meant to last forever. In many ways, the human body is just a physical machine. In concert with this last point, *der Bewegungsapparat,* the German compound noun often used for "the musculoskeletal system," appropriately conveys "the machinery, or apparatus, of movement" as a conceptual nuance.

People of faith need to be kinder to themselves and to each other concerning outcomes associated with disabilities, disorders, and diseases.

There will be more on the topics of natural healing and supernatural healing in the following chapters.

Chapter Questions

This section is intended to facilitate learning by providing relevant activities, exercises, and experiences to aid students of divine metaphysics in their quest for grasping spiritual concepts, integrating them into their own belief systems, holding them more

---

97 *Via Dolorosa* is Latin for "Way of Grief" or "Way of Suffering" and refers to the specific pathway in the Old City of Jerusalem that Jesus took to his crucifixion on Calvary (the hill that resembled a skullcap, or *calvarium*).

assuredly, and making them more practical in daily life.

The following questions should be answered after reading each titled section. To answer a few of the questions, students may need to consult outside resources or external references. Students are also encouraged to answer these questions with others during group discussions.

Introduction to the Skeletal System

1. What other phrases are used in this textbook for *unfallen man?*

2. What other phrases are used in this textbook for *fallen man?*

3. How do muscular contractions and gravity contribute to normal development and maintenance of the skeletal system?

4. Why was a bony skeletal system unnecessary for original Man?

Connective Tissue

5. What are the four general categories of connective tissue?

6. (a) Using an outside resource, briefly explain the difference between spongy bone and dense bone. (b) Give four examples each of where spongy bone and dense bone are located in the human body.

7. (a) Using an outside resource, explain how metallurgy and metallography relate to calcium deposition in bone. (b) Using an external reference, find and list calcium's nearest neighbors on the periodic table.

The Stellate Nature of Original Man

8. Why does the author describe original Man as *stellate* and six-pointed?

9. What is one factor that causes human beings to appear grossly (i.e., macroscopically) different from extraterrestrial biological life forms?

10. Using an articulated human skeleton at a local museum or in a laboratory classroom, visually identify the thirty different bones in the arm and the thirty different bones in the leg by naming them. To receive credit for this question, it will be sufficient for you to give the name and address of the location where you viewed the articulated human skeleton.

11. What do the six points of the Star of David represent?

12. Are created beings on track to become equal to the Creator? Please explain.

13. How does the somatic identity of original, unfallen man differ from the somatic identity of fallen, corporeal man?

14. Briefly discuss the *soul* and *spirit* of a person.

15. When does literal anthropomorphization of Deity occur?

16. (a) What supports the notion that the invisible God has a somatic identity? (b) Does this contradict the Biblical truth that God is Spirit (John 4:24)? (c) In what ways should we seek to understand God the Father's somatic identity? (Think creatively in answering this question.)

The Head and the Skull

17. Construct a list of what the human head represents metaphysically.

18. Memorize Deuteronomy 6:4-5 and repeat the verses from memory to at least one other person.

19. In Heaven, what names will be emblazoned on our foreheads?

The Cranial Cavity and the Mercy Seat of God

20. (a) What does the Mercy Seat of the Ark of the Covenant represent? (b) Where is a vestige of the Mercy Seat found in the human body? (c) Explain the structural relationships between and among the following: cranium, sphenoid bone, sella turcica, and hypophyseal fossa.

21. Construct a table that includes the following areas of the sphenoid bone in one column and state what each area represents metaphysically: (a) hypophyseal fossa, (b) sphenoidal sinuses, (c) greater and lesser wings, and (d) pterygoid processes.

22. Why are prayers recognized by the Creator as a sweet savor?

The Vertebral Column

23. Consulting an external reference, construct a list of all bones in the axial skeleton and all bones in the appendicular skeleton.

Disclaimer

24. Briefly explain why human anatomic structures are not "the verities-in-themselves."

Articulations

25. Consulting an external resource, learn how to demonstrate the following movements: flexion, extension, hyperextension, abduction, adduction, rotation, and circumduction.

26. What is the functional difference between *ligaments* and *tendons?*

Medical or Metaphysical Treatment?

27. Should students of divine metaphysics be embarrassed or feel guilty about their own joint-related disorders or the joint-related disorders of others they are treating prayerfully and metaphysically? Why or why not?

28. In what ways can chronic pain and swelling be useful?

29. Give examples of joint-related conditions that might require treatment by a medical practitioner.

30. How does the path of suffering experienced by Jesus Christ on the Via Dolorosa relate to the embarrassment and guilt experienced

by people of faith when spiritual healing does not occur?

Chapter Four
Divine Metaphysics of the Nervous System

Commit your works to the LORD, and your thoughts shall be established.

PROVERBS 16:3 KJV (PARAPHRASE)

The Supraconsciousness of God

The neocortex is the outer layer of the human cerebrum and is divided into the four lobes shown in Figure Ten. Of all the various brain regions, the neocortex of the cerebrum especially represents the supraconsciousness that original Man had in God before the Adamic Fall. The tripartite nature of the Godhead is even seen in the three general areas of the cerebrum that fit into the anterior cranial fossa[98] (formed by the frontal bone), the middle cranial fossa (formed by the sphenoid and temporal bones), and the posterior cranial fossa (formed by the occipital bone). Although not

---

[98] A skeletal *fossa* is generally a depression or concavity that may be superficial or deep. (*Fossae* is the plural form of the Latin noun *fossa*.)

labeled, these depressions (or *fossae*) are seen in Figure Seven from the previous chapter on divine metaphysics of the skeletal system.

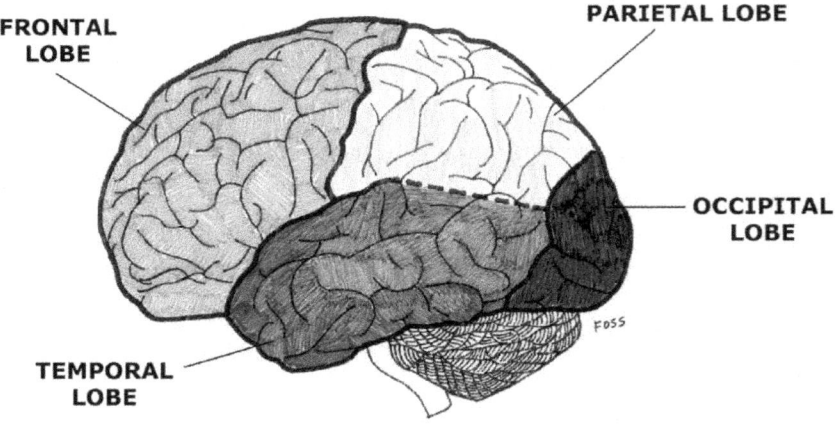

Lobes of the Cerebrum
Figure Ten

The neocortex of the human cerebrum also represents the cloud of God's Glory, or *Shekinah,* that periodically hovered above the Ark of the Covenant housed within the Holy of Holies, or Most Holy Place, in the Wilderness Tabernacle as well as in the Jerusalem Temple. The "tent" of the Tabernacle and the "house" of the Temple are represented by both the cranium and the dura mater, or outer "tough membrane," that covers the human brain.

Because original, unfallen man was made in God's complete image and perfect likeness, the seat of God's Holy Spirit (i.e., His *Soul)* is represented metaphysically by: (1) the hypothalamus, (2) its downward evagination that makes up the infundibulum (or stalk of the pituitary gland), and (3) the neurohypophysis (or posterior pituitary gland). These structures are illustrated in Figure Eleven:

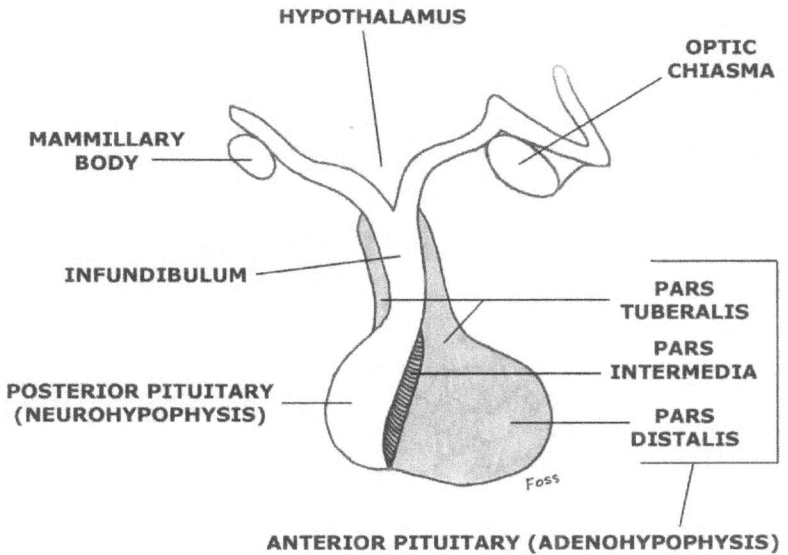

The Hypothalamus and the Hypophysis
Figure Eleven

As discussed in the chapter on the skeletal system, it is the hypophysis, or pituitary gland, that fits into the hypophyseal fossa of the sphenoid bone. The hypophyseal fossa metaphysically represents the place where God's Soul communicated with the soul of original, unfallen man. This place is also represented by the Mercy Seat of the Ark of the Covenant, where God communed with the High Priest in the Holy of Holies.

God's Holy Spirit communed supernaturally with original, unfallen man via invisible pathways. In human anatomy, remnants and vestiges of these pathways are represented by the various nerve tracts originating in the hypothalamus as well as by the various hormones and releasing factors[99] produced in the hypothalamus. In

---

99 Although it is now more common to refer to these "releasing factors" as "releasing hormones," the present author uses the older terminology ("releasing factors") merely to help distinguish between: (1) "releasing hormones" produced by the hypothalamus that stimulate the release of hormones produced in the adenohypophysis; and (2) those hormones produced by the hypothalamus that travel through the hypothalamic-hypophyseal tract and are eventually released by the neurohypophysis.

human physiology, (1) at least two of these hormones move to the neurohypophysis (or posterior pituitary) from the hypothalamus through the hypothalamic-hypophyseal tract in the infundibulum (or stalk) of the pituitary; and (2) the releasing factors move to the adenohypophysis (or anterior pituitary) via capillary flow from the hypothalamus.

Although Rene Descartes (1596-1650 A.D.) postulated that the pineal gland (see Figure Twelve) is the seat of man's soul, the pars distalis of the adenohypophysis (or anterior pituitary gland) actually *represents* that seat. And, metaphysically speaking, the pars intermedia (or so-called "intermediate lobe" of the pituitary gland) is where God's Soul (represented jointly by the hypothalamus, infundibulum and neurohypophysis) meets man's soul (represented by the pars distalis) through the shed blood of Jesus Christ (represented by the blood in the vasculature of the pars intermedia). Please refer back to Figure Eleven for the structural relationships of these various regions.

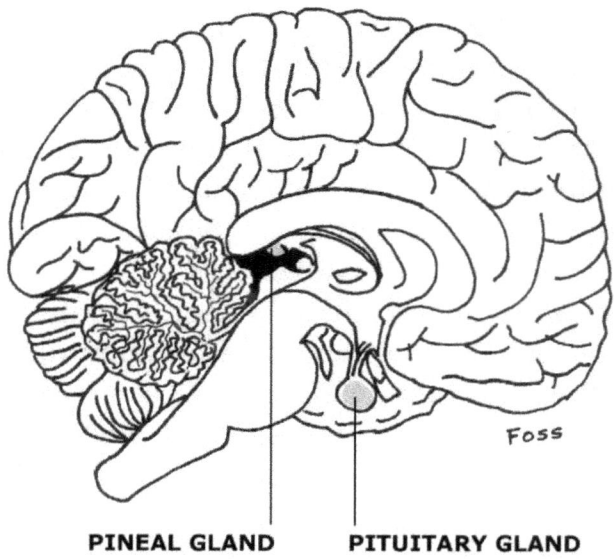

PINEAL GLAND   PITUITARY GLAND

*The Pineal Gland in Relationship
to the Pituitary Gland
Figure Twelve*

Although Rene Descartes was inaccurate in his conclusion about the pineal gland being the seat of man's soul, through histologic and comparative anatomic observations of the pineal gland, it is accurate to conclude that the pineal gland metaphysically represents the "third eye" by which spiritually-enlightened man peers into the world of the invisible when that world is opened to man by God and God alone. It is important to emphasize here that human beings do not open the door to the world of the invisible because that would be unseemly. *For example,* human beings *never* initiate or control communication from the Holy Spirit and *never* initiate or control contact with departed souls in Heaven. Those who say they do are *always* perpetrating a hoax.

Since the dot, mark, or jewel on the forehead worn by some Jains, Buddhists, Hindus, and Jews (Ezekiel 16:12) represents the energy center of inner sight that aligns with the pineal gland, it is easy to understand why this area on the forehead is sometimes referred to as "the third eye."

Disclaimer

It is important to emphasize as well as regularly reiterate to the readers of this book that the modern human anatomic structures are themselves no longer what they represent metaphysically. *For example,* the hypophyseal fossa is *no longer* the Mercy Seat of God; the hypothalamus, infundibulum, and neurohypophysis are *no longer* where God's Soul (or His Holy Spirit) is found; the anterior pituitary gland (vis-à-vis its pars distalis) is *no longer* the actual seat of man's soul, etc. All of these structures simply represent a supernatural reality that existed within original, unfallen man as well as exists within the etheric body double of every restored soul (i.e., saved human being).

The invisible and etheric body double for each saved person is a shadow or type of electromagnetic impression — more specifically, a spiritual *alto relief* (or high definition image) — of immortal man's original somatic identity. (This is in contrast to the spiritual *bas relief* — or low definition image — found in unsaved persons.)

Just as the photograph of a person only represents the person, so do modern human anatomic structures merely represent higher spiritual verities. Just as the photograph of a person is not the actual person, so are modern human anatomic structures *not* the verities-in-themselves.

The Limbic System ("The Emotional Brain")

Assumptive beliefs determine the direction that analytical thinking takes. That is why two or more intelligent and rational people, or two or more groups of intelligent and rational people, can be widely divergent in their views on emotionally-charged issues, each person or group claiming that the other person or group is not thinking "clearly" or accusing the other person or group of not being rational or of disregarding certain "self-evident" and "obvious" truths.

Assumptive beliefs are convictions, or positions, that are held to be true regardless of the existence or nonexistence of supportive evidence or contradictory evidence. If they are negative, assumptive beliefs may actually prejudice their holders deleteriously because they taint objectivity and critical analysis. Negative assumptive beliefs interfere with (that is, *bias* or *slant*) deductive and inductive reasoning in harmful ways. And, because *assumptive beliefs* are grounded in emotions as well as provide for emotional grounding, those beliefs that are negative *bind* intellectual processes too tightly. On the other hand, positive assumptive beliefs *tether* intellectual processes but do not bind them.

Because *assumptive beliefs* are related to emotions and memory, their "seat" is found in the so-called limbic system of the brain, also known as "the emotional brain" (portions of which are illustrated in Figure Thirteen). I write "so-called" to simply acknowledge that there is academic debate among neuroscientists concerning what is included and what is excluded in this system as well as the appropriateness of the word "limbic." Regardless, many neuroanatomists and neurobiologists would at least include the hypothalamus, thalamus, hippocampus, amygdala, and fornix as parts of the limbic system[100] — all of which form a structural central core of the brain, which core is deep to (that is, below and inside) the neocortex of the cerebrum and above the brainstem.

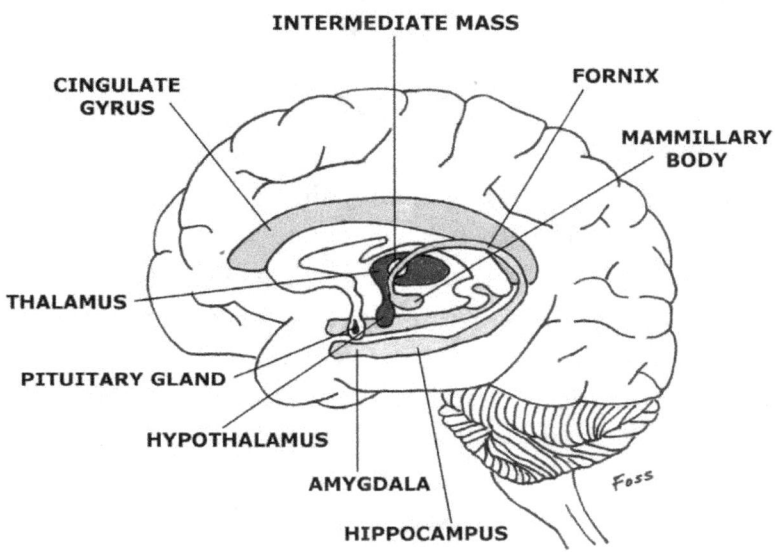

The Limbic System
Figure Thirteen

For academic discussions of the anatomy and physiology of the limbic system and other structures that may be included within it by neuroscientists, please consult the most recently published general textbooks of anatomy and physiology as well as the most current medical textbooks and journal articles specifically related to the neuroanatomy and neurophysiology of the limbic system.

---

100 Many neuroscientists also include the prefrontal cortex, the rostral anterior cingulate cortex (rACC), the olfactory cortex, and other cortical regions as well as the mammillary bodies (often considered parts of the hypothalamus), the pineal gland (i.e., epiphysis), and the olfactory bulbs. The intermediate mass shown in Figure Thirteen is part of the thalamus. (*Mammillary* is also correctly spelled *mamillary*.)

Metaphysically speaking, the limbic system represents the spiritual-emotional self not only of original, unfallen man but also of the Creator. (Remember, we were originally created in the complete image and perfect likeness of God.) In the human being, the limbic system also represents the *fallen* spiritual-emotional self, which must be overridden, or consciously redirected, by the prefrontal cortex of the cerebrum if the restored spiritual self (or *saved soul)* is to reign over conscious and unconscious (i.e., subconscious) thoughts, feelings, and actions. Thus, the prefrontal cortex metaphysically represents the seat of free will, self-control, or individual volition in original, unfallen man.

In the etheric body double of every human being, the *fallen* spiritual-emotional self "hovers" over the vestige of God's Mercy Seat: (1) misdirecting emotional-visceral responses; and (2) driving inappropriate thinking, feeling, and behavior in the natural, corporeal, or carnal self. Only the Spirit of God that lives in the restored spiritual self of each saved soul has the power to override or consciously redirect emotions away from spiritually-unhealthy desires and responses toward spiritually-healthy desires and responses. *For example,* only the Holy Spirit can override and replace the desire to indulge sinful and addictive behaviors with the desire to please the Creator in prayer, praise, adoration, and holy living. Only the Holy Spirit is the prime mover in spiritual falconry. (See the section entitled *Metaphysical Treatment of Disability, Disorder, and Disease* in Chapter Two for a discussion of spiritual falconry.)

The Spirit of God has the power to "bump" the *fallen* spiritual-emotional self out of its position of control and replace it with the higher emotional identity of the restored spiritual self. If the restored spiritual self has control over the limbic system of the etheric body double (the invisible counterpart to the physical limbic system), then this energy pathway in the human body is cleared for the supraself of the individual — which includes the Supraconsciousness of God — to be in the position of controlling the conscious functioning self, which simply steps aside in acquiescence to such control.

In individuals compromised by active addiction,[101] demonic forces also have the power to "bump" the spiritual-emotional self out of its position of control. In this case, however, a primal and primitive consciousness is in the position of control — to what degree and at what interval and duration depends on the nature of each person's susceptibility and the kind and level of addiction. (Also see additional sections in this chapter that cover addictions and susceptible channels.)

The seat of fear is also found in the limbic system and is, thus, greatly related to the level of what one is experiencing as anxiety, pain, sorrow, suffering, anger, rage, pleasure, satiety, affection, memory, and affect (or mood). Because fear has great relevance to the spiritual self, and because fear is often defined too simplistically, I will now discuss it.

Too often, spiritually-minded people think of fear as being universally negative. That is not true. Some forms of fear have a survival advantage, or edge, and some forms of fear accompany reverence for the Creator and awe of things divine.

Fears can be rational, irrational, and/or supernatural. Some rational fears can go wild to become irrational fears and some irrational fears can be mitigated to become rational fears. And some irrational fears can be influenced by demonic forces to become supernatural fears. To be sure, not all supernatural fears are demonic. Supernatural fears also include an utmost reverence for God and an awe of the magnificent things God has created.

Rational fears influence us to take protective measures and proactive steps against possible harmful events. In contrast,

---

101 As used in this book, addiction not only includes the abuse of external agents absorbed after their ingestion, inhalation, or injection but also chemical agents naturally produced by the body in response to danger, fear, alarm, pain, hunger, satiety, sexual arousal, and olfaction of aromatics that are pheromones or pheromone-like. These naturally-produced, addictive agents include certain neurotransmitters and hormones as well as less complex chemicals such as glucose, oxygen, carbon dioxide, and various ions. Human beings can become addicted to changing levels of their own naturally-occurring, internal chemicals as well as external chemicals they ingest, inhale, or inject.

irrational fears, or phobias, can incapacitate us and keep us from doing what needs to be done for successful daily living. As indicated previously, the category of supernatural fear includes both reverence and intense respect for God as well as awe of spectacular events and majestic views of God and things created, designed, and orchestrated by God; supernatural fear also includes intense foreboding that is, more often than not, demonically-engineered and satanically-engendered.

The following acronym of unknown origin is sometimes used to represent fear: *F*alse *E*vidence *A*ppearing *R*eal. Although that phrase is useful to describe irrational fears that are of organic origin and supernatural fears that are of demonic origin, the statement does not represent rational fears necessary for practical daily living or the supernatural fear of God or legitimate awe of things divine, divinely-inspired, or majestically-created. In other words, this *F-E-A-R* acronym is too simplistic.

Antidotes for fear include: (1) practical preparation for successful daily living in responding to rational fears; (2) medication, psychological therapy, and education in counteracting irrational fears; and (3) understanding and applying Biblical truth in counteracting supernatural fears. Trust in God should be the major ingredient that accompanies the application of each of these antidotes. Trust in God includes abiding faith, abiding hope, and abiding confidence in God. It also includes fleeing to God to take refuge even during times of seeming peace in addition to times of open attack. (Review the section entitled *Psychic Attack and the Wicked Smart* in this chapter.)

If the tiny ungerminated mustard seed represents faith in God,[102] then the huge mustard tree represents trust in God that is fully rooted, flourishing, and producing fruit in Him. Trust in God does not include the "name-it-and-claim-it" or "confess-it-and-possess-it" types of super silly and supercilious belief systems so often endorsed by "prosperity" and "word-of-faith" Christian preachers that emerge in every generation. Rather, trust in God includes affirmations that declare God's goodness and

---

102 Matthew 17:20; Luke 17:6

righteousness as well as His Providence.

Understanding God's Providence begins in understanding Romans 8:28 (KJV Paraphrase):

All things work together for good to those who love God and who are the called according to His purpose.

Christians are taught to "not be anxious about anything, but in every situation, by prayer and petition with thanksgiving, present their requests to God."[103] This directive presupposes that we place our trust in the Will of God to do good always for those who belong to God and are, therefore, "the called according to *His* purpose."

What sits enthroned in the limbic system of the etheric body double determines our reactions to fear. Either the Spirit of God sits enthroned in our spiritual-emotional self or the spirit of Satan (sometimes called "mortal mind" in the language of Christian metaphysics) sits enthroned in our spiritual-emotional self. (Either one or the other sits enthroned but not both and certainly not at the same time.) If the Spirit of God sits enthroned, then the supraself of the individual directs the conscious functioning self to relinquish control, allowing the supraself to direct our thinking, feeling, and reactions based on them. If the spirit of Satan sits enthroned in the limbic system, then an emotionally-depraved "lower self" directs the thinking, feeling, and behaviors of the individual.

When the Spirit of God is in control, naturally intuitive and spiritually discerning people are able to be precise and accurate in their feelings and impressions concerning the world of the invisible. When the spirit of Satan is in control, then intuited and discerned information is jumbled, mismatched, misperceived, and imprecisely understood by such gifted people. In other words, the purity of the channel (in this case, *accuracy)* depends on the purity of the channel (in this case, *holiness).*

It is important to point out that pain and suffering are processed and interpreted on an emotional-visceral level by the limbic system and, then, processed and interpreted on a cognitive level in the

---

103 Philippians 4:6, King James Version (Paraphrase)

neocortex of the cerebrum.

Sometimes, we erroneously interpret that pain and suffering constitute punishment from God when they do not. Of course, pain and suffering *can* be punishment from God, but they do not always constitute punishment.

Earlier, I wrote that "the limbic system represents the spiritual-emotional self not only of original, unfallen man but also of the Creator." Thus, because original, unfallen man was created in the complete image and perfect likeness of God, God's emotions are also seated within His supernatural limbic system. This is where God experiences love, joy, affection, pleasure, satiety, and patience as well as hatred, anger, disaffection, displeasure, dissatisfaction, and wrath. As you may have already concluded, the only emotion that God does not experience is fear. (God withdraws from places where evil abounds not out of fear but out of respect and reverence for His Own Holy Name.) However, God does understand fear experientially through the palpable fears felt by Christ Jesus in the Garden at Gethsemane. (For the sake of clarity, Christ Jesus was never afraid of evil; Christ Jesus was afraid of what he knew he would experience on the cross at Calvary.)

Eternal hope, and not despair, springs within the emotional brain of the human being when God is in control. Eternal hope is irrational and unrealistic optimism. Eternal hope is irrational and unrealistic because it exists despite current human conditions and the seemingly certain consequences of those conditions.

When metaphysically understood, our memories of the past heighten our imagination of the future. In the world of God, not only are all good things possible, they are probable. Moreover, in the world of God, not only are all good things probable, they already *are* (that is, they already exist in the reality of God). Divine metaphysics seeks to bring into human reality what already exists in the reality of God, which is a spiritual and supernatural reality.

Depression and despair, and not optimism, are engendered by negative thinking. However, not all so-called negative thinking is actually negative. Some so-called negative thinking helps us to avoid making the same mistakes in the future as well as helps us to avoid various forms of disruption, pain, and suffering in our lives.

God understands that we will make mistakes, but He wants us to learn from our mistakes. When we learn from our mistakes, we please Him. (Pleasing God involves obeying God and abiding by His Will.)

Eternal hope springs from the mind of Christ and eternal despair springs from Satan's mortal mind and its fleshly servant, carnal mind. Our hope is an eternal hope because it is alive in Christ Jesus.

Carnal Mind versus the Mind of Christ

The mind, or creative consciousness, is different from the brain in that the mind can override and redirect the brain. Spiritually speaking, the mind functions independently of the brain. The mind is metaphysical and the brain is physical. The mind includes morality and ethics in relationship to free will, volition, self-control, and *being*.

The brain cannot *know* beyond what it observes and experiences physically, cognitively, and emotionally. In contrast, the mind experiences spiritually, supernaturally, and metaphysically and is, therefore, capable of grasping invisible realities in the spiritual universe of God. The brain is only capable of grasping natural reality derived strictly from the physical senses and interpreted cognitively and emotionally. The brain seeks to experience pleasure as well as avoid discomfort. The mind, however, transcends pleasure and discomfort based on its understanding of their spiritual, supernatural, and metaphysical import. In this way, the mind overrides the brain and is capable of redirecting the brain's thinking and feeling.

"Carnal mind" is discussed in the Eighth Chapter of the Apostle Paul's Epistle to the Romans:

> *{6} For to be carnally minded [that is, fleshly-minded or walking after the flesh] is death; but to be spiritually minded [that is, divinely-minded or walking after the Spirit] is life and peace. {7} Because the carnal mind*

[or the mind operating according to fleshly desires] is enmity against God, it is not subject to the law of God neither, indeed, can it be.

ROMANS 8:6-7 KJV (PARAPHRASE)

The noun phrase *mortal mind* describes the spirit and intelligence of Satan. The noun phrase *carnal mind* describes the selfish desires and lusts of our own flesh. Carnal mind includes the so-called *rat brain*, or mesolimbic,[104] portion of the human brain. The phrase "rat brain" is a figurative expression describing those areas of the human brain that collectively drive an individual to involuntarily and repeatedly seek pleasure, comfort, and satiety as well as avoid unpleasantness, discomfort, and hunger. So-called *rat brain* activities are often monitored in experimental animals by recording their responses to positive and/or negative chemical, electrical, and thermal stimuli. Among other things, the "rat brain" provides a practical neurobiological disease model for understanding human addictions related to sinful thoughts, feelings, and activities generated by the carnal mind.

Satan's mortal mind seeks to work through each individual's carnal mind in two major ways: (1) by masquerading as our own imagination; and (2) by projecting unholy thoughts and feelings onto the screen of our unconscious (i.e., subconscious) mind. In both cases, Satan's mortal mind hopes that we will embrace unholy thoughts, feelings, and desires and act them out as if they were our own. Unfortunately, the unholy thoughts, feelings, and desires do become our own as soon as we act on them.

Although demonic activity always tempts human beings to indulge their carnal mind, indulging carnal mind may or may not trigger demonic activity. The existence of demonic activity depends on the extent to which an individual indulges his or her own carnality as well as on that individual's susceptibility to influences from invisible spiritual realms. To be sure, not all people

---

104 *Mesolimbic* refers to an inner, central pathway that especially regulates memory and emotion as they relate to desire, motivation, reward, and avoidance.

are susceptible to demonic activity and not all susceptible people are equally susceptible to demonic activity.

Although there may be momentary relapses, souls restored (i.e., *saved*) through the shed blood of Jesus Christ ultimately do not walk after the ways of the flesh or carnal mind but after the ways of the Spirit because they have "the mind of Christ."[105] However, from time to time, even saved souls in fleshly bodies will yield to carnal thinking and feeling if they are not daily submitting themselves to the mind of Christ by living in a state of contrition (LSC).

To what extent do saved souls on Earth have the mind of Christ? Saved souls on Earth have the mind of Christ to the extent that they: (1) permit the mind, or spirit, of Christ access to their souls; (2) submit themselves to the mind, or spirit, of Christ; (3) focus on yielding to the Will of God; and (4) activate their prefrontal cortex to override base, or ignoble, instincts.

> *Let this mind be in you that was also in Christ Jesus.*
>
> PHILIPPIANS 2:5 KJV (PARAPHRASE)

> *Be not conformed to this world; but be transformed by the renewing of your mind that you may prove the good, and acceptable, and perfect will of God.*
>
> ROMANS 12:2 KJV (PARAPHRASE)

> *Create in me a clean heart, O God; and renew a right spirit [i.e., right mind] within me.*
>
> PSALM 51:10 KJV (PARAPHRASE)

Here, it is important to point out that the Hebrew word *ru'-akh* [H7307 in Appendix Table A] — translated as "spirit" in Psalm 51:10 — also means "mind." Thus, one can accurately interchange the phrase "mind of Christ" with the phrases "spirit of Christ" and

---

[105] 1 Corinthians 2:16, King James Version

"Spirit of God." (Remember, Jesus Christ was God in the flesh.[106])

The religion of Satan seeks for us to abrogate our free will, self-control, and individual volition by handing ourselves over as prisoners to Satan to appease him. In contrast, the religion of the Lord God Almighty seeks for us to fulfill our free will, self-control, and individual volition by embracing the mind of Christ to please God. Although Satan can never be appeased, God can certainly be pleased.

Conscience Matters

The conscience of individuals interprets what is right and what is wrong not only for the individuals themselves but also, correctly or incorrectly, for others. Except for people with certain neurological conditions, unusual biochemical imbalances, and/or specific genetic disorders, every human being is born with the capacity to learn differences between what is right and what is wrong. This capacity is linked not only to the ability to learn and remember what one has learned but also to the ability to process and value what one has learned.

Determining differences between right and wrong is learned by children through nature, nurture, peer pressure, social interactions, training, and education. However, the conscience of a child who grows up in an environment that might be characterized as abusive, violent, and vulgar may or may not be different from the conscience of a child who grows up in an environment that might be characterized as supportive, loving, and refined. It depends on how each child internalizes, accepts, and rejects what it is exposed to.

The concept of conscience is an invention of the human mind to explain an individual's ability to interpret and determine right from wrong. There is no specific locus for the conscience in the human brain although there are brain centers, areas, and pathways related to learning, decision-making, judgment, memory, intelligence, and

---

106 Colossians 2:9 and 1 Timothy 3:16

reason — all of which contribute to the shaping and exercising of one's conscience. In other words, the conscience is a function of the mind (which can only be understood metaphysically) and not one structure within the human brain.

If the conscience is an individual's moral compass, then absolute truth is the metaphysical, magnetic north pole that determines the direction in which the compass should be pointing. But absolute truth can only determine that direction when God's Holy Spirit resides within the individual and has the freedom to reign. God's Holy Spirit provides the magnetic field and lines of flux to keep one's moral compass pointing in the right direction. Without God's Holy Spirit residing within an individual, a person's conscience can only be based on subjective criteria interpreted from — and determined by their acceptance or rejection of — cultural, social, familial, and peer group norms.

God's Holy Spirit teaches us the difference between right and wrong in relationship to God's Will for us all individually, collectively, and corporately. God's Holy Spirit provides the "still, small voice"[107] from within and the "light to enlighten"[108] the soul in order that we know in which direction we should be traveling.

Often, an individual's conscience is in conflict with God's Will for us all. However, as we grow in faith and trust in the Lord God Almighty, we learn to yield to His Will at the same time that we learn to resist employing the arbitrary values of right and wrong that we have learned culturally, socially, familially, and interpersonally. (Do not interpret this to mean that everything we have learned is disharmonious with absolute truth.)

The human conscience commends and condemns erroneously; only God has the authority and omniscience to accurately commend and condemn. The human conscience rewards in feelings of self-pride and self-integrity and it has remorse for what has been done that it perceives as wrong; however, only God can reward us for what we have done that is pleasing to Him, and only God can determine what is sin and convict us of our need for

---

107 1 Kings 19:12, King James Version
108 Luke 2:32, King James Version (Paraphrase)

repentance. Again, we can only know accurately what is right and what is wrong through the continuing instruction of God's indwelling Holy Spirit.

There are those who might say that human beings are born with a conscience — that is, the innate ability to know the difference between absolute right and absolute wrong. The kernel of truth in that comes from the soul's far memory of its origin and past; but, unless the soul is able to apply that memory to the present, such memory is of null effect. To be sure, only God's Holy Spirit imparted to the saved sinner possesses complete knowledge of absolute right and absolute wrong. So, we cannot tap into that knowledge unless God's Holy Spirit indwells us. Even when God's Holy Spirit indwells us, we can still impose our own subjective values and erroneous conclusions to obfuscate what God's Holy Spirit tries to teach us. Paradoxically, we can only sort through all of this by yielding to the authority and omniscience of God's indwelling Holy Spirit.

As a footnote to this and every section, it is important to remind the reader that God's Holy Spirit cannot indwell us until we have accepted God's only-begotten Son, Jesus Christ, as personal Savior and Savior of the world. Without an acknowledgement of the divinity of Jesus Christ, divine metaphysics is neither divine nor metaphysics.

The Role of Trust in Matters of Conscience

All iniquity, all sin, all erroneous thinking and feeling, all activity inconsistent with God's Will, and all submission to temptation is the direct result of displaced trust. It is as if each person has been given a *100X* capacity to trust — the same quantity of the quality that represents the foundation for all of our earthly thoughts, feelings, words, and actions. We can place all *(100X)* of our trust in God and act like it. Or we can place all *(100X)* of our trust in noumena and phenomena other than God. To be sure, we can also place some *(from 1 to 99X)* of our trust in God and the remainder *(from 99X to 1X)* of our trust in noumena and phenomena other than God.

Some of us trust in ourselves and nothing else. Some of us trust in others and not God. Some of us trust more in chance, coincidence, and circumstance and less in divine direction, intervention, and intercession. Some of us trust more in people doing the wrong thing and less in God influencing people to do the right thing. Some of us trust more in humanism and a social conscience and less in God's goodness and the ongoing guidance of His Holy Spirit.

Although God gives each one of us a full complement of trust, God does not force us to trust in Him.

Adam and Eve yielded to temptation because they did not trust God completely. Jezebel threatened to kill the Prophet Elijah because she trusted in a false god. Judas yielded to the temptation to betray Jesus because he trusted in himself and not in God. Ananias and Sapphira yielded to temptation because they trusted in their own riches. You and I continue to yield to temptation because we trust in something else more than we trust in God. The lesson we all must learn during our human experience is to place, or replace, *all* of our trust in God and to trust in nothing and no one else other than God. As long as some of our trust remains displaced away from God, we will continue to think the wrong thoughts, feel the wrong emotions, say the wrong words, and do the wrong things. Unless we learn to trust in God completely, we will continue to disappoint God as well as ourselves.

It is not wrong to trust other people, but it is wrong to trust them completely. It is unrealistic. They will disappoint us by not living up to our expectations of what we think they should do or who we think they should be or become. They will disappoint us because they will not always have our best interests at heart. However, God will never disappoint us. Although He may not always do what we expect Him to do or what we think He should do, God always has our best interests at heart.

If we trust in God completely, we permit God's Holy Spirit to direct our moral compass toward His absolute truth and allow God's Will for our lives to be fulfilled in us.

I must confess that I daily fail miserably in trusting God

completely, but I do absolutely trust that God forgives me for my considerable failings. How? I know Him to be Who He says He Is — that is, full of grace and mercy. (Of course, it would be sinful to try to prove God's grace and mercy by purposely continuing to sin.)

It is true that, after we are saved, we can only disappoint God by disappointing ourselves. Unfortunately, I have experienced this myself. Fortunately, we can learn from our mistakes. Indeed, there is always hope when we trust in God.

Living in a state of contrition includes being continually aware that we have the power to disappoint God. We disappoint God when we fail to trust in Him for all our needs in every situation.

Chemical Addiction as a Thorn in the Flesh

All sin is addiction. Because we are all sinners (regardless of whether we are saved or not), someone who *is not* a substance abuser has no basis for feeling superior to someone who *is* a substance abuser. Substance abuse is a complex issue and always has been. Some people are predisposed to substance abuse because they suffer from an anxiety disorder or from endogenous depression. Other people have a condition that is akin to having a "thorn in the flesh" in their limbic system. It is this last group of people about which I will now comment.

To be sure, no human being has the right to accuse, judge, or condemn another human being for any reason. If someone you know has an intestinal parasite, you certainly would not accuse, judge, or condemn that person because having the parasite would not be his or her fault. For that matter, you really could not even judge the parasite since the parasite simply would be doing what it was created to do.

In his Second Epistle to the Corinthians, the Apostle Paul explains that he had a "thorn in the flesh" from "a messenger of Satan" that had been sent to "buffet" him — which is to say, *fight against* him (2 Corinthians 12:7 KJV). Although the Apostle Paul asked Christ Jesus to remove the thorn in his flesh, he was told that the Lord's grace would be "sufficient" for him and that the Lord's "strength is made perfect in weakness" (2 Corinthians 12:9 KJV).

The Apostle Paul could take no personal responsibility for the infirmity caused by the thorn in his flesh because it was God's Will that he have it. Although many people think that they may know in which area of his physical body that the Apostle Paul had his "thorn in the flesh," *they really do not know*. They can only speculate because the Holy Bible is never specific about how or where the Apostle Paul's thorn manifested in his flesh. This uncertainty is especially helpful for the metaphysical understanding and treatment of various conditions caused by thorns in the flesh from messengers of Satan. In other words, the Apostle Paul's thorn has a more universal application to disease processes, physical disabilities, and demonic attacks for certain people instead of just a specific application to one ailment or a single difficulty.

The Apostle Paul's thorn in the flesh serves as an example that there are some disease processes, physical disabilities, and demonic attacks for which the afflicted have no personal responsibility because they are neither the cause of the affliction nor the reason for its permanency or residual effects. However, the afflicted always have responsibility for seeking God's grace in dealing with the affliction and for modeling Christ in their actions and reactions to the affliction. And they also have the responsibility to share their pain, suffering, and adversity with Christ, with other people who love them, and with medical or psychological practitioners and spiritual intercessors.

This spiritual truth has great relevance for substance abusers because some addicts have a thorn in the flesh, specifically in their limbic system via a dopaminergic pathway. Metaphysically speaking, this thorn in the flesh is like an invisible parasite that has burrowed into, and affixed itself to, the emotional brain. This thorn in the flesh creates an insatiable desire for opiates, opioids, and opioid-like substances as well as for other addictive substances (like alcohol, benzodiazepines, nicotine, and psychostimulants) that lessen the physical and emotional pain caused by the condition itself.

Just as the Apostle Paul identified that his own thorn in the flesh was from an invisible messenger of Satan, so also are the invisible parasites that cause addictions in certain individuals not only spiritual but have their origin in Satan, too. These demonic parasites fix their hooks deeply in the vulnerable flesh of the host's limbic system and are virtually impossible to remove. The only thing that victims and their loved ones can do is pray for the strength to endure the physical and emotional pain and suffering from these thorns in the flesh. All addicts must learn to use their pain and suffering to become increasingly reliant and dependent on the Lord God Almighty. If their trust and hope is in God, then, despite having such a troubling condition, they bring more glory, praise and honor to God's Holy Name. Although the condition is abhorrent, its victims are not abhorrent. In fact, their disease can be used to bless the Name of the Lord through their endurance, perseverance, and faithfulness.

Please do not misinterpret that I mean to suggest that all chemical addictions are due to thorns in the flesh or that no thorn in the flesh will yield to spiritual, supernatural, and metaphysical healing treatments. If there is not the slightest remission after multiple treatments of prayer, fasting, meditation, praise, and affirmation, then the spiritual practitioner should assume that the condition is due to the existence of a thorn in the flesh from Satan. The condition should then be viewed and treated as such by praying for God's strength to be made manifest in the victims that they are able to not only endure but also triumph over the agony of their conditions.

Although it might be easy to conclude that substance abusers who have this peculiar thorn in the flesh are self-indulgent, such may not be the case. And, although it might be easy to conclude that these substance abusers are possessed by unclean spirits, this is rarely the case. Whereas unclean spirits possess people's souls and are cast out by calling upon the Name of the Lord (specifically, by praying "for Thy Name's Sake"), messengers of Satan that cause thorns in the flesh are responsible for specific problems that may be allowed by the Lord God Almighty. Their conditions can remain for a short time, a long time, or a lifetime. To be sure, the Book of Job in the Holy Bible details the struggle of a righteous man tormented and troubled by Satan with permission from God. Job's friends, who were quite intelligent and well-intentioned, speculated as to why Job experienced what he did. However, Job's friends were inaccurate in their assumptions and analyses concerning his afflictions. Similarly, we should not be so certain of our personal diagnoses concerning people who have chemical addictions. We must pray to God for guidance concerning their diagnosis and treatment.

The Cerebellum

The cerebellum (the labeled region at the base of the brain in Figure Fourteen) is responsible for the unconscious (i.e., subconscious) coordination of muscular movements with the energy-based spatial input from auditory and visual stimuli. (Olfactory and gustatory stimuli are chemically-based rather than energy-based.) In this coordination, the cerebellum also helps to maintain equilibrium, posture, and balance. Tracts of white matter within the cerebellum are collectively referred to as the *arbor vitae* (literally, "the tree of life," seen in Figure Fourteen).

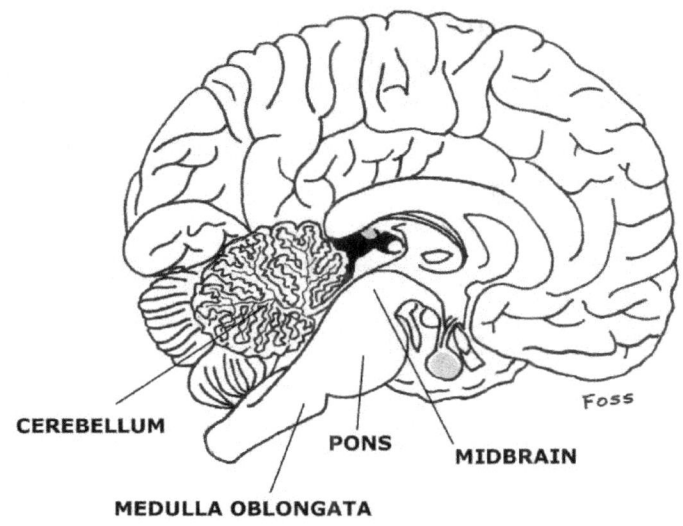

Cerebellum and Brain Stem
Figure Fourteen

Metaphysically speaking, the *arbor vitae* of the cerebellum is a visual reminder of God's "Tree of Life," originally found within the Garden of Eden, or Heavenly Paradise, from which man was expelled at the time of the Adamic Fall. (Fortunately, God's real "Tree of Life" is found within the city of New Jerusalem, where redeemed man is fully restored.[109])

In the glorious Presence of God, members of the Body of Christ involuntarily flex, extend, and hyperextend their appendages in coordinated mass movements designed to worship their Creator. In God's supernatural reality (called "the Spiritual Universe" in the present author's two prequels to this book), we not only function (1) individually but also (2) collectively as one spiritual, social organism and (3) corporately as one spiritual body. Our involuntary movements in praise of God are not only executed at (1) the individual level, they are also executed in unison at (2) the spiritual-social level as well as (3) the spiritual-corporate level. Such movements in individuals are coordinated by one of the energy vortices in redeemed, restored man that is analogous to the cerebellum in the anatomy of fallen, corporeal man.

It is in the praise of God that we find the source of all life as well as fulfill the role that we were intended to fulfill within God's spiritual universe.

As a footnote here, although I have written that the movements associated with praise are "involuntary" in the spiritual state, I do not mean to suggest that they are outside of our own volition, consent, or control. Rather, these collective movements are involuntary because they are the supernatural reflex responses of created beings to the Presence of their Creator. Indeed, in a spiritually-glorified state, we freely and fully agree to such worshipful movements in intimate communion and communication with our Creator.

---

[109] Genesis 2:9, 3:22 & 24; Revelation 22:2 & 14

The Brain Stem

The brain stem consists of the midbrain, pons, and medulla oblongata (all illustrated in Figure Fourteen). The brain stem contains various relay and involuntary reflex centers associated with respiration, heartbeat, and blood vessel diameter as well as involuntary movements associated with visual and auditory stimuli. Activities of the brain stem can be overridden physiologically by higher brain centers (such as the forebrain) and metaphysically by the supraself (the supraconscious mind of one's etheric body double).

In an oversimplification, the phrases "brain stem" and "reptile brain" (or "reptilian brain") are used synonymously. The so-called reptile brain is that part of the human brain responsible for some major involuntary reactions and instinctual responses to changes in the environment that potentially impact one's survival.

Energy Centers (Vortices) and the Central Nervous System

Throughout recorded history, various people, groups, philosophers, theologians, religionists, and healing arts practitioners have tried to interpret and elaborate their own intuitive sense of energy centers related to the human body in various systematic bodies of knowledge. *For example,* descriptions of the Kabbalistic (Cabalistic) Sephirot, or Sephiroth (singular *Sephira* or *Sephirah*), and the Hindu Chakras attempt to define energy centers related to the human body in very complex ways. However, all such attempts to make the unknown known have obfuscated the simple metaphysical reality that original, unfallen man was made in the complete image and perfect likeness of God and that human beings now possess a fallen, corporeal somatic identity and, therefore, reflect a distorted image and imperfect likeness of God. These elaborate and complex attempts often relegate simple spiritual truths to the dark and mysterious realms of the occult, where hidden or concealed knowledge is only available to a chosen few and only after much study of obscure, and often trite, information for a student to become one of the so-called *initiated*.

Although there are those who might take some of what has been written in this book and present it as knowledge requisite for any spiritual advancement, they will have missed the point that understanding who we now are, as well as who we used to be, comes only through our accepting the shed blood of God's only-begotten Son for our salvation. All spiritual advancement is found only in the acceptance of this truth. Unfortunately, for most people, that truth is either arcane itself or archaic and purposeless. They have decided that the Creator's requirement of a blood sacrifice for sin, as elaborated and fully explained in the Old and New Testaments, is borne of the human psyche's need to devise an unnecessary primitive action to ritually remove individual and collective guilt, shame, and self-condemnation. Indeed, they are wrong. They misunderstand our Creator's intent. And they misunderstand the gracious benevolence of His Plan of Salvation through Jesus Christ.

Without true understanding and acceptance of the following two passages from the Holy Bible, all study of divine metaphysics is useless and a waste of time:

> *For God the Father so loved the world that He gave His only-begotten Son that whoever believes in the Son should not perish but have everlasting life.*
>
> JOHN 3:16 KJV (PARAPHRASE)

> *Without the shedding of blood, there is no forgiveness of sins.*
>
> HEBREWS 9:22B KJV (PARAPHRASE)

The absolute truth of the entire Holy Bible rests on the truth expressed in John 3:16 and Hebrews 9:22b. Without understanding this truth, a discussion of divine metaphysics is purely academic and belongs to the realm of useless and obscure mystery religions. The crucifixion and resurrection of Jesus Christ is the crux of all history and of all spiritual reality. Jesus Christ is not just "the Wayshower" or "the Waymaker," Jesus Christ is the very Way itself:

> *I am the Way, the Truth, and the Life: no person comes to the Father, but by me.*
>
> JOHN 14:6 KJV (PARAPHRASE)

Pain and Suffering

I have opted to include a section on pain and suffering in this chapter because pain and suffering are experienced by the brain, and because so many Christians who seek healing spiritually through intercessory prayer and metaphysical treatment are embarrassed by the existence of pain and suffering when they need not be. Embarrassment comes either because of ignorance or because one is unable to control outcomes; and one is unable to control outcomes either because one is ignorant or because one is not willing to submit to the one who has all power, God.

Simple physical pain in itself is not evil since it can have therapeutic value for an injured body part or can direct us, reflexively, to move away from potentially harmful situations *(for example*, when we withdraw a hand as soon as we touch a hot stove or when we move a foot as soon as we step on a sharp object). Unless actual nerve damage has been sustained, the prolonged simple physical pain of a body part is usually due to swelling, which stimulates both pressure receptors and pain receptors.

Prolonged pain can have therapeutic value because it causes us to move cautiously to avoid further injury to an area and not interrupt its healing (that is, if we are healing normally). The fear of physical pain has practical benefits, too. *For example,* one of the reasons that we move away from an oncoming motorized vehicle is to avoid potentially painful and damaging consequences from being hit by the force of a heavy, moving object. Thus, simple physical pain in itself and a healthy fear of physical pain are not evil. In fact, they help to provide each of us with a physical survival advantage and edge.

Prolonged intense physical pain alerts us to potentially life-threatening situations that need to be prayed for, diagnosed, and treated successfully or accepted as ongoing conditions. Prolonged intense physical pain causes mental and emotional suffering. But such suffering can be used by our Creator for spiritual purposes. *For example,* God will use suffering to discipline people who are unwilling or unable to discipline themselves. If we refuse to discipline ourselves by refraining from sin, then God will do it for us — not because of His Wrath but because of His Love for us. Indeed, all circumstances, including pain and suffering, are at God's disposal to use in helping us to mature spiritually. Our spiritual maturation is God's secondary goal for us; our salvation is His primary goal. Students of divine metaphysics need to understand the difference between: (1) God's Wrath toward those who worship false gods, shed innocent blood, and reject His only-begotten Son; and (2) God's chastening of those who belong to Him.[110]

God can also use pain and suffering to help us learn important lessons in life, including becoming more compassionate toward others who experience pain and suffering. And God can use thorns in the flesh[111] to help people shift their focus away from the physical toward the spiritual, supernatural, and metaphysical with increasing trust in, and dependence on, Him.

Aside from paranormal events that can happen spontaneously to any person, true spiritual visionaries often contend with daily pain and suffering. Indeed, pain and suffering can *help* to open a window of the soul to the unseen. *Help* is italicized in the previous sentence to emphasize that pain and suffering alone do not cause us to become spiritual visionaries or more spiritually-minded

---

110 **Revelation 3:19, King James Version**
111 **2 Corinthians 12:7-10**

people. Also, spiritual visionaries and spiritually-minded people must learn how to separate delusions and illusions that *are not* God-ordained from visions, dreams, and impressions that *are* God-ordained. God-ordained visions, dreams, and impressions provide us with allusions and metaphors of spiritual reality and are, therefore, ways for us to understand the divine. They help us to better understand God and who we are in Him.

Sometimes, God permits pain and suffering to help us to see spiritual truths more clearly as well as learn how and when to apply them (either now or sometime in the future) to our own reality as well as to the reality of others.

Intermittent or continuous pain and suffering can be short term, long term, or lifelong. Here is how God has used pain and suffering in my own life:

1. To correct, discipline, and chasten me.

2. To strengthen me by causing me to grow spiritually (and, thus, helping me to stand on my own two feet).

3. To initiate and develop my compassion for others who experience pain and suffering.

4. To help me fix my gaze on spiritual truths and to learn how to apply them to my own condition as well as to the conditions of others.

5. To enable me to gain spiritual insights, glimpse spiritual truths, and have spiritual dreams and visions.

6. To keep me from entertaining, indulging, and acting on sinful desires.

7. To help distract my attention away from intense emotional stress, worry, and anxiety.

8. To help me learn that there are things beyond my control.

Lest anyone misconclude that I am trying to present myself as a model for others by sharing the previous eight points, please know that Jesus Christ is your first, last, and only model. The present author is not your role model.

The most profound way in which the Lord God Almighty can use pain and suffering is to keep us from sin. How? "The person who suffers in the flesh no longer lives to fulfill the lusts of the flesh by sinning but, instead, lives to fulfill the Will of God."[112]

I doubt that most readers have ever heard a sermon on the topic of pain and suffering as gifts from God because it would be an unpopular one and probably misunderstood. Sometimes, God permits pain and imposes suffering on us so that we no longer entertain or indulge the desires of a carnal mind, which desires include lusts related to our fallen somatic identity. And, when given the free will choice by God, we may even consciously choose pain and suffering for the benefits they present. For some people, persistent pain and suffering are a combination of both imposition by God and conscious acceptance in order for them to avoid sin. (It is not my intent to endorse or honor self-injury, self-abuse, addiction, sadomasochistic tendencies, false martyrdom, or any other personality disorder by referring to the "conscious acceptance" of beneficial pain and suffering.)

Personally, when I am in the throes of pain, I do not think about sinning. When I am in constant pain, I simply am not tempted to sin. If I was given a choice by our Creator to be healed of the chronic pain that keeps me from sinning, I would decline such healing (unless, of course, I had permanently overcome my desire to sin). I prefer the healing of my spiritual self over the healing of my physical body as well as the heightened spiritual focus and spiritual vision that my chronic pain allows. Over-the-counter medications do not mitigate my pain. And it is my choice not to use anything stronger to lessen it. In other words, the pain I am experiencing is spiritually therapeutic. That is why God and I are in complete agreement concerning its existence. Please do not misinterpret the previous statement to mean that I direct God; rather, I yield to God's direction of me. And please do not misinterpret that I am advocating that you should not seek medical, psychological, and/or spiritual treatment to lessen pain. Indeed, I am not endorsing false martyrdom or self-pity for myself

---

112 1 Peter 4:1b-2, King James Version (Paraphrase)

or anyone else.

Interestingly, when I am in the midst of using my creative consciousness — *for example,* in writing this book — I am not aware of pain. Experience has taught me that when we use our brains to focus on things supernal, there is no room for our brains to simultaneously experience pain. Additionally, I have observed that our brains often experience the greatest physical pains that we have at the same time that they dismiss any lesser physical pains we might also have. The explanation is that human brains are capable of experiencing only a few stimuli at the same time. Our brains experience the greater physical pains to direct our attention toward the areas of greatest need in case we can change the circumstances that are causing the pain. Why? Normal and healthy brains are oriented toward ensuring our physical survival. Our brains focus on the greatest immediate threats to our physical survival.

Pain and suffering are also useful to us as we approach the time for our transition from the physical realm to the spiritual realm through the process we call death. Pain and suffering help us to want to lay down our earthly burdens and deteriorating bodies. Therefore, they prepare us to yield to the passing of our souls from this world to the next. We become too weak to fight to stay alive. We become too weak to continue to hate (if, in fact, we have held on to hate). We even become too weak to withhold forgiveness. Our will to live in fleshly existence wanes, diminishes, disintegrates, and eventually disappears. Thus, we are better prepared to make the transition as this life ends.

When pain and suffering are not God-ordained, they should be treated physically, psychologically, and spiritually. It is most unfortunate that many who rely on spiritual healing reject any and all physical and/or psychological treatment. And it is equally as unfortunate that many who rely on physical and/or psychological treatment distance themselves from spiritual healing. Physical and psychological treatment and spiritual healing do not need to be mutually exclusive. The idea of mutual exclusion has come from an ignorance of when one modality should supersede the other as well as the erroneous idea that we need to wholly commit ourselves to one or the other in order for the chosen modality to have maximum efficacy. To rely radically on spiritual, supernatural, and metaphysical healing should not require us to decline having a wound cleansed and bandaged or a broken bone realigned and wrapped since that would be resisting common sense and eschewing practicality. Rather, cleanse the wound and reset the broken bone while you are praying as well as proclaiming God's goodness and your wholeness in the Lord — even if spiritual healing is the particular modality that you have chosen for primary treatment.

Unfortunately, most physicians and psychologists are neither educated nor trained in the spiritual healing arts and most Christian metaphysicians are neither educated nor trained in the science of physical healing or in diagnosing and treating mental disorders. Hence, practitioners within each category often regard each other with suspicion, contempt, and disdain and refuse to work together. Because of their ignorance of other modalities, they misconclude that choice of treatment is an "either/or" question. They do not consider the possibility of blending, shifting, and reshifting treatment based on changing physical, psychological, and spiritual needs. For this reason, I am proposing a new category of healing practitioner — which is to say, a "metapractitioner." (The definition for *metapractitioner* is given in the section of Chapter One entitled *The Vocabulary of Divine Metaphysics*.)

Metapractitioners should be educated and trained to diagnose and treat disabilities, diseases, and disorders through combined methodologies from medicine, psychology, and divine metaphysics. They should be educated and trained to work with other specialists in medicine, psychology, and divine metaphysics. They themselves should each have a specialty in one or more of these three areas. Thus, although *metapractitioners* might take on the role of coordination, their expertise would extend into the arena of treatment itself. Their involvement should be far beyond simple case management.

Concerning treatment modality, the idea is not to convince ourselves or others of what is right but to recognize what is right and apply it to the situation. *For example,* it is not necessary to refute the existence of pain and suffering to radically rely on divine healing. In fact, refuting the existence of pain and suffering sometimes represents dysfunctionality, which is antithetical to spiritual healing. Rather than refuting the existence of pain and suffering, acknowledging their existence and moving forward — unhindered and unfettered despite their existence — is the preferred spiritual alternative.

Regardless of whatever else is done for pain and suffering, pain and suffering should always be brought before the Mercy Seat of God, where intimate communion and authentic communication with God take place.

Either pain and suffering have power over you or you have power through Christ Jesus over pain and suffering. It is that simple. There can be no amalgamation or sharing of power. If pain and suffering have power over you, they will control you by sapping your strength and deterring you from your daily responsibilities and spiritual purpose. To have control over pain and suffering through Christ Jesus means, minimally, that you submit them to God moment by moment and, maximally, that you are completely free from their deleterious effects. Here, freedom does not necessarily mean that you are no longer experiencing pain and suffering (although it can mean that). Metaphysically speaking, freedom means that you are no longer controlled by pain and suffering or by fear induced from their presence or potential presence.

The Church historian Eusebius Pamphili (263-339 A.D.), Bishop of Caesarea, detailed how Christian martyrs tortured to the point of death were often able to find that spiritual inner place where they could endure pain and suffering without recanting their commitment to Jesus Christ.[113] In this way, they were able to complete and fulfill their unique personal witness of Jesus as their Savior. Indeed, they were graduated to Heaven with *summa cum*

---

113 *Eusebius – The Church History: A New Translation with Commentary,* Kregel Publications, Grand Rapids, 1999. (See pages 172, 175, 177, 210, and 235 for examples of early Christian martyrdom.)

laude honors! As I see it, Christian martyrs are the greatest saints of God. Yielding to impending martyrdom flies in the face of everything physical, including "fight or flight" response mechanisms. (Do not misinterpret that I am advocating that you should seek martyrdom. That would be presumptuous of us both.)

In addition to Christian martyrs, true spiritual visionaries, mystics, seers, oracles, and prophets are often able to find that place of resolve, commitment, and communion in their individual souls as they journey with God while they are experiencing pain and suffering. Do not misinterpret that such people control when God speaks to them. That would be unseemly. God is omnipotent. God is not subject to control by anything or anyone or by any set of circumstances or by any specific formulas. We do not control God. All control belongs to God. For that reason, we need not be afraid of anything that is beyond our control.

Here are five questions that should be asked and answered relative to pain and suffering in yourself or others:

1. Is the probable cause of the pain and suffering physical, psychological, and/or spiritual?

2. What do physicians, psychologists, and metaphysicians say concerning the cause?

3. What do physicians, psychologists, and metaphysicians say concerning the treatment?

4. How shall we pray concerning the cause and treatment of the condition?

5. What combination of treatments should be used and in what sequence?

Hopefully, during *the Millennium*, you will be able to visit a *metapractitioner* for accurate diagnoses and recommendations for treatment concerning all disabilities, diseases, and disorders with referrals to the appropriate specialists.

The Role of Prayer in Healing

Prayer is communion with God — specifically, communication *to* God. However, prayer not only includes making requests *to* God but also waiting for responses *from* God. Praying without ceasing[114] includes: (1) the constant desire to yield to, and act upon, the Will of God; and (2) the constant desire to please God in every thought, in every word, and in every deed. Prayer includes making a commitment to always seek, as well as yield to, God's Will.

It is not sufficient to know the truth. It is not sufficient to articulate the truth. God's hand must always be involved in the application of the truth and the timing of the application. Without God's involvement, your "knowing" the truth and articulating the truth are of no avail. They are useless. We must invite God's involvement into our daily activities through prayer, which includes desiring God to be at the helm of all of our activities.

The spiritual, supernatural, and metaphysical treatment of physical and psychological problems requires that we never lose sight of the efficacy of the shed blood of Jesus Christ. All spiritual healing power rests in applying that blood to the problem or challenge at hand. Without the assertive and proactive knowledge of the shed blood of Jesus Christ and its efficacy, all metaphysical dialogue is just so much claptrap.

Because the causes of many physical and psychological problems are multivariate, we should never be disappointed when such problems do not yield to spiritual, supernatural, or metaphysical treatment in the ways that we think they should. Despite persistent problems, let us continually grasp the truth that God's love is consistently unfaltering and consistently unfailing.

Prayer is not only the first line of defense but also the first line of offense to counteract Satan's attacks on our physical, psychological, and spiritual well-being. The spiritual healing of unhealthy physical, emotional, mental, and spiritual conditions includes intercessory prayer as well as metaphysical treatment. Intercessory prayer is the verbal articulation to God of a personal

---

114 1 Thessalonians 5:17

desire — in this case, for healing. In contrast, metaphysical treatment to resolve an unhealthy condition includes recognizing, acknowledging, applying, affirming, and proclaiming — that is, laying claim to the truth by declaring — who we really are in God through Christ Jesus. (More on comparing and contrasting intercessory prayer and metaphysical treatment will be shared in following chapters.)

Understanding the Special Physical Senses

All special physical senses originate in the human head. They include: vision (seeing), olfaction (smelling), audition (hearing), and gustation (tasting). Touch, pressure, pain, and temperature receptors are not only found in the head but throughout the entire human body; consequently, they are not considered "special senses" and will not be discussed in this section.

Metaphysically speaking, God sees, smells, hears, and tastes. In contrast, man-made gods "neither see nor hear nor eat nor smell."[115]

Vision (Seeing)

Key words in the Bible: *eye/eyes, see/seeing/sight, vision, "apple of the eye"*

The eye reveals the focus of the viewer — which is to say, what is important to the observer. To be sure, we are the "apple of God's eye" because God's sight is fixed on us. Here, the word *apple* connotes "object of intense desire" as demonstrated by the image reflected in the pupil as well as the relative diameter of the pupil, which inversely relates to the degree of one's interest (i.e., the greater the interest, the more constricted the iris and the smaller the pupil). *Apple* also connotes "what one favors or looks upon with favor." To be sure, God has intense desire for the people of His Earth. In fact, we are "the pupil" of God's extraordinary eye. We are

---

115 Deuteronomy 4:28, King James Version

His created. That is why His eye is fixed on us. And God extends His favor and mercy to all for whom He has a "tender eye."

The truth be told, the apple Satan offered to Adam and Eve simply represents that they were tempted by something attractive and desirable to them (i.e., something that found favor in their eyes). The same is true for us today: Satan can only tempt us with what we desire — which is to say, an "apple of our eye."

God's eye is upon all who fear, or revere, Him because they constitute the righteous people of God. This is why He watches over them and has mercy upon them. As recorded in the Book of Revelation, the "seven eyes" of the Lamb of God represent the sevenfold Spirit of God that searches the hearts and minds of all people to know what is within them.[116] (Remember, God is omnipresent but not in a pantheistic sense.)

Concerning the vision of human beings, people only possess their own individual perspectives and nothing else. For people who belong to God, even *possessing* our own vision is questionable since it is God Himself, through His Holy Spirit, Who permits us glimpses of His truth and glory:

> *The hearing ear, and the seeing eye, the LORD has made them both.*
>
> PROVERBS 20:12 KJV (PARAPHRASE)

In other words, the people of God on Earth can only see God to the degree that He permits them to see Him. Nevertheless, we must still look for God by focusing on His spiritual truth and the principles contained within His Holy Bible. Also, we must desire to see Him. (Remember, prayer *is* desire.)

As mentioned in Chapter One of this book, "the eye has not seen the things that God has prepared for those who love Him."[117] There are spiritual, supernatural, and metaphysical truths that human beings cannot and will not understand until they arrive at

---

116 Revelation 5:6
117 1 Corinthians 2:9, King James Version (Paraphrase)

that point in time when they have been sufficiently prepared by God to understand them.

Christ Jesus declared that "the light of the body is the eye; therefore, if your eye is single, your whole body shall be full of light."[118] The metaphysical import of this statement is that, when our spiritual sight is fixed on knowing God, only then will we be enlightened by His truths. However, if our sight is fixed on indulging our carnal selves, then we will be in the dark concerning God's existence and His seemingly mysterious ways. (See also Matthew 6:23.)

Without the Spirit of God residing within us, we cannot see spiritual truth. We may see physically but be blind spiritually. In contrast, we may not see physically but have spiritual sight (i.e., supernatural insight, hindsight, and foresight). And, although the saved of God can see God, they can only see God to the extent that He permits them to see Him. Regardless, we will never see God inexhaustibly — except, perhaps, at the time of the end, when He infuses us all with His glory.[119]

Let us become more like Job, who took custody of his eyes that he not look upon things to lust after them:

> *I made a covenant with my eyes; why then should I think upon a maiden?*
>
> JOB 31:1 KJV

Olfaction (Smelling)

Key words in the Bible: *nose, smell, odor, incense, savor, sacrifice*

God smells the "sweet savor" or "sweet incense" of our earnest prayers to Him.[120] The smell of acceptable sacrifices and oblations

---

118 Matthew 6:22, King James Version (Paraphrase)
119 1 Corinthians 15:28, King James Version
120 Luke 1:9-10; Revelation 8:3-4

of praise are well-pleasing, or sweet-smelling, to God.[121] It is recorded in Amos 5:21 (KJV) that God said to the reprobate children of Israel: "I will not smell in your solemn assemblies." In other words, because of their idolatrous practices, He would not accept their sacrifices. Interestingly, the Hebrew word for both "smell" and "acceptable odor" is *ru'-akh* [H7306 in Appendix Table A], which is the primitive root for the Hebrew word for human "spirit" and human "mind" as well as for God's Holy "Spirit" and God's "divine Mind" [see H7307 in Appendix Table A].

To be sure, God's Holy Spirit is the breath of our life, or what sustains us. In the reality of God, we inspire and expire God's "living water," which is His Holy Spirit. Before the Adamic Fall, we were not only indwelt by God's Holy Spirit, we were completely immersed in His Holy Spirit. When we get to Heaven, we will again be completely immersed in His Holy Spirit. At the present time, saved people on Earth are infilled by His Holy Spirit. Therefore, let us always *seek* to be continually infilled by God's Holy Spirit as well as demonstrate such infilling in thought, word, and deed. As the innocent unborn fetus inhales and exhales amniotic fluid, so does the reborn soul inhale and exhale God's Water of Life (i.e., His Holy Spirit). (See also the chapter entitled *Divine Metaphysics of the Respiratory System*.)

Audition (Hearing)

Key words in the Bible: *ear/ears, hear/hears/heard, hearken, listen, comprehend*

Metaphysically speaking, the two ears on both sides of the head act as if they are scales with the brain in between to "weigh" both sides of what is heard. This association for "ears" and "scales" is corroborated by these two Hebrew heteronyms:[122] (1)

---

121 Philippians 4:18b
122 Hebrew heteronyms are words that are spelled identically but pronounced differently because they each have different vowel points (that is, different cues for vowel sounds).

o'-zen [H241 in Appendix Table A], which means "ear;" and (2) *a-zan'* [H239 in Appendix Table A], which means "weigh," "test," "prove," and "consider."

Every member or individual, or group of similar individuals, within the body of Christ has a different gift and function. Even individuals within a group that have the same gift or similar function demonstrate diversity based on variance. Metaphysically speaking, "the ear" in the Body of Christ receives divine revelation. Therefore, "the ear" includes both Old and New Testament prophets. Generally speaking, all people who belong to the Lord God Almighty are to "give ear" to Him by obeying His Will and listening for His "still small voice" (1 Kings 19:12 KJV). No one who belongs to God should neglect his or her God-given prophetic gift, which comes from God through His Holy Spirit.

When God inclines His ear, He is attentive to those who speak to Him. God is not attentive to those who are arrogant. In fact, He disinclines His ear away from those who are prideful. God is not attentive to those who whine or grumble; He does not pay attention to complaints. However, God is attentive to those whose lives praise Him by blessing His Holy Name. (See Exodus 32:18.) Today, God inclines His ear toward the brokenhearted and toward those who authentically use the Name of His only-begotten Son, regardless of which language they may use to say it or how they might pronounce it.

The double entendre in the Hebrew word from which the English word *Samuel* has been transliterated provides additional understanding for *audition*. The Hebrew *shem-u-al'* [H8050 in Appendix Table A] not only means "heard of God" but also "he who hears God." In other words, true communication with God is *two-way* communication. God hears those who hear Him — which is to say, He pays attention to those who demonstrate, by doing His Will, that they are paying attention to Him.

When we seek to do God's Will, He opens (or "unstoppers") our ears and grants us the knowledge of salvation as well as continued guidance throughout our spiritual journey based on that knowledge. Because their ears are "uncircumsized," people who refuse to accept Jesus Christ as God's only-begotten Son refuse to listen to the Lord God Almighty. Thus, they cannot understand Him because they refuse to hear Him. An expression in the King James Version of the Holy Bible — "those who hearken not unto the LORD" — refers to people who refuse to obey God even though He has spoken to them directly. Although many in the world would state that God has not spoken to them directly, He has spoken directly to us all through the life, death, resurrection, and ascension of His only-begotten Son, Jesus Christ, and He has spoken to us through the truths contained within His Holy Bible.

We should never doubt that God can speak to us through His Holy Spirit whenever He wants. However, we should be cautious in believing what we have heard is from God or that we are accurately interpreting the significance of what we have heard. Passage of time will always confirm or disconfirm that we have heard from God or that we have interpreted accurately what we have heard.

Not everyone is able to understand Bible prophecy simply and clearly. For this reason, the following blessing is recorded in God's written Word:

> *Blessed is the person who reads, and they who hear [or understand] the words of this prophecy, and keep [or ponder, value, and treasure in their hearts] those things that are written therein: for the time is at hand.*
>
> REVELATION 1:3 KJV (PARAPHRASE)

All understanding comes from the Lord God Almighty in accordance with His Will, which is always pure, and His timing, which is always perfect:

> *The LORD has not given you a heart to perceive, and eyes to see, and ears to hear, until this very day.*
>
> DEUTERONOMY 29:4 KJV (PARAPHRASE)

Gustation (Tasting)

Key words in the Bible: *tongue, taste/tastes/tasted, sweet, sour, salty, bitter*

Metaphysically speaking, *tasting* in the Bible refers to *experiencing*:

> *O taste and see that the LORD is good: blessed is everyone who trusts in Him.*
>
> PSALM 34:8 KJV (PARAPHRASE)

> *And Jesus said to them: "Indeed, I say to you that there are some who stand here who shall not taste death [i.e., experience the full ramifications of their evil] until they have seen the Kingdom of God come with power."*
>
> MARK 9:1 KJV (PARAPHRASE)

> *{4} For it is impossible for those who were once enlightened, and have tasted of the heavenly gift, and were made partakers of the Holy Ghost, {5} And have tasted the good word of God, and the powers of the world to come, {6} If they shall fall away, to renew them again unto repentance; seeing they crucify to themselves the Son of God afresh, and put him to an open shame.*
>
> HEBREWS 6:4-6 KJV (PARAPHRASE)

In addition to touching the things that they see with their hands and feet, infants and toddlers also put new things into their mouths to experience them. Metaphysically speaking, adult human beings also do the same thing with new ideas. We "taste" them to see: (1) if they are compatible with our current belief systems; (2) if they can be accommodated and assimilated into our current belief systems (thereby enlarging those systems); or (3) if they are incompatible and must be rejected permanently or mentally shelved for future reevaluation and reconsideration. Successful students of divine metaphysics always use their extensive knowledge of the Holy Bible as a filter for thoughts and ideas new to them. Without compatibility to the metaphysical principles contained within the Holy Bible, new thoughts and ideas must be rejected outright or retooled, reoutfitted, and refined to ensure compatibility to a belief system that is consistent with God's written Word. (The Holy Bible is God's only written Word.)

Coupled with olfaction, gustation grants us a special experience of the things that we are about to "swallow." If the physical things that we place in our mouths are savory and pleasant to the chemical senses of olfaction and gustation, we ingest, chew, and swallow them. In contrast, if the things are unsavory and unpleasant to these senses, we never ingest them, never chew them, and never swallow them but quickly spit them out. The same is true for metaphysical concepts, principles, and ideas.

Metaphysically speaking, negative thoughts and unseemly ideas are not to be ingested, chewed, or swallowed but spit out. Even if cake has only a little manure in it, we must spit out the whole mouthful because all of it has been spoiled. New thoughts and ideas must be pleasant to our spiritual, supernatural, and metaphysical sensitivities and sensibilities in order for them to be chewed and swallowed (which is to say, cogitated upon by our mind and incorporated into our *Weltanschauung,* or worldview). Even if what we are offered is 99 per cent truth and only 1 per cent error, the whole has been spoiled and, therefore, cannot be accepted without some reservations and qualifications.

Christ Jesus told those who belong to the Lord God Almighty that they are "the salt of the earth" because salt adds flavor and savor to what is eaten. Jesus said:

> *You are the salt of the earth: but if the salt has lost its savor [or distinctiveness], how shall it be salted [or made unique]? It is thenceforth good for nothing, but to be cast out, and to be trodden under foot.*

MATTHEW 5:13 KJV (PARAPHRASE)

In the Holy Bible, offerings to God and covenants with Him are often accompanied by salt. Metaphysically speaking, holy commitment is "salt" to God. Without holy commitment, sacrifices and promises to God have no meaning. For this reason, the written Word of God states: "Let your speech be always with grace, seasoned with salt [or holy commitment], that you may know how you ought to answer everyone."[123] Metaphysically speaking, holy commitment preserves us and keeps us from being corrupted by the ways of the world like salt preserving foodstuffs in corning, brining, and pickling.

The prayers of the saints are sweet and pleasant to God both in taste and in smell. They delight Him. God experiences joy when His children pray to Him. Their prayers bless His Holy Name by acknowledging Him as their Sovereign Creator and their only Provider, Rewarder, and Blesser. The Supraconsciousness of God is flooded with joy upon hearing the prayers of His people.

In contrast to salt water and poisoned water, both of which are described in the Holy Bible as "bitter," fresh water in the Holy Bible is often labeled as "sweet." Thus, the living water of God (i.e., His Holy Spirit) is also considered sweet because the Spirit of God refreshes those who have already been washed clean by the shed blood of Jesus Christ. And, like a hose with water continually rushing through it, the Spirit of God constantly and continually infills those who open themselves up to Him by living in a state of contrition (LSC).

Although the Hebrew word *meh'-lakh* [H4417 in Appendix Table A] is generally translated as "salt" in the King James Version of the Holy Bible, "ash" would have been a better word to use in Genesis 19:26. When Lot's wife looked back at her past life because she longed to return to it, she really wasn't reduced to just a pillar of sodium chloride, she was reduced to a pillar of ash (which includes sodium chloride) and, in this way, resembled the pillars of fossil salt that are found in regions surrounding the Dead Sea.

---

123 Colossians 4:6, King James Version (Paraphrase)

Concerning a sour taste in our mouths, just as unripened grapes are sour, so are thoughts that are immature both sour and unpleasant to God as well as to the spiritually mature people of God. Immature thoughts, ideas, and feelings are all sour because they have not yet been made ripe through the process of spiritual maturity, which requires time in addition to understanding. Although the fruit of the vine may ferment to produce wine, the wine must rest for it to mature. Mature wine, like understanding, has greater definition because it is more refined. That is why we must "let patience have her perfect work in us, that we may be complete and whole, lacking nothing."[124]

Understanding the Psychic Sense

Although the psychic sense is also a special sense, it is not recognized as such by most people. Due to ignorance of genuine paranormal phenomena and slanted, skewed, and biased interpretations of the Holy Bible relative to communications from the "here-beyond" as well as the existence of numerous fake healers, false mediums, and self-deluded "fortune tellers," the word *psychic* has taken on a negative connotation for most intelligent, authentic Christian believers.

Both the Biblical Hebrew word *neh'-fesh* [H5315 in Appendix Table A] and the Biblical Greek word *psu-khay'* [G5590 in Appendix Table B] mean "soul" or "mind." Indeed, *psu-khay'* is the Greek word from which the English words *psychic* and *psychology* have been derived. Thus, just as the word *psychology* means "the study of the *mind,*" so does the word *psychic* mean "*mind* reader" in a general sense. In its purest sense, the word *psychic* goes well beyond describing functions of the cerebrum as detected by brain wave activity during exercises of extrasensory perception. And, in its most spiritual sense, the word *psychic* describes sensing activity in the invisible, electromagnetic, and supernatural realm by gifted and talented "sensitives" or "susceptible channels." Metaphysically speaking, to be

---

124   James 1:4, King James Version (Paraphrase)

a *psychic* means that one "reads the soul" (i.e., receives impressions) and can transcend relative space-time to sense aspects of the past, present, and future.

Psychic Attack and the Wicked Smart

The wicked smart are usually people with remarkable abilities, including lightning speed and multi-track cognitive abilities as well as terrific forensic and oratory skills (which is to say, great speech communication and debating abilities). Although they themselves may be tactless and rude, they know when and how to employ flattery and rules of courtesy — and even charm — to manipulate and deceive others into believing that they are basically good people who will eventually grow to be better people over time when given the opportunity to do so.

To get their own way, the wicked smart will assassinate the character and integrity of those who pose a threat to them. (They do not waste their time and energies on those who do not pose a threat to them.) To do this, they try to inject doubt into others about their intended victim's character, integrity, motives, and behaviors. This usually takes place during their communications with those they seek to build alliances. Unless you are sensitive electromagnetically, psychically, or spiritually to the hidden motives of others (and, thus, are already able to identify the wicked smart through discernment), regular negative communications directed toward others will help you to identify the wicked smart in their operations of psychic attack. Unlike the wicked smart, people who simply have a negative and/or contrarian disposition will have something negative to say equally about almost everyone. Although they may eventually slander everyone in a small group, the wicked smart usually target only one, or just a few individuals at a time, in order to discredit them.

Interestingly, the wicked smart only build alliances with other people for the purpose of neutralizing threats from those who dare to go against their self-absorbed and prideful wills. Sometimes, others become willing allies because they recognize that the wicked smart could become dangerous to them personally. Thus, some people end up choosing to serve in the capacity of ally to, rather than victim of, the wicked smart. Often, however, allies of the wicked smart are simply trusting, passive, ignorant, and/or lazy individuals who neither have had much experience in discernment or fighting foes metaphysically nor the inclination, interest, or need to do so. It is usually a waste of time, effort, and energy to try to convince these allies about the heinous motives of the wicked smart. Most often, the allies will end up questioning your motives for saying something negative about the wicked smart; or they will just simply respond that they don't want to get involved. Your silence to others about the wicked smart, except for sharing with well-seasoned Christian brothers and sisters, is usually the best approach (in addition to prayers for protection) when you are under psychic attack.

Written and/or spoken character assassination in itself is a form of *psychic attack* (i.e., "mental malpractice" in the language of Christian metaphysics and "witchcraft" in the language of the Holy Bible). However, silent psychic attack can be far worse than attack out in the open. Silent psychic attack is more formidable because it seeks to occupy the time of the victim and cripple the victim's psychic defense mechanisms through electromagnetic entanglement, mental/emotional preoccupation, and spiritual assassination — all generally undetectable to unconcerned and/or spiritually dull bystanders.

Just like psychic attack, psychic defense mechanisms are also electromagnetic, mental, and spiritual in nature. These defense mechanisms include: (1) prayer by the intended victim or victims as well as by others on their behalf; (2) authentic prayers of forgiveness for the wicked smart (acknowledging them as mere tools of the Devil); (3) meditation on spiritual truths articulated in the Holy Bible; (4) mentally envisioning hedges of protection that circumscribe the intended victim or victims; (5) silent and spoken affirmations of truth, declarations of well-being, comfort, or safety, and proclamations of victory by expressing trust in the Lord God Almighty's omnipotence, omniscience, and omnipresence; and (6) spiritual falconry. Psychic defense mechanisms may also include some healing arts practices regarded as nontraditional to help relax the physical body and soothe frazzled emotions during periods of psychic attack and distress.

How can you tell the difference between the wicked smart who are immature and those who are well-seasoned? Those who are emotionally immature and childish will walk away from you in their attempts to hurt you; they will want to hurt you through their departure and, in their minds, punish you by their absence. In contrast, those who are highly skilled will walk toward you in their attempts to attack and parasitize you. They will want you to feel intimidated and fearful. Regardless of the maturity level of the attacker, you should never demonstrate fear. Why? The spirit of fear and of powerlessness and of an unsound mind is the antithesis of "the spirit of love and of power and of a sound mind" (2 Timothy 1:7 KJV Paraphrase).

Unless they have an ego-inversion, the fate of the wicked smart is unpleasant. After their lives are over, their souls become unclean spirits (also known as "devils," "evil spirits" or "demons" in the Holy Bible) that wander invisible realms for the purpose of attacking and attaching to the souls of human beings who themselves are vulnerable "sensitives" or "susceptible channels."

Susceptible Channels

The noun phrase "susceptible channels" is used in this book for people who are unusually sensitive to invisible, electromagnetic, and spiritual stimuli. Unless they are protected spiritually by the shed blood of God's only-begotten Son, susceptible channels are especially vulnerable to Satanic influence, attack, and control. Not all people are equally vulnerable to demonic influence, attack, or control because not all people are susceptible channels and not all people who are susceptible channels are equally susceptible.

The *majority* of people who wander the streets muttering to themselves, or who have been long-term residents in psychiatric institutions, are susceptible channels possessed (that is, inhabited) by unclean spirits. They are subject to demonic direction and control and may even attack others physically. To be sure, some diagnosable psychiatric conditions are entirely organic; some are entirely demonic; and some are a combination of organic and demonic in varying degrees. Medical practitioners, mental practitioners (including psychiatrists, psychologists, and trained counselors), and metaphysical practitioners should work together jointly concerning diagnosis and treatment of susceptible channels who are under demonic influence, attack, and control. All practitioners should receive education and training in this area.

Physical Homeostasis and Metaphysical Equipoise

Because the brain is incapable of distinguishing between and among various types of stressors, the same set of physical responses may occur for stressors that are physical, emotional, mental, or spiritual in origin. Depending on the type, strength, and duration of the stressor, the following physical stages may occur: (1) an *alarm reaction,* which is a short-term burst of "fight-or-flight" responses; (2) a *resistance reaction,* which is a delayed but sustained set of responses; and (3) *exhaustion,* which is a set of responses that may damage the body when stressors are unduly prolonged.

Sustained physical, emotional, mental, and spiritual stressors all stimulate the hypothalamus as well as other associated regions of the limbic system to cause: (1) the sympathetic division of the autonomic nervous system to increase output of epinephrine and norepinephrine by the adrenal medulla during the *alarm reaction;* (2) the adenohypophysis (or anterior pituitary gland) to increase output of thyrotropic stimulating hormone (TSH), growth hormone (GH), and adrenocorticotropic hormone (ACTH) during the *resistance reaction;* [125] and (3) hypokalemia (lower blood potassium levels) and eventual cellular death during lengthy periods of

---

125 In turn, ACTH stimulates the adrenal cortex to increase its production of mineralocorticoids, glucocorticoids, and gonadocorticoids; and TSH stimulates the thyroid gland to increase its production of T3 and T4.

physiologic *exhaustion*.

Personal conflicts with God, conflicts within oneself, and conflicts between oneself and others — as well as psychic attacks from other human beings and/or evil discarnates[126] — all induce the same set of physical responses and resulting conditions of disequilibria in the human body. Generally speaking, equilibrium in one's physical state of being is referred to as *physical homeostasis*. And, in this book, equilibrium in one's spiritual state of being is referred to as *metaphysical equipoise*.

To combat deleterious effects from sustained stress responses — including disease, cellular deterioration, and eventual death — each person needs to learn how to resolve conflict and transcend stress experiences to maintain, or return to, physical homeostasis through the tranquility and peace that comes from metaphysical equipoise.

In metaphysical equipoise, one is content regardless of the state in which one finds oneself.[127] Metaphysical equipoise leads to physical homeostasis and the presence of mind to endure sustained stress.

Resolving Conflict to Restore Equilibrium and Equipoise

Steps for resolving conflict with the Lord God Almighty:

1. Acknowledge Jesus Christ as the only-begotten Son of God, only Savior of the world, and your one true and only personal Savior.

2. Confess sins to God, repenting of them, and asking for forgiveness for them in the name of Jesus Christ.

---

126 Evil discarnates are also referred to as *devils, demons, evil spirits,* and *unclean spirits* in various translations of the Holy Bible.

127 Philippians 4:11, King James Version

3. Pray to the Lord God Almighty that His Will[128] be done in the name of Jesus Christ.

Steps for resolving conflict within yourself:

4. Make sure that you have completed Step 1 and are regularly repeating Steps 2 and 3.

5. Regularly ask others to prayerfully intercede for you. (James 5:16)

6. Continually trust that God has heard your prayer and is answering your prayer in accordance with His Will, which is always pure, and in accordance with His timing, which is always perfect. (1 John 5:14-15)

7. Regularly "meditate" on God's written Word by reading and pondering passages in the Holy Bible. (Psalm 1:1-2 KJV)

8. Regularly memorize passages from the Holy Bible.

9. Regularly set time aside to listen for God's "still small voice from within" (1 Kings 19:12 KJV Paraphrase).

10. Continually ask for God's guidance in terms of which thoughts and feelings are *pleasing* to Him and, then, think on those thoughts and feelings. (Philippians 4:8)

11. Continually ask for God's guidance to identify which thoughts and feelings are *displeasing* to Him.

12. Continually reject thoughts and feelings that are *displeasing* to God.

13. Continually combat carnal mind by taking captive every carnal thought and feeling by placing them under the feet, or authority, of Jesus Christ. (Matthew 28:18; Romans 8:28; 2 Corinthians 10:5)

---

128 God's Will for each individual includes different possible choices, activities, and outcomes. God's Will does not lock us into choosing for ourselves only one activity or only one area of interest. God's Will for us includes different possible trajectories in our lives with some different possible outcomes that are all within His Will for us.

14. Regularly recognize that there are certain conditions in you and in others over which you or others have absolutely no control but over which God has complete, absolute, and perfect control. (Daniel 7:14; Matthew 28:18)

15. Regularly recognize that there are certain conditions in you and in others which you and/or others did not cause.

16. Regularly recognize that there are certain conditions in you and in others which you and/or others cannot cure.

17. Regularly recognize that there are certain conditions for which there is no cure except natural physical death. (2 Corinthians 12:9)

18. Regularly recognize that certain conditions do not require that their cause be sought for them to be treated effectively and healed. (John 9:2)

19. Continually remember to incorporate gratitude to God and humility throughout all of your activities. (Psalm 69:30; Proverbs 22:4)

20. Continually remain in hope through the knowledge that God is always in control even when circumstances seem dark and outcomes appear to be bleak. (Proverbs 3:5)

21. Regularly correct and reject error in your thinking by evaluating it alongside of God's truth within the Holy Bible. (2 Corinthians 10:5)

22. Periodically rebuke evil and cast out demons. (Matthew 10:8) [Don't invent demons or imagine that they are involved when they are not.]

23. Regularly resist the Devil. (James 4:7)

24. Regularly recognize the extent of your own limitations. (Psalm 50:21)

25. Continually give up control to God. (Matthew 6:10)

26. Continually seek to bless and promote God's Holy Name and not your own name or the name of any other created being or person. (Psalm 96:2)

Additional steps to foster physical, mental, emotional, and spiritual healing within yourself and others include the following:

27. Regularly have periods of healthy physical activity that are both age-appropriate and ability-appropriate.

28. Regularly fulfill physical therapy when prescribed.

29. Regularly change your diet to eat well-balanced and healthier meals.

30. Regularly take dietary supplements responsibly by following the advice of your medical practitioner; and regularly educate yourself about the supplements with accurate and up-to-date information.

31. As appropriate and/or required, seek treatment from qualified medical, psychological, and healing arts practitioners, including Christian spiritual advisors. (When the day comes that they exist, consult a metapractitioner.)

32. Regularly take prescribed medication until your medical and/or psychological practitioner tells you that they are no longer needed.

33. In conjunction with Step Seven from this list, regularly incorporate into your daily routine other forms of meditation that are compatible with Christianity.

Speaking Truth Aloud

Key words in the Bible: *mouth, speech, speak, groanings, pray, prayer, praise, shout, cry out*

For the overwhelming majority of people, the mouth provides the major means for us to express ourselves to God as well as to bless His Holy Name not only directly to Him through prayer and praise but also indirectly by extolling His virtues to others. For this reason, the mouth is the second most important part of the head after the brain. The mouth not only receives and experiences food through ingestion and gustation, it vocalizes our thoughts and feelings to and about God through oral expression.

As indicated earlier in this book, spiritual healing includes intercessory prayer as well as divine metaphysics. In intercessory prayer, we speak our requests to God vocally or subvocally. In divine metaphysics, we declare, affirm and proclaim our wholeness in God. In both intercessory prayer and metaphysical treatment, we use oral expression.

Before the Adamic Fall, created beings expressed themselves about God, and to God, through many different forms of oral expression. I write "many different forms" because from the mouth of every created being issued an individual's worshipful thoughts about, as well as feelings toward, God — not only in heavenly languages but also in music and in "groanings."

All languages have their own specialized vocabulary, grammar, and syntax that help to convey meaning. Musical compositions have their own specialized vocabulary, grammar, and syntax that help to convey meaning, too. Musical notes, especially when played together as chords at graded intensities and varying rates of succession, can resonate meaning within our cognitive, emotional, and spiritual frameworks. Thus, regardless of whether they come crashing, echoing, or lilting down upon us, the notes of a musical composition can convey special meaning to our cognitive, emotional, and spiritual selves. Through certain types of music, our hearts and minds can soar to God by transcending corporeal existence. Indeed, music has its own vocabulary, grammar, and syntax, whose collective meaning is especially conveyed to those who are able to understand and feel the values expressed by it. It is easy to see as well as hear why some music has therapeutic value. Unfortunately, although music can be therapeutic, it generally falls outside of the current boundaries for medical, psychological, and metaphysical treatment.

Unlike language and musical composition, spiritual "groanings" do not have vocabulary, grammar, and syntax comprehensible to human understanding. That is why the groanings of the Holy Spirit, the groanings of each individual soul, and the collective groanings of all creation can only be understood in the realm of Spirit.[129] Spiritual "groanings" are utterances that the human brain does not comprehend. The Bible states that the Holy Spirit makes "intercession for us with sounds that cannot be expressed in words [or understood by hearing]."[130]

During sleep, I once heard God's Holy Spirit interceding in prayer for me in my own native language. I asked the Holy Spirit: "Why are you praying in English rather than in a heavenly language, or *groanings?*" God's Holy Spirit answered by responding: "So that you would understand what is being prayed for." In other words, God's Holy Spirit wanted to comfort me in a very special way by allowing me to understand what was being prayed for on my behalf.

Without God's indwelling Holy Spirit, human beings will not understand the meaning behind any heavenly language. (Here, when using the expression "heavenly language," I am not writing about nonsense words that are fabricated because of ignorance, peer pressure, and/or manipulation from a so-called spiritual leader but about genuinely unknown spiritual "tongues" or languages.) Sometimes, as the Apostle Paul indicated, it is "not lawful" for human beings to repeat heavenly tongues or interpret them because it would be unseemly to do so.[131] However, when God's Holy Spirit intentionally gives heavenly speech to human beings, He always makes known its meaning through interpretation. Because charlatans and spiritually immature people well-versed in the Holy Bible know this, they often make up interpretations to satisfy this requirement.

Created beings live on the food of God. Metaphysically speaking, the food of God is the spiritual truth of His Being expressed to us through His living voice, which is the voice "of many waters."[132] That is why Jesus said that "human beings shall not live by bread alone but by every word that proceeds out of the mouth of God" (Matthew 4:4 KJV Paraphrase). Spiritual truth is the food that God provides to sustain us. Ironically, spiritual truth is

---

129 Romans, Chapter Eight
130 Romans 8:26, King James Version (Paraphrase)
131 2 Corinthians 12:4, King James Version
132 King James Version of Ezekiel 43:2 and Revelation 1:15

also the two-edged sword that proceeds out of God's mouth to slay His enemies (Revelation 19:15).

Spiritual truth is powerful. Thus, our power in God is in speaking His spiritual truth with an emphasis, first and foremost, on the gospel of salvation. That is why we should declare His righteousness and affirm His goodness, grace, and mercy in our daily living — not only to ourselves individually but also to each other.

We give back to God through our prayer to, and praise of, Him. Indeed, prayer is a form of praise because it, in effect, acknowledges God's Sovereign Deity. (Why else would we pray to God unless we recognized His Sovereign Deity?) To be sure, without diaphragm, intercostal muscles, lungs, respiratory tract, and larynx, human beings would not be able to sound out their love for God from their physical beings. Similarly, without the life force of God residing within their souls, heavenly beings would not be able to utter their love for God either. In the final analysis, the energy necessary for each utterance of prayer and praise is divine in nature and supplied to us by God through the harmonics of a living and breathing spiritual universe.

Metaphysically speaking, living souls are the very breath of God. When God created us, He breathed (that is, spoke) His Life[133] into us. And, in prayer and praise, we speak, or breathe, His Life back to Him. In this way, the flow of God's Life is rhythmic and cyclic in nature.

Jesus said to his followers: "Now you are made clean through the word [or spiritual truth] that I have spoken to you" (John 15:3 KJV Paraphrase). Thus, when we speak aloud the written Word of God, souls are calmed, physical bodies are healed, and lusts of the flesh are quelled. In other words, as we speak spiritual truth aloud using the language of divine metaphysics, the mind of Christ is actualized within us and, thereby, enabled to be in full possession of our limbic system while God's healing virtue courses through our entire *being*.

---

133 In Hebrew, *life* is *Khi* [H2416 in Appendix Table A]; in Chinese, *life* is *Qi* (*Ch'i*).

Intelligence, Memory, and Learning

Both intelligence and memory are necessary for learning. Intelligence is the ability to process, analyze, and interpret information; and memory is the capacity to store information, including the by-products from continually processing, analyzing, and interpreting information.

Intelligence and memory are dependent on: (1) the numbers and kinds of neurons that exist within the human brain; (2) the numbers and kinds of interconnections (synapses) between and among these neurons; (3) the numbers and kinds of synaptic discharges and neurotransmitters released between and among these neurons; (4) the numbers and kinds of proteins associated with these neurons both on their cell surfaces as well as within them; (5) the permeability of neuronal cell membranes to various ions — in particular, potassium, sodium, and calcium; (6) the concentrations of those ions intracellularly (i.e., within the cell) and extracellularly (i.e., outside of the cell); and (7) the overall immediate availability of other nutrients, especially glucose, to neurons in the brain.

Anything that impairs or disturbs any one of the previous seven factors will impact the ability to learn. If nature and nurture are harmful or even less than ideal during childhood, the negative aftereffects on learning can be lifelong. Indeed, infants and toddlers need to regularly receive appropriate sensory stimuli and positive emotional feedback for each of them to develop their own individual, maximal aptitude for learning.

Metaphysically speaking, the one hundred billion or so neurons in each human brain represent the stars within the physical universe. And the stars within the physical universe, in turn, represent the living stars in God's spiritual universe as well as the stellate nature of original, unfallen man (described and pictured in the chapter entitled *Divine Metaphysics of the Skeletal System*). Currently, the living stars in God's spiritual universe include created beings who never fell as well as created beings who have been restored to their original spiritual state through the shed blood of Jesus Christ. Indeed, the brain (especially the granular layers of its neocortex) represents the Supraconsciousness of God, which contains within it all the living stars of God who communicate to each other instantly and instantaneously via the pulsating bundles of spiritual energy they emit from the vortices along their central *axes* (plural of *axis*).

Like their Creator, in whose complete image and perfect likeness they had been created, every original, unfallen individual had a control center, or brain. The original brain was a vortex (i.e., "wheel" in the language of the King James Version of the Holy Bible) composed of spiritual energy and *astral gelatinous*™ material. At the time of the Adamic Fall, the coalescence of spiritual energy and concretioning of *astral gelatinous*™ substance in this central control vortex manifested the brain's current grey and white matter. Not so ironically, grey and white matter imparts to the contemporary brain its translucent and gelatinous qualities. These qualities provide a hint of the original *astral gelatinous*™ nature of this main energy vortex within the incorruptible body before its corruption. During the Adamic Fall, the *astral gelatinous*™ brain was transformed from a major spiritual "wheel" (or energy vortex) to a physical brain.

Concerning the interchangeability of spiritual "wheel" with "vortex" in Chapters One, Three, Ten, and Eleven of the King James Version of the Book of Ezekiel, the word *wheel* is translated from the Hebrew *o-fan'* [H212 in Appendix Table A]. The Prophet Ezekiel was only able to describe each energy vortex that he saw in his visions as a *wheel* because he had no other referent to label a whirling confluence of spiritual energy and heavenly light.

Ion channels that exist as integral parts of brain neuronal cell membranes are very important relative to allowing the passage of ions from one side of each neuron's cell membrane to the other. Because nerve impulses are generated after ion channels open, anything that causes the opening of these protein pores — via their molecular, three-dimensional reconfiguration — will impact nerve impulse generation and self-propagation as well as subsequent synaptic transmission to other neurons. Because prayer, meditation, fasting, authentic praise (not just highly animated activity), and metaphysical treatment all stimulate an increased opening of some of these ion channels, the brain becomes more sensitive to the thoughts of God (or "the mind of Christ") because of those activities. Additionally, the distribution, number, and concentration of ion channels within neurons of the brain also contribute to whether an individual is more sensitive to electromagnetic and thermal field influences from the world of the invisible. This is the physical reason that some people are more sensitive or susceptible to electromagnetic and thermal field changes from various realms of the unseen. This is also the reason that such sensitivity or susceptibility may run in families. There is a genetic contribution to — or an inheritance component of — the distribution, number, and concentration of ion channels within the cell membranes of brain neurons. This is one reason why levels of native intelligence are inherited, too.

The opening of ion channels in the cell membranes of brain neurons is caused by myriad stimuli, including electromagnetic and thermal influences that change the molecular, three-dimensional configuration of the proteins comprising these membrane pores. The neurons within the limbic system of some psychiatric patients are especially vulnerable to spontaneous firings (that is, self-generated action potentials), which result in delusions and imagined events as perceived by various sensory regions within the neocortex. *For example,* some schizophrenics are especially vulnerable to attack from evil discarnates (also known as devils, demons, evil spirits, and unclean spirits in the Holy Bible) because their neuronal ion channels are more sensitive, or susceptible, to electromagnetic and thermal influences from the spirit world. This does not mean that they are possessed or will be possessed. It means that they are more sensitive to demonic influences and more susceptible to possession. Sensitive, or susceptible, channels that abuse addictive substances *(for example,* opiates, opioids, opioid-like substances, alcohol, benzodiazepines, and psychostimulants) are more likely to have psychotic episodes and become (1) schizophrenic if they are saved or (2) possessed if they are not saved. To be sure, neurological abnormalities other than schizophrenia provide additional insights concerning brain-related activities that are linked to intelligence, memory, and learning as well as sensitivity of the brain's neurons to invisible forces.

Analytical Thinking

What does the author of this book know personally about analytical thinking?

Analytical thinking is a brain-based activity that includes deductive and inductive reasoning. Analytical thinking is binary. Analytical thinking is only bound by an inactive imagination, a suppressed imagination, or an active imagination that is without grounding in spiritual truth. Imaginations are suppressed by egocentrism coupled with belief systems that imprison rather than liberate thinking.

As a child, I was aware that my brain-based thinking was binary (although I did not then know the word *binary*). Today, I recognize that at any particular moment in time my brain-based thinking is figuratively composed of tens of thousands of switches (or hundreds of thousands, depending on the topic), some of which turn "on" while others turn "off" in a series of simultaneous, sequential, and/or circular "if-then" statements, all of which leads me to not only frame questions but also make conclusions about and formulate answers to the framed questions.

I also know that there are "sets" of switches with overlap between and among the sets (somewhat like a multi-dimensional Venn diagram) with greater or lesser overlap depending on the correlation of categories and topics related to each set as well as their overarching "supra-sets" and subsumed "infra-sets." It is the intersection of heretofore non-overlapping sets that creates new ideas, new thoughts, and new knowledge for the individual as well as for the entire human race. In other words, new ideas, new thoughts, and new knowledge are uniquely new intersections of previously known pieces of information that have never been brought together before.

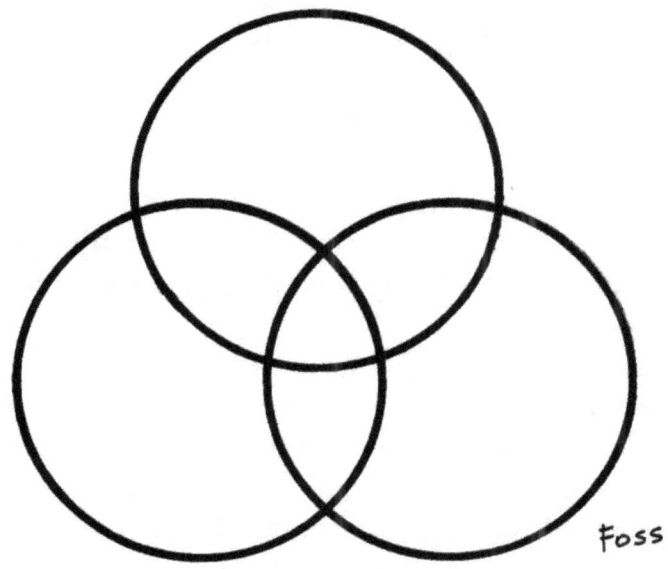

Example of Venn Diagram
Figure Fifteen

I know that the levels and degrees of analytical thinking are dependent on: (1) the number and kind of brain neurons; (2) the number and kind of synapses between and among the various neurons; (3) the action potentials fired by certain neurons at any particular time (the "on" switches); (4) the inhibition of action potentials by other neurons at the same time (the "off" switches); and (5) the multivariate nature of the experiences that one has during one's lifetime. To be sure, the action potentials referenced in (3) and (4) are dependent on the concentrations and kinds of: ions, membrane pores, neurotransmitters, and synapses.

Although I am aware of the sets of switches turning on and off in my own simultaneous, sequential, and circular thinking, I purposely shift my focus away from such activities to not preoccupy my thoughts with unnecessary clutter and noise. Instead, I metaphysically handle the concepts (those created from within as well as those from external sources) to better familiarize myself with them, grasp them, and make them more practical for spiritual understanding in relationship to daily living.

Nerve Trunks

Except for an oblique reference to nerve trunks in Footnote 38 (where nerve trunks are included in my remarks on sinews), my comments on nerves thus far have only been about individual nerve cells, or neurons, and not about nerve trunks, which are bundles of neurons — or, more specifically, bundles of nerve fibers (i.e., either dendrites or axons).

Nerve trunks either bring impulses toward the central nervous system (i.e., the brain and spinal cord) or away from the central nervous system. If they bring impulses toward the central nervous system, they are referred to as sensory and afferent. If they bring impulses away from the central nervous system, they are referred to as motor and efferent. If they bring impulses toward and/or away from the brain, they are *cranial nerves.* If they bring impulses toward and/or away from the spinal cord, they are *spinal nerves.*

Cranial Nerves

It is no accident that there are twelve pairs of cranial nerves (i.e., twenty-four altogether), whose nerve fibers and/or associated nerve tracts all radiate away from and toward areas of the brain close to the hypophyseal fossa of the sphenoid bone. In particular, the areas of the brain in association with cranial nerves include the thalamus, midbrain, pons, and medulla oblongata. In the chapter on the skeletal system, I mentioned that the hypophyseal fossa of the sphenoid bone metaphysically represents the mercy seat on the Ark of the Covenant, or God's throne, which is the place where the Creator communes with His created.

Exiting and entering the brain near the hypophyseal fossa, the twenty-four cranial nerves represent the twenty-four elders, or patriarchs, who encircle God's throne in Heaven:

> *And around the throne were twenty-four seats: and upon the seats I saw twenty-four elders sitting, clothed*

in white clothing[134] *and they had on their heads crowns of gold.*

REVELATION 4:4 KJV (PARAPHRASE)

In five of the six verses of Revelation[135] that mention the twenty-four elders,[136] it is clear that their major role is to worship God in their spoken praise and through their actions, including: (1) casting their crowns down before Him; (2) falling on their faces before Him; and (3) offering up the prayers of the saints to Him. The worship of God is a pleasant sensory experience for Him because it is praise directed toward Him (which is, of course, *afferent*).

Three of the twelve pairs of cranial nerves are entirely sensory and afferent. Nine of the twelve pairs of cranial nerves are mixed, meaning they are composed of both sensory, afferent nerve fibers as well as motor, efferent nerve fibers. Consequently, although five of the nine mixed pairs have mostly motor, efferent nerve fibers, all twenty-four cranial nerves have sensory, afferent nerve fibers.

Motor activities initiated through the motor, efferent branches of the cranial nerves are responsible for expressive actions such as: speech; eyelid and eye movements; secretion of tears, saliva, and digestive fluids; facial muscle movements; head and neck movements; and muscle contractions associated with the respiratory, circulatory, and digestive systems. Metaphysically speaking, the motor functions of the nine pairs of cranial nerves that are mixed represent that God expresses Himself through His elect, or those who belong to Him (although not exclusively so).

The Spinal Cord and Spinal Nerves

Together, the brain and the spinal cord constitute the central

---

134 White clothing represents the righteousness of the saints, or the elect, of God. (All saved people are the saints, or the elect, of God.)
135 Revelation 4:4 & 10; 5:8 & 14; 11:16; 19:4
136 The twenty-four patriarchs, or elders, in this heavenly Sanhedrin may collectively represent the twelve sons of Israel from the Old Testament and the twelve Apostles from the New Testament.

nervous system (CNS). Metaphysically, the central nervous system represents God's Tree of Life with its trunk (the spinal cord), its branches (cranial and spinal nerves), and its flourishing elements (i.e., "leaves" representing the healing balm of salvation, and "fruit" representing works of the Holy Spirit that result from salvation).

As the brain has twelve pairs of cranial nerves (i.e., twelve branch pairs of the Tree of Life), so does the spinal cord have thirty-one pairs of spinal nerves (i.e., thirty-one branch pairs of the Tree of Life). And, as the brain is housed in the cranium with its hypophyseal fossa (metaphysically speaking, this means that the Supraconsciousness of God is housed in the temple of God, which contains His Mercy Seat), so is the spinal cord protected by the vertebral column (i.e., the encircling bark on the Tree of Life).

Together, the skull and the vertebral column comprise the axial skeleton, which is distinct from the shoulder and pelvic girdles and their associated appendages, which altogether comprise the appendicular skeleton. The vertebral column is composed of: (1) the cervical region with seven cervical vertebrae, (2) the thoracic region with twelve thoracic vertebrae, (3) the lumbar region with five lumbar vertebrae, (4) the sacrum with five fused vertebrae, and (5) the coccyx with two or three fused vertebrae.

The seven cervical vertebrae represent the sevenfold Spirit[137] of God. The twelve thoracic vertebrae simultaneously represent: (1) the twelve sons of Jacob — each son a patriarch, or elder, of the twelve tribes of Israel; (2) the nation of Israel with her twelve tribes, shown as the crown of twelve stars upon the head of the woman in Chapter Twelve of Revelation;[138] (3) the twelve gates of the city of New Jerusalem in Chapter Twenty-One of Revelation;[139] and (4) each of the three dimensions (in *stadia*[140]) of the city of New Jerusalem (12,000 stadia x 12,000 stadia x 12,000

---

137 Revelation 1:4; 3:1; 4:5; 5:6 (See also Isaiah 11:2.)
138 Revelation 12:1
139 Revelation 21:12 & 21
140 One Greek *stadion* (plural *stadia*) is equal to 600 Greek feet, 625 Roman feet, or 606 ¾ British feet.

stadia).[141] The twelve elements that make up the lumbar, sacral, and coccygeal regions combined (5 + 5 + 2 = 12) simultaneously represent: (1) the twelve foundations of the city of New Jerusalem, each foundation representing one of the twelve Apostles;[142] (2) the twelve fruits of the Tree of Life;[143] and (3) the twelve basic months of the Jewish calendar, which is based on a solilunar year.[144] The *total number* of vertebral bony elements (7 + 12 + 5 + 5 + 2 = *31)* is repeated in the *total number* of pairs of spinal nerves: 8 cervical nerve pairs, 12 thoracic nerve pairs, 5 lumbar nerve pairs, 5 sacral nerve pairs, and 1 coccygeal nerve pair (8 + 12 + 5 + 5 + 1 = *31)*.

God's Tree of Life is also represented in the "Ten-Numbered Name of God"[145] embedded in the Kabbalistic (Cabalistic) Sephiroth[146] (Figure Sixteen) with the trunk (i.e., Central Nervous System) of that Tree demonstrated by combining Sephirah 1 (the brain and crown), Sephirah 6 (the spinal area near the heart), and Sephirah 9 (the generative area near the base of the spine). To be sure, there are more than ten Hebrew names for God in the Old Testament. The following Ten-Numbered Name of God is merely one attempt to systematically represent ten of them:

---

141 Revelation 21:16
142 Revelation 21:14
143 Revelation 22:2
144 Revelation 22:2
145 Adapted from "The Sephirothic System of Ten Divine Names" from *An Encyclopedic Outline of Masonic, Hermetic, Qabbalistic, and Rosicrucian Symbolical Philosophy* by Manly P. Hall, H.S. Crocker Company, San Francisco, 1928, plate CXXIII (page 123).
146 *Sephirah* [H5615 in Appendix Table A] is the singular for "number," and *Sephiroth* is the plural for "numbers."

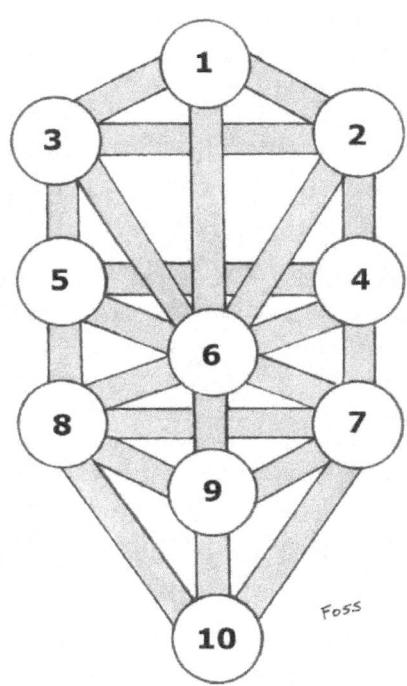

KEY

1 = אהיה = EHYaH = "I AM"
2 = יה = YaH (JaH)
3 = יהוה אלהים = YaHWeH ELoHIM = "LORD God"
4 = אל = EL = God
5 = אלהים = ELoHIM (divine plural) = God
6 = יהוה = YaHWeH = "LORD"
7 = יהוה צבאות = YaHWeH TsaBAOTh = "LORD of Hosts (armies)"
8 = אלהים צבאות = ELoHIM TsaBAOTh = "God of Hosts (armies)"
9 = אלחי = EL-ChaY = "Mighty Living One"
10 = אדני = ADoNaY = Lord ("Sir," a title of respect & reverence)

The Ten-Numbered Name of God
Figure Sixteen

The Name of God associated with Sephirah 1 in Figure Sixteen is *EH'-YaH* [H1961 in Appendix Table A], which form of the verb "to be" is translated in Exodus 3:14 (KJV) as "I AM" but may also be translated as: (1) "I BECOME," (2) "I WILL BECOME," or (3) "I WILL BE." Although the Book of Revelation is not written in Hebrew (it is written in Greek), the following italicized expression in Revelation 4:8 (KJV) captures the meaning of *EH'-YaH:* "Holy, holy, holy, Lord God Almighty, *which was, and is, and is to come.*" The essence of the crowning Hebrew word *EH'-YaH* is the eternality and Self-Existence of our Creator, the one true and only real God. Consequently, *EH'-YaH* represents the Supraconsciousness of God, which He imbues to His created through the mind of Christ in those who are spiritually restored to Him through their personal salvation. It is *EH'-YaH* from which the names *Yahweh, Yehova, Yahowa,* and *Jehovah* are derived.

Metaphysically speaking, the central nervous system represents the confluence of spiritual energy between the Creator (the Source of all spiritual energy) and His created, who are conduits for that energy. In this sense, God's Tree of Life is the spiritual backbone, or central axis, for every created person. This spiritual backbone was fully actualized in original Man but is now only in the process of being reactualized in spiritually restored man. (Keep in mind that spiritual restoration of fallen, corporeal man occurs only through the remission of sins by the shed blood of the only-begotten Son of God, Jesus Christ.)

Spiritual energy is effluent through efferent pathways in the branches of God's Tree of Life (represented in fallen, corporeal man as the motor portions of the spinal nerves) and influent through afferent pathways in the branches of God's Tree of Life (represented in fallen, corporeal man as the sensory portions of the spinal nerves). As mentioned previously, all spinal nerves are *mixed* (at least at the point of their exit from the vertebral column) — which is to say, each spinal nerve has both sensory and motor portions. Thus, just as action potentials move from the spinal cord through the motor portions of the spinal nerves and such nerve impulses move from the sensory portions of the spinal nerves back to the spinal cord, so does spiritual energy move, or flow, from the trunk of God's Tree of Life through its effluent branches to all parts of spiritually restored man and ebb, or return, through its influent branches back to the trunk of that Tree. This spiritual energy rhythmically ebbs and flows, contributing to the pulsing emanations that radiate from the electromagnetic body double of spiritually restored man.

Principles similar to those elaborated here form the bases for Tantric Yoga and Kundalini Yoga, which are ritualized systems that often incorporate pagan practices and magical thinking. Although the physical practices of yoga can produce benefits conducive to spiritual development, all belief systems that have man as the center of his own universe — capable of controlling God and initiating his own spiritual evolution — should be rejected. Man's responsibility for his own spiritual development rests solely in his responsiveness to the opportunities that God creates for him and not in the creation of his own opportunities. Similarly, that we are to "work out our own salvation with fear and trembling"[147] relates to our responsiveness to those opportunities and does not mean that we are responsible for saving ourselves. To be sure, understanding God's Work and our own work requires a delicate balance. It is easy to see how unstable people can lose footing and go off in the wrong direction. For unstable people, this delicate balance proves presumptive, precarious, and precipitous.

A more rational system of therapeutic measures based on energy ebb and flow is to be found in educated and trained practitioners of acupuncture and acupressure who use these techniques for analgesia and not anesthesia. Although there is no evidence-based research for acupuncture meridians and acupuncture points, there is much scientific evidence for the existence of dermatomes, which are areas of the skin that are innervated by specific spinal nerves.

A typical dermatome map is shown in Figure Seventeen. Although the outlines of the dermatomes might suggest to the casual observer that each dermatome is precisely delineated, there can be considerable innervation overlap between contiguous dermatomes:

---

147   Philippians 2:12, King James Version (Paraphrase)

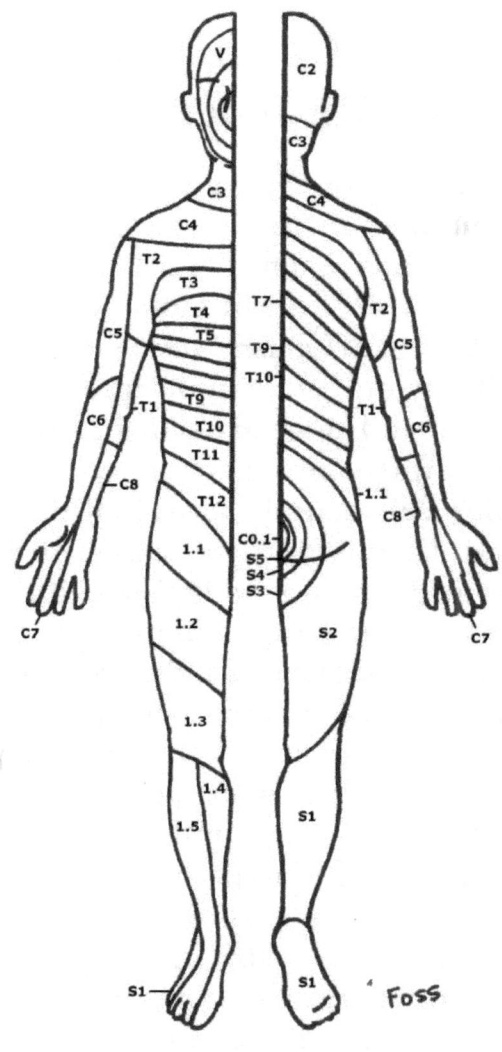

**Dermatome Map
Figure Seventeen**

Acupuncture and Networking Neurological Disorders

Although there is a dearth of evidence-based research concerning the existence of acupuncture meridians and acupuncture points, much scientific work has been done in human anatomy and physiology to prove the existence of biological neural networks. As used in this book, *biological neural networks* are neuronal circuit boards that go well beyond the simple interconnections of a few neurons in a reflex arc and that, instead, involve multiple neurons associated throughout the central nervous system in complex ways. *For example,* biological neural networks are involved in the accommodation and assimilation processes of the brain that are associated with learning (and relearning) specific fine motor skills.

The relevance of biological neural networks to the discussion at this juncture is that acupuncture is efficacious not because of the stationary presence of acupuncture needles but because of the movement of acupuncture needles through epidermal, dermal, hypodermal, and myofascial tissues during the needle insertion process as well as subsequent manipulation[148] of those needles. In other words, the stationary presence of acupuncture needles does not change or deflect life energy (known as Qi or Ch'i), but the act of moving acupuncture needles through superficial tissues of the body helps the brain to refocus its attention away from focal points of pain toward points where acupuncture needles are being inserted and manipulated. This is somewhat analogous to situations in which the brain focuses primarily on an area in the body where pain is acute and, concomitantly, shifts attention away from areas in the body where pain is less intense. *For example,* someone who has chronic bilateral knee joint pain may become unaware of that pain when more intense pain is experienced in a tibiotalar joint (the major ankle joint) due to gout. The shift in the attention of one's brain helps to explain why acupuncture has a demonstrable analgesic or pain mitigating effect. Acupuncture

---

148 Devitt, Michael. "Needle manipulation may hold the key to acupuncture's effects." *Acupuncture Today,* February 2002, Volume 03, Issue 02.

draws the brain's attention away from other areas of the body toward the insertion points of the acupuncture needles.

To move acupuncture from the arena of analgesia to actual therapeutic treatment of disease requires a greater understanding of specific points on the body from future remapping of acupuncture meridians and acupuncture points (i.e., not depending on maps previously established and currently used) based on acupuncture effects relative to specific "networking neurological disorders."[149] Indeed, an understanding of acupuncture — greater than what we have now — must be researched and developed.

Determining whether a neurological disorder is "networking" or "non-networking" would depend on the disorder's response to therapeutic acupuncture treatment. *For example,* aphasia is a recognized neurological disorder that involves impaired language ability. To determine if aphasia is "networking" or "non-networking" would require experimental treatment to see if a biological neural network can be found that causes any one of the various types of aphasia to favorably respond to acupuncture treatment. Of course, this opens a whole new arena for evidence-based research concerning potential therapeutic effects of acupuncture. At the time of this writing, humankind has barely scratched the surface in understanding acupuncture for therapeutic benefits. What is currently used is mostly based on ignorance, mysticism, magical thinking, coincidence, and accident.

I propose that future experimental work on the therapeutic effects of acupuncture be conducted using the established dermatome map shown in Figure Seventeen to establish new dermal referents for acupuncture insertion points in the treatment of networking neurological disorders.

---

[149] There are hundreds, if not thousands, of different networking neurological disorders. A few examples are Parkinson's disease, amyotrophic lateral sclerosis (ALS or Lou Gehrig's Disease), and multiple sclerosis (MS). As an additional note, it is not the venom from a bee sting that has a favorable effect on multiple sclerosis; it is the actual process of stinging that favorably impacts the nervous system by stimulating it in a most unusual, unique, and unconventional way.

Principles of Metaphysical Practice

Applying metaphysical principles to physical, emotional, mental, and spiritual problems requires seeking that our Lord God Almighty's Will be done on Earth as it is already being done in Heaven. Naturally and supernaturally, this requires us not only to do our Lord's Will but also to seek that His Will be done in our lives (regardless of our not knowing what He specifically wants done concerning a problem we might have). Seeking that our Lord's Will be done does not necessarily mean that we will know all the specifics of our Lord's Will for our lives even though we will always know the generalities of our Lord's Will for our lives. To be sure, these generalities include knowing that "all things come together for good for those who love God, and who are the called according to His purpose."[150]

We do not need to pray that all things come together for good, and we do not need to affirm that they will come together for good, for them to do so because it is God's spiritual law that they will, regardless of our asking for them to do so, and regardless of whether or not we affirm that they will. Using divine metaphysics, we should just simply *know* that they are already coming together for good and that we are already the called according to His purpose because we love the only-begotten Son of God. *Knowing the truth* is a key for successfully applying metaphysical principles to earthly problems that need solution and require resolution. Healing results from resolution, which necessitates clarifying spiritual truth for ourselves individually, collectively, and corporately as well as applying that truth to life's difficulties.

Another important principle for successful metaphysical practice in our daily lives is in recognizing not only that we already know who we are but also that we already know who we are supposed to be and what we are supposed to become. In other words, in the depths of our souls, we know who we are (meaning, what strengths and weaknesses we have), and we know who we are supposed to be by employing our strengths and overcoming our

---

[150] Romans 8:28, King James Version (Paraphrase)

weaknesses as we become what the Lord God Almighty has destined for us to become. Our destiny includes performing our specific roles and purposes in this earthly life as well as in the next life (that is, our heavenly life or "afterlife").

We should live each day on Earth as if it is our last day. And we should live each day on Earth as if we will have many, many more days that follow. Assessing what we do, what we care to do, and what we will do (as well as not do) requires mentally maintaining this particular delicate balance in daily living.

"Seeking our LORD's face"[151] means seeking His Presence. How do we seek our Lord's Presence? We seek our Lord's Presence by seeking that His Will be done on Earth as it is already being done in Heaven. In order for His Will to be done on Earth requires that He be present in our lives. We do not *will* God to be present (that is, *command* Him to be present). Instead, we pray, or ask, for His Presence by seeking His Will and by seeking to be within His Will. As we seek that God's Will be done, He is instantly present and His Will actualizes for us on Earth in the same way that it is always actualized in Heaven. This is one way in which our thoughts become things and materialize for us here on Earth.

Successful metaphysical practice requires overcoming weaknesses, which includes overcoming temptations. We do not overcome temptations by simply saying "I will not do *this*" or "I do not have the desire to do *that.*" Instead, overcoming temptation requires us to seek the Lord God Almighty's Will within our lives by living in a state of contrition (LSC). In doing so, temptation is both naturally and supernaturally overcome. Simply refuting temptation or the desire to sin does not enable us to overcome. Rather, seeking God's desires for us places us in the physical, emotional, mental, and spiritual framework that permits us to overcome temptation and our own individual desires to sin. The next time you desire to sin, and every time thereafter, focus on what God's desire is for you. Then, you will no longer seek pleasing

---

151 King James Version of 1 Chronicles 16:11; 2 Chronicles 7:14; Psalm 24:6, 27:8, 105:4; Proverbs 7:15; and Hosea 5:15.

yourself because you will be seeking to please God.

When you choose to live in a state of contrition, you will find that, whenever you are tempted to go against God's Will, you are required to make a conscious choice to do so or not do so; for that reason, you will do so less often or not at all. In other words, living in a state of contrition (LSC) gives pause to your every thought, feeling, and action.

Concerning all unhealthy conditions that need to be healed, it is important to treat the real person and not the image of the person that we have in front of us. In a sense, the earthly image that we have in front of us is no more than a holographic image projected, or *pushed,* onto the framework of the relative space-time that we know. If there were an imperfection in a holographic image, you would not paint over or alter the projection, you would seek to correct the source of that image so that the desired image would show through. In the metaphysical treatment of unhealthy conditions, *working with the real person and not the projected earthly image of that person* is equally as important as working with the source of a holographic image to alter what is projected. See?

Chapter Questions

This section is intended to facilitate learning by providing relevant activities, exercises, and experiences to aid students of divine metaphysics in their quest for grasping spiritual concepts, integrating them into their own belief systems, holding them more assuredly, and making them more practical in daily life.

The following questions should be answered after reading each titled section. To answer a few of the questions, students may need to consult outside resources or external references. Students are also encouraged to answer these questions with others during group discussions.

The Supraconsciousness of God

1. (a) How many hemispheres comprise the cerebrum? (b) How many lobes are found in each cerebral hemisphere? (c) Why is the outer layer of the cerebrum called the *neocortex?*

2. Create a table of structures in the human brain and name what they metaphysically represent in the invisible reality of God. (This table should represent all structures addressed throughout this chapter.)

3. What structures of the hypophysis are embryologically related to the hypothalamus?

4. Define (a) *histology* (adjective: *histologic)* and (b) *comparative anatomy.*

Disclaimer

5. Restate the disclaimer in your own words and explain why the disclaimer should be important to students of divine metaphysics.

The Limbic System

6. What are *assumptive beliefs* and how do they impact analytical thinking?

7. Research the origin of the word "limbic" as a descriptor of the emotional brain. Present your findings.

8. Name the brain structures that are generally included in the limbic system.

9. How is the desire to indulge sinful and addictive behavior overridden and replaced with the desire to please God?

10. In what way(s) can fear be positive?

11. What are the three main categories of fear?

12. (a) How is the *F-E-A-R* acronym accurate and helpful? (b) How is the *F-E-A-R* acronym inaccurate and unhelpful?

13. What are the antidotes for fear?

14. Why does it matter who sits enthroned in the limbic system of the etheric body double (or electromagnetic body double)?

15. (a) Explain the following statement: "The purity of the channel depends on the purity of the channel." (b) To whom is the previous statement referring?

16. Do pain and suffering constitute punishment from God?

17. (a) Name the emotions we experience that God also experiences. (b) Which emotion does God not experience?

18. Contrast eternal hope and despair.

Carnal Mind versus the Mind of Christ

19. Using outside resources and external references, research and describe the differences in the "reptilian brain," the "rat brain," and the neocortex as they relate to human brain structures and functions.

20. Discuss the "rat brain" as it relates to a neurobiological disease model for addiction.

21. Contrast differences between the terminology "mind" and "brain."

22. (a) Using a concordance to the King James Version of the Holy Bible, write out the verses that use the noun phrase "carnal mind." (b) Write a definition for the phrase "carnal mind" based on its context within the Holy Bible. (c) According to the present author, in what way is "carnal mind" not the same as "mortal mind?" (d) In what way is "carnal mind" not the same as "Satan?"

Conscience Matters

23. What is the conscience and how does it relate to God's Holy Spirit?

24. Who and what determines absolute truth, absolute right, and absolute wrong?

25. In what ways is the human conscience arbitrary and subjective?

The Role of Trust in Matters of Conscience

26. What does it mean to trust in God completely?

Chemical Addiction as a Thorn in the Flesh

27. (a) Discuss personal responsibility relative to physical disease and emotional disorders. (b) Are there any physical diseases or emotional disorders for which those afflicted have no personal responsibility? (c) Choose one physical disease and one emotional disorder and discuss personal responsibility relative to these two conditions.

28. Discuss the Biblical basis for "thorns in the flesh."

29. As you read/reread the Book of Job in the Holy Bible, list the inaccurate assessments of Job's condition that were given by his friends.

30. (a) Distinguish between being "active" or "in recovery" concerning addiction. (b) Discuss the accuracy of the following statement: "All active addictions lead to a state of drunkenness."

Cerebellum

31. Briefly discuss the location, structure, and function of the human cerebellum.

32. Compare and contrast the terms *voluntary, involuntary, reflexive,* and *volitional.*

The Brain Stem

33. List and describe the three major brain areas associated with the brain stem and summarize their individual functions.

34. Using outside resources and external references, research various views on the "reptile brain" *(reptilian brain* or *reptilian complex)* and share which brain structures are generally included, and which brain structures may also be included, depending on source consulted. (Remember to cite the source.)

Energy Centers (Vortices) and the Central Nervous System

35. Using outside resources and external references, define these terms: *Kabbalah (Cabbalah), Sephirot/Sephiroth, Chakra,* and *Theosophy*. (This question is not meant to imply an endorsement of the systematic theologies associated with any of these terms.)

36. (a) According to the present author, which two verses in the Holy Bible are the two most important for understanding divine metaphysics? (b) Memorize these two verses and repeat them to at least one person.

Pain and Suffering

37. Should people who rely on spiritual healing through intercessory prayer and metaphysical treatment be embarrassed if they do not experience a healing?

38. Name ways in which human beings may benefit from pain.

39. Explain the difference between God's Wrath and God's chastening.

40. Explain ways in which God can use pain and suffering to benefit His people.

41. (a) According to the present author, what is a "metapractitioner?" (b) In what ways can patients and their advisors combine medical, psychological, and spiritual healing?

42. (a) What is a Christian martyr? (b) In what ways are Christian martyrs the greatest saints of God?

The Role of Prayer in Healing

43. What does prayer mean to you personally?

44. What is the difference between using intercessory prayer and using metaphysical treatment concerning the healing of unhealthy conditions.

Understanding the Special Physical Senses

45. What four human senses are considered *the special senses?*

46. What does it mean to be "the apple of God's eye?"

47. What is the difference between earthly sight and spiritual vision?

48. What is the significance of incense offered to God in the Holy Bible?

49. (a) What is the difference between hearing and listening? (b) How do hearing and listening relate to comprehending?

50. Briefly discuss the metaphysical meaning of tasting.

Understanding the Psychic Sense

51. Briefly explain the existence of biases against the psychic sense.

Psychic Attack and the Wicked Smart

52. (a) What is psychic attack? (b) Who are the wicked smart?

Susceptible Channels

53. (a) What are the characteristics of a susceptible channel? (b) Who should work together in the treatment of demonic possession?

Physical Homeostasis and Metaphysical Equipoise

54. What are the three potential stages of prolonged stress?

55. What is the difference between physical homeostasis and metaphysical equipoise?

Resolving Conflict to Restore Equilibrium and Equipoise

56. Name causes for conflict and discuss ways to resolve the causes named.

Speaking Truth Aloud

57. Name and describe the different ways in which one can speak truth aloud.

Intelligence, Memory, and Learning

58. (a) What are ions? (b) What are ion channels? (c) Describe how ion channels are involved in nerve impulses, or action potentials, in neurons.

59. In what ways are intelligence, memory, and learning dependent on neurons in the brain?

60. Why is the word *wheel* used in the King James Version of the Holy Bible to describe an *energy vortex?*

Analytical Thinking

61. In general, why is analytical thinking important relative to daily living?

62. In what ways are neurons involved in analytical thinking?

Nerve Trunks

63. What is a nerve trunk?

64. (a) What do the number of cranial nerves represent? (b) What do the functions of the cranial nerves represent?

65. What do the regions of the vertebral column represent relative to the spinal nerves?

66. How many energy vortices are represented by the Kabbalistic (Cabalistic) Sephiroth?

67. What are dermatomes and how do they relate to spinal nerves?

Acupuncture and Networking Neurological Disorders

68. Briefly describe biological neural networks.

69. According to the present author, how might some neurological disorders relate to biological neural networks?

Principles of Metaphysical Practice

70. Based on this section, construct a list of principles of metaphysical practice. Upon finishing this entire book, redo the answer to this question to include all principles of metaphysical practice detailed throughout this book.

Chapter Five
Divine Metaphysics of the Cardiovascular System

If you will seek the LORD your God with all of your heart and soul, you will find Him.

DEUTERONOMY 4:29 KJV (PARAPHRASE)

Metaphysical Matters of the Heart

Metaphysical matters of the heart involve several important aspects at our spiritual core: (1) desire, (2) expressiveness, (3) reasoning, (4) concern, and (5) pulse.

Desires of the Heart

Metaphysically speaking, the heart is the central core of an individual. What the heart of an individual desires depends on the individual's spirit, which determines the individual's personality, mentality, emotions, attitude, character, interests, and motives.

Either the spirit of an individual desires to please the Creator or the spirit of an individual desires to please itself or other people instead of the Creator. Either the motives of one's heart are pure or they are impure. Motives that are *completely pure*[152] involve seeking only to do the Will of God. Motives that are impure, or less than pure, involve seeking to do our own will or the will of other people. The more interested that a person is in enacting his or her own will or the will of other people, the more impure are that person's motives.

The greatest obstacle to purity in this life is temptation. That is because temptation plays upon the weaknesses, frailties, and infirmities of human flesh. The human mind yields to temptation because the human mind is flesh (i.e., the brain is corporeal). Purity is achieved by human beings only as they turn to God to resist temptation. In fact, only the pure in heart see God,[153] which means that only people who regularly resist temptation can apprehend and apperceive God on a daily basis. (This does not preclude God's intervention for people who are on the wrong path.)

The desires of a person's heart are in alignment with the desires of God's heart when that person yields his or her own will to God's Will. When this happens, both God and the individual want the same things. When God's Will indwells and permeates us, we find ourselves desiring what God desires for us, which desires are naturally[154] blessed by God because they are His desires. If we are ever unsure about the origin of our desires, we should look to their origin in spiritual realms. If the desires of our heart are to please God in accordance with His Will, then we can be assured that those desires originated in the very heart of God Himself.

---

152 Although the word "completely" is not necessary to modify the word "pure," it has been used here to reinforce the quality of purity being discussed. To be sure, what is pure is pure without qualification. Of such is the nature of purity. Purity has no degrees, in contrast to impurity, which does have degrees.
153 Matthew 5:8, King James Version
154 The word *naturally* is used here in the sense of "consequently" and not in the sense of "corporeally" or "biologically."

We were created to please God. As we seek to please God, we demonstrate our restoration to His complete image and perfect likeness through the shed blood of Jesus Christ. On the other hand, if the desires of our heart are to please ourselves, then we should assume that those desires originated in a carnal mind, which always opposes God. Unfortunately, Satanic evil, or mortal mind,[155] stands ready to fuel the desires of a carnal mind.

As we seek to do the Will of the Lord God Almighty, His Will supplants our own. He does not impose His Will on us. It is not a conscious effort or act of His. His Will simply becomes our own will. Thus, what God wants for Himself and for us individually, collectively, and corporately become what we want for Him and for ourselves individually, collectively, and corporately. What I am describing is that, when we begin to think and feel in God's terms, His terms become our own terms. There comes a point in our spiritual progress when we no longer distinguish between "His Will" and "my will" because the two have become synonymously one and unequivocally equivalent. Such a point of agreement is not in a physical place but in a metaphysical space-time that has neither singular locus nor individual location. That point is in the here-beyond, where there is no beginning and no end. Thus, that point is *in* the Self-Existent One, Who is the one true and only real God as well as the sole Creator of *all-that-is*.

When the desires of the heart of God become our own desires, we find ourselves wanting what is best for us all, which includes wanting God to purge the Earth of all unrighteousness not only through the efficacy of the shed blood of Jesus Christ but also

---

155 Although the phrase "mortal mind" may be used to describe "Satanic evil," it is important to remember that Satan is an entity with consciousness, volition, and free will. Satan is not just an impersonal force; he has intelligence and personality. The noun phrase "mortal mind" is not used synonymously with "carnal mind" in this book. "Carnal mind" includes fleshly, material, and prideful human desires — all of which are worldly and, therefore, nurtured and inflamed by mortal mind. (See 1 John 2:16.) In this book, it is important to understand and remember that "mortal mind" is really "Satan's mortal mind" — the mind that permeates all demonic thinking, feeling, and acting.

through His Wrath (i.e., His justified Anger).

Expressions from the Heart

Sooner or later, we always express what is in our heart. What is in our heart eventually bubbles out even when we are trying to hide what we actually think or what we really feel. Eventually, we let our guard down and what is within us surfaces and becomes apparent to others. In the final analysis, we cannot hide who we really are. Even Satan, who falsely appears as an angel of light,[156] cannot hide his motives from God or from those who love God.

Out of the heart, the imagination takes shape, the mouth speaks, the arms and hands act, and the legs and feet move. When we love the Lord God Almighty, we cannot be other than who we are and who we are meant to be. Who we are meant to be is determined by our intent, which is borne in and by our heart. That we are to pray specifically to our heavenly Father to "lead us not into temptation"[157] recognizes that without God's causality and leadership, our hearts can only lead us back to iniquity and sin. Consequently, we must ask God to steer us away from places where a desire to sin starts taking shape in our imagination and then is enacted by us in word and deed. The desires of our heart remain depraved when we seek to function independently of God.

Salvation is dependent on what we first believe in our heart and then confess with our mouth (or declare with our hands when using the language of the hearing impaired). Metaphysically speaking, the heart represents the seat of our emotions. Of course, from the standpoint of human anatomy and physiology, the seat of our emotions is in our brain. The human heart originally became identified as the seat of emotions because reverberations from powerful emotions like shock, rage, grief, sorrow, fear, anxiety, embarrassment, joy, and peace are often "felt" by (or *in*) the muscular organ known as the heart. This is partly because

---

156 2 Corinthians 11:14, King James Version
157 King James Version of Matthew 6:13 and Luke 11:4

responses to powerful emotions — generated through the brain's limbic system — trigger action potentials (i.e., nerve impulses) in either: (1) the sympathetic division of the autonomic nervous system (ANS); or (2) the parasympathetic division of the ANS, both of which have branches that innervate the heart. These action potentials are responsible for either excitation or inhibition of rate, duration, and strength of cardiac contractions. This explains why the human heart has been erroneously identified as the physical seat of human emotions. *(For example*, when we are shocked emotionally, our heart may skip a beat.)

Although there is a correlation between human emotions and cardiac activity, human emotions do not originate in the human heart. When we speak of emotions felt by the human heart, we are actually speaking about: (1) the limbic system and its interactions with other parts of the brain, including the cerebrum, cerebellum, and brain stem; and (2) physiologic activities mediated by the autonomic nervous system.[158]

Metaphysically, the emanation of emotions in the center of our etheric body pulses from its central core — which corresponds to Sephirah 6 in Figure Sixteen and to Anahata, which is the heart chakra (minus all associations with pagan deities, of course).[159]

Our hearts become weary only when we do not believe that God causes all things to come together for good for the called according to His purpose. Our hearts faint prematurely — that is, before the time appointed for them to stop — when we trust only in ourselves. Lack of belief, faith, and trust is the reason that we become frightened and that our hearts stop out of fear. Souls in dust are

---

158 The autonomic nervous system (ANS) influences heart activity specifically through its sympathetic division via cranial nerve X (the vagus nerve) and through its parasympathetic division via postganglionic nerve fibers associated with specific cervical and thoracic ganglia. A *ganglion* (plural *ganglia*) is a cluster of nerve cell bodies. (A nerve cell body contains the nucleus of a neuron and its surrounding cytoplasm, or *neuroplasm*.)

159 Coincidentally, Anahata is often represented with two intersecting triangles similar in configuration to the Star of David. (For the sake of clarification, yogic traditions would never describe this configuration using the nomenclature "Star of David.")

fainthearted because they are fearful. Hearts tremble and melt out of fear when people do not trust in the Lord God Almighty. (Sometimes, however, souls in dust are fainthearted when they encounter the power of God.)

God punishes hardened hearts and chastens hardening hearts in the hope that they will become soft enough to generate gratitude, humility, repentance, and forgiveness. Interestingly, when God sees fit, He can even harden hearts by casting a caul, or veil, over our understanding in order that we not see clearly (i.e., not interpret correctly) and, as a result, confuse what is right with what is wrong. Although God is not a puppeteer, God sets the world stage for His Will to be enacted not only in the hearts of those who love Him but also in judgment of those who despise His Sovereignty and, therefore, reject His Plan of Salvation through His only-begotten Son, Jesus Christ.

God sends His plagues and pestilences (i.e., enacts His curses) upon the hearts of those who will not repent for three reasons: (1) that His Wrath, or justified Anger, might be expended, or spent, as it strikes its fill; (2) that those with hardened hearts might find a reason to turn to Him in the time of their trouble and woe; and (3) that the world might become purified of unrighteousness and evil. God will not force us to choose Him. God will, however, create conditions for good seed to germinate within us, which germination sometimes must be preceded by conditions associated with frost or fire (i.e., unpleasant, extreme circumstances).

What is on our minds is first within our hearts because the heart is the seat of will and purpose as well as the source of intent and direction. To know what is on God's mind is to first know what is within His heart. And, without heart, it is impossible to have an intimate relationship with God. To care about God and His feelings is not possible without heart. We expect God to comfort us yet we do not seek to comfort Him — especially during these dark days of hatred toward God and outright rejection of Him as well as complete indifference to His feelings and emotions.

We know the hearts of others only when we have experienced what they have experienced. We cannot know the hearts of those who are oppressed and victimized unless we ourselves have first experienced oppression and victimization. We cannot feel the pain of others unless we have first felt pain. We cannot have sympathy for those who are in darkness unless we have experienced darkness firsthand for ourselves.

Our offerings to God should be free will offerings — meaning, they should be given from the heart, not out of guilt or a sense of obligation but with the emotions of gratitude and joy. When the high priest, beginning with Aaron, went into the Most Holy Place (i.e., Holy of Holies) within the inner sanctuary, he was instructed to wear the breastplate of judgment with the names of the twelve tribes of Israel over the area of his heart as a continual memorial before the Lord God.[160] This served as a reminder that all children of God are dear to God's heart.

As children of God, we are not to discourage each other but, instead, encourage each other to enter into the Lord God's Presence and to enter into that which He has promised to those who belong to Him, which includes peace, joy, comfort, and good counsel (i.e., wisdom). As children of God, we should seek to comfort and console the hearts of others.

The hearts of the wicked are hardened, but the hearts of the righteous are tender. The hearts of the prideful and arrogant are puffed up and swollen, but the hearts of the humble are strong and resilient.

The words of God are inscribed upon the tablets of the heart in people who belong to Him. Those who love God keep His commandments. And, if we seek God's face early (that is, from our youth), then we will also learn early that He will never break His covenant with us or the specific promises He has made to us. God keeps His word. His written Word (i.e., the Holy Bible) contains His promises — from which He will not repent (i.e., change His mind or heart). You and I can depend on the promises of God because they are from His heart.

The Holy Bible is clear that, whenever our hearts turn away from the Creator, we end up worshiping false gods. Regardless of the idol worshiped, all idols are merely outer representations of

---

160 Exodus 28:29, King James Version

inner false gods; thus, such worship is always egocentric and, at the same time, consciously or unconsciously (i.e., subconsciously) directed toward Satan. Yes, we worship ourselves whenever we fail to worship the one true and only real God. Egocentrism and the worship of false gods actually feed Satan and help him to grow more powerful within us and, therefore, within the world.

Spiritual Reasoning and the Seed of Concern

In general, reasoning is the mental process whereby we come to know ideas, facts, concepts, principles, and truths. *Human reasoning* includes both inductive and deductive analytical processes. *Spiritual reasoning,* however, includes perception and discernment, which allow a person to see through and hear beyond the things of this world to the things of the world of God (i.e., His spiritual universe).

Spiritual reasoning enables us to know the truth without having to depend on mere speculation, hypothesis, or opinion. *Spiritual reasoning* permits an individual to know — from within himself or herself — divine ideas, spiritual facts, metaphysical concepts, Biblical principles, and truths of *being*.

Those who regularly focus on, consider, and inquire as to their "divine nature"[161] are privy to information in Christ that is unavailable to those unconcerned about spiritual matters. The former eventually come to ascertain, discern, and determine who God is and who they are in Him. Spiritual truth becomes resolved *to* them as well as *for* them. And they are sure of the truth of what they perceive and discern because they know that they have yielded their spiritual eyes and ears to the Lord God Almighty, Who has become the Sovereign of their souls. God's Sovereignty should always be utmost in our hearts. We should be eternally thankful that our Creator is Who He is. And we should forever praise our Creator that He is Who He said He is.

Spiritual reasoning is a process of the heart and not the head. When the caul of spiritual darkness has been removed from off the

---

161 2 Peter 1:4, King James Version

heart, when the heart has been circumcised of selfishness, when the commandments of God have been inscribed upon the fleshly tablets of the heart, and when a soul seeks out ways for God's love to be expressed through its heart, then — and only then — is the individual ready to apprehend and apperceive divine ideas, spiritual facts, metaphysical concepts, Biblical principles, and truths of *being*. Until that time, an individual is either asleep to the purpose and meaning of life or spiritually dead.

How does one get *spiritual reasoning?*

Spiritual reasoning requires a softening of the heart. Such softening begins in mortals when they come to believe in the Lord God Almighty. In other words, mortals are required to become open to God's spiritual universe before the elements of that universe can be both seen and heard by them. *Spiritual reasoning* also begins and ends with our love for God and concern for others. "Concern for others" is defined here as a demonstrable love for others in contrast to an abstract love. "Concern for others," or demonstrable love, is what the King James Version of the Bible most appropriately calls "charity."[162]

Sensitivity is the ability to receive impressions of thoughts, feelings, concepts, and ideas from a source outside of one's self. True sensitivity is a godlike quality, a quality that God shares with those who are like Him — which is to say, those who are made (i.e., *recast)* in His complete image and perfect likeness. Sensitivity is a gift from God to those whose hearts are open to Him. In varying degrees, many human beings possess sensitivity. But whether our sensitivity is finely tuned to the thoughts, feelings, concepts, and ideas of God and relatively free from the static of carnal mind and the evil that inflames it, or coarsely focused and subject to the interference of that mind's noisome pestilence, depends on the objects of our concern. Thus, what happens to the spiritual gift of sensitivity depends on the individual who possesses it. Genuine love for God and concern for others refine sensitivity. Excessive concern for one's mortal self and human identity

---

162 For example, in the Thirteenth and Fourteenth Chapters of 1 Corinthians (King James Version).

perverts sensitivity to touchiness, defensiveness, and unhealthy vulnerability.

If souls are to labor more productively in this Earth's harvest field, they need to have a fuller sense of what concern for others is by cultivating it within themselves. To be sure, such growth can occur independently of the written or spoken word, but it cannot occur without the earnest pursuit of understanding that thoughts and ideas originate either from the mind of God, such mind immortal and divine, or from the mind that is opposite, opposing, contrary, and contradictory to it, such mind no real mind at all (i.e., in the metaphysical sense).

Though most human beings would claim that they are the originators of the thoughts and ideas that pass through them or the feelings they experience, they are, in fact, transponders, receivers, and conduits of them. What we receive and transmit depends greatly on the objects of our concern and the degrees to which we are concerned about those objects. Souls in the earth plane of consciousness who feel a wide-open concern — that is, a demonstrable love — for others freely receive the thoughts, ideas, and feelings of God. However, souls who feel a huge concern for the false and distorted image they have of themselves, or the image they would like others to have of them, close themselves off to divine thoughts, ideas, and feelings and, concomitantly, open themselves up to demonic attack. The dichotomy is just that sharp and distinct. Two different and separate worlds are present side by side: the perfect world of God and the nether-world of self-will and self-pride. The two worlds represent two different states of mind. From which world we receive thoughts, ideas, and feelings depends on which world we are more open to through our concern.

In the truest metaphysical and highest spiritual sense, the heart of an individual is its concern. If an individual is mostly concerned with the false image it has of itself, then its heart may be described as "foolish," "proud," "hardened," "stubborn," or "uncircumcised." If an individual is solely concerned with the mortal or "dead" self it has in front of it (i.e., its human identity), then its heart may be described as "evil" or "having been turned to stone."

The heart of our dear Savior, Jesus Christ, may be referred to as "bleeding" because of his total concern for the well-being and salvation of others. The heart of Christ may also be referred to as "sacred" because the love of God tabernacles within it. Those in the earth plane of consciousness who strive to become "pure in heart" — that is, unconcerned with matters of self-will — receive the thoughts, ideas, and feelings of God in proportion to their concern for the things of God. According to their degree of selflessness, hearts may be described as "melting," "contrite," "understanding," and "soft."

Though souls in dust travail to be delivered from their iniquity and sin, they should not be of "heavy heart." Rather, their hearts should be glad that the substantive nature of God is revealed to them through "hearts broken" of self-will. In the metaphysical reality of God, His children have one heart, "whole" and "circumcised" in its dedication to good. Thus, at the heart of the children of God is their love for God and concern for one another. When those emotions are lost, children of God turn themselves into something that cannot *be* — in other words, they turn themselves into that which cannot exist in the absolute reality of God. They lose the spiritual gift of sensitivity to the things of God as well.

Selfless love — the highest degree of demonstrable concern that we can have for others — is indicated by humility, which is an expression of our gratitude for the opportunity we have to be returned to our Creator. Though it may sound abhorrent to a corporeal sense of self, humility should be an obsession to those who seek to please God. Why? No one can do greater in the earth plane of consciousness than walk with an inner, quiet love of God and express concern for others by serving the Creator as He meets their needs. No one on Earth can hope to do greater than put others before his or her own human self. "Greater love has no one than this: that they lay down their life for their friends."[163] "Laying down our life" includes living a life of daily

---

163 John 15:13, King James Version (Paraphrase) In this context, the word *friends* means "covenant partners in and through Jesus Christ."

self-sacrifice in addition to the willingness to give up one's life to protect others.

It is important to add that humility — or being "lowly in heart"[164] — never draws attention to itself. If individuals feel the need to inform others of their humility, then they have fallen to the cunningness of self-will. That one can be humble at the same time one is telling others of his or her own humility is a self-evident absurdity. However, the meekness of humility should never be confused with weakness — just as submission to God's Will should never be confused with giving up one's identity. God the Son demonstrated his true identity in perfect meekness and complete submission to the Sovereignty of God the Father. Yet Christ Jesus openly rebuked evil despite the consequences. Although he was humble, the Lord Jesus remained unafraid of evil throughout his entire sojourn on Earth.[165] In the same way, we should be unafraid of evil as well.

Most people who say that they are spiritually-minded do not agree completely with each other because they really do not have the same concern for others that they have for themselves individually. If any of us are ever to be healed of divisiveness or reconcile any of our personal differences, we must see eye to eye on the weightier matter of concern for others. It is through this concern that souls are known in Heaven as true children of God and real members of the body of His Christ.

Just how important to *spiritual reasoning* is concern for others? The heart is the observatory of the soul. The larger the heart, the bigger the space in which the individual dwells, and the more of God's perfect world the soul can see and hear. Remember, God's heart is so large that it spans the entire spiritual universe, which is His *all*. Let us, then, strive to be like God by loving others as He loves us — that we might hear and see Him more clearly and help others to hear and see Him more clearly as well.

---

164 Matthew 11:29, King James Version
165 In the Garden at Gethsemane, Christ Jesus was not afraid of evil; he was afraid of what he would experience on the cross at Calvary.

The Pulse of Life's Ebb and Flow

The Holy Bible is clearly in agreement with biological science that the human heart pumps life throughout the human body — "for the life of the flesh is in the blood" (Leviticus 17:11 KJV). And, just as blood circulates throughout the human body in blood vessels, so does spiritual energy ebb and flow throughout the spiritual body in influent and effluent energy conduits. Just as blood recirculates throughout the human body by returning to the heart over and over again, so does spiritual energy pulse from and return to the central energy core of one's etheric body double in a repetitious and rhythmic fashion.

In the chapter on the skeletal system, I mentioned that blood is one of the connective tissues. Many cultured and educated people prefer to overlook the importance that God has placed on blood in the Holy Bible, where it is clear that: (1) blood is synonymous with life itself;[166] (2) atonement is not possible without the shedding of innocent blood;[167] and (3) God's Wrath is especially dispensed on those who are responsible for spilling innocent blood.[168] People who fancy themselves as intellectual or progressive assume that blood sacrifices are unnecessary, primitive, and even barbaric. Concomitantly, they think that because God is divine Love,[169] He does not hate and, therefore, can have no Wrath. They fail to realize that God's Anger is justified and that what especially justifies His Anger is the murder of innocent people (i.e., the spilling of innocent blood) in sacrifice to false gods. If God were not angry about this, He would not be a just God. If God, in return, did not spill out His justified Anger, or Wrath, upon those who have murdered innocent people to venerate the false Islamic god or any other pagan deity, He would not be a just God.

---

166 Genesis 9:4; Leviticus 17:11 & 14; Deuteronomy 12:23
167 Leviticus 17:11; Hebrews 9:22
168 Deuteronomy 19:10-13, 21:8-9; 2 Kings 21:16, 24:4; Psalm 106:38; Proverbs 6:17; Isaiah 59:7; Jeremiah 22:3, 26:15; Joel 3:19; Jonah 1:14
169 1 John 4:8,16

Indeed, vengeance belongs to God, and it belongs to God alone.[170] This is not to say that God will not withdraw His curse from murderers, sex traffickers, and child abusers who come to understand that what they have done is wrong, confessed that wrong to Him, and repented of their ways by dedicating the remainder of their lives to doing His Will.

As to why God has placed such importance on blood, we may inquire of Him so that we might be taught why, but we are not to question Him in an accusatory tone (i.e., ask Him to justify His actions). Why? He alone is God, and He does what pleases Him as well as what is just. It would be unseemly to ask God to justify His actions. (The importance and meaning of blood are also discussed in the chapter entitled *Divine Metaphysics of the Lymphatic System and Immunity*.)

It is important that we build our belief systems upon the foundations of truth that are found in the Holy Bible. In doing so, we must be careful to not misrepresent or mischaracterize God, to not misrepresent or mischaracterize what He has said, and to not misrepresent or mischaracterize what He has implied. Instead, we should pray that God corrects our understanding concerning who He is, what He has said, what He means, and how what He means should apply to various situations. Unfortunately, throughout most of human history, people have misinterpreted God to be what they want Him to be and, in such self-deception, they have misrepresented what He has said and what He means to bolster their own views. *For example,* during my own lifetime most people who claim to be "full gospel" are, in fact, "partial gospel" (including some of the people who might nod "yes" to this statement). And most people who claim to have certain spiritual gifts are either fooling themselves or they are seeking to fool others. (Obviously, they cannot fool God.) And they conclude erroneously that God will bless them for their less-than-whole views of Him and for their own self-deception and deceit.

Although blood contains antibodies as well as cells that phagocytize (i.e., surround and engulf) foreign elements and

---

170 Deuteronomy 32:35 & 43; Psalm 94:1; Isaiah 63:4; Nahum 1:2-3; Romans 12:19, 13:4

cellular debris, the most important role of blood is in carrying life-giving oxygen to the cells of the body.

Metaphysically speaking, oxygen represents the spiritual energy that (1) nourished the body of original Man, (2) nourishes the etheric body double of saved man, and (3) will nourish the restored somatic identity of every saint of God. Metaphysically speaking, oxygen is the fruit from the Tree of Life in the Garden of Eden. And, just as oxygen is produced from water by the leaves of trees on Earth, so, too, is spiritual energy produced from the Spirit — or "Living Water" — of God, Who is Himself the foliage on that Tree of Life and the balm within its leaves. The "-gen" suffix in the word *oxygen* means "begetter." Thus, in a figurative sense, oxygen is the *begetter* of human life. Just as no human being can live without oxygen, so, too, can no spiritual being live without the Spirit of God because God is Life.[171] Of course, God, and not oxygen, is the real *begetter* of all true life.

Coincidentally, oxygen has an atomic number of eight on the Periodic Table, which means that each of its atoms has eight protons. The number eight is the number of perfection and completion: when turned sideways, the number "8" can represent eternity.

Biochemically speaking, oxygen molecules move from one type of protoporphyrin ring to another — *for example,* from the protoporphyrin ring in chlorophyll in the cells of leaves on trees to the protoporphyrin ring in hemoglobin in red blood cells (i.e., erythrocytes) as well as to the protoporphyrin ring in myoglobin in muscle fibers (i.e., myofibers). Such movement of oxygen symbolizes the continuity of all life not only in a carbon-based global ecosystem but also in the metaphysical ecosystem of the spiritual universe of God, where spiritual energy flows from the Creator (i.e., the Tree of Life) through His created (i.e., all living beings made in His complete image and perfect likeness), empowering all actions there, everywhere.

Although readers of this book may find the abundance of physical to metaphysical analogies a bit tedious, it is important for

---

171 Deuteronomy 30:20

them to know that everything that exists in corporeality has a counterpart in the world of Spirit and that everything that exists in the world of Spirit has a counterpart in corporeality. (As you look for connections, you will discover them for yourselves.)

In the reality of God, the entire spiritual universe is living and alive with God as its heart. However, God's heart is not only the center but also the circumference of His spiritual universe.

If you ever feel that your speech and vocabulary are inadequate, it is especially important to know this metaphysical truth: *When the heart speaks, it is always understood by those who have heart.*[172] In other words, when you speak from the heart, others with heart will always understand you!

Treating Cardiovascular Ailments Metaphysically

Like the section entitled *Treating Malignancies Metaphysically* in Chapter One, this section gives the present author an opportunity to discuss the metaphysical treatment of a human organ system (i.e., the cardiovascular system) that is relatively straightforward and easy to understand for beginning students of human anatomy and physiology who might also like to apply metaphysical principles in seeking to correct disabilities, diseases, and disorders.

Remember, the object of this book is not to get you to think like its author but to help you to learn how to think metaphysically and intelligently at the same time. As stated previously, thinking metaphysically and thinking intelligently should not be mutually exclusive processes.

A great disadvantage for most practitioners of divine metaphysics is that they have not received an education in human

---

172 Eddy, Mary Baker. *Miscellaneous Writings* in *Prose Works other than Science and Health with Key to the Scriptures.* Boston: The First Church of Christ, Scientist, 1953, Page 162: lines 10-12. (Although the present author's sentence is not a direct quote, it is based on a nuance of the metaphysical truth expressed in this specific footnoted reference.)

anatomy and physiology. Due to this lack of education, they tend to think about the human body in mysterious ways, often with magical thinking, misconclusions, and/or sweeping generalizations. In such ignorance, practitioners of divine metaphysics might conclude that ignoring an unhealthy physical condition will help to expunge it from existence. Unfortunately, as a result of ignoring the condition, they unwittingly and unnecessarily complicate (i.e., make worse) their lives or the lives of the people they are treating metaphysically.

For example, coronary artery disease is an easily understood condition of the heart. One can't really ignore coronary artery disease for it to go away. In fact, ignoring coronary artery disease only permits it to get worse. For that reason, coronary artery disease should be medically diagnosed and treated as soon as possible. This is not to say that the condition of coronary artery disease can't be handled prayerfully and metaphysically while it is treated medically. Rather, it is to say that, once the disease has been diagnosed accurately by a medical practitioner, the condition should receive medical treatment while the patient is receiving spiritual treatment. The same is true for many, if not most, diseases.

What are the benefits of prayer and metaphysical treatment if the disease is already being handled medically? Certainly, prayer helps us to be at peace with — or not be afraid of — unhealthy physical conditions by reminding us that we belong to God, the Source of all peace. And metaphysical treatment helps us to be at peace with an unhealthy physical condition by reminding us who we really are in God and that our true identity is in Him. In prayer, we ask God that an unhealthy physical condition be removed from us and not recur. In metaphysical treatment, we declare: (1) that we are already complete, whole, and perfect in God; and (2) that God does not visit sickness upon those who are doing His Will. Simultaneously, we proclaim our gratitude to God in anticipation of His healing. Prayer invites God's active participation in our healing. Metaphysical treatment uses the tools that God has given to us for our return to a healthy equilibrium and equipoise. Prayer asks God for supernatural intervention (i.e., a miracle). Like prayer, divine metaphysics includes faith and trust in

God but divine metaphysics also includes realization and application of God's truth through affirmation, declaration, and proclamation of His goodness. To be sure, prayer and divine metaphysical treatment go hand in hand in responding to unhealthy conditions.

Concerning the cardiovascular system, students of human anatomy and physiology learn: (1) that the structures and functions of the human heart are easy enough to understand and remember; (2) that the circulatory pathways and their blood flow patterns are straightforward; and (3) that the general functions of the circulatory system and the connective tissue (i.e., blood) that flows through its vessels are simple enough to grasp. From the structural standpoint, even the specific names of many blood vessels are easy to remember because their names are derived from their locations within the human body. And the general nomenclature of blood vessels — which is to say, arteries, arterioles, capillaries, venules, and veins — are determined based on: (1) the direction of blood flow relative to the heart; (2) the presence or absence of certain histological[173] elements within the walls of the blood vessels; (3) the size (i.e., diameter) of the passageways; and (4) the function of each vessel.

The peripheral nervous system (that part of the nervous system outside of the central nervous system, including both somatic and autonomic nervous systems) and the circulatory system are closely aligned. Generally speaking, except for some superficial areas of the body, each artery is accompanied by a vein and a nerve, all three constituting a *triad*. (Such a triad is called a *neurovascular bundle*.) A fourth element often near each triad is a lymphatic vessel that contains lymph. It is no accident that all four structures are involved in flow, including: (1) blood flow away from the heart in arterial vessels; (2) blood flow toward the heart in venous vessels; (3) lymph flow toward the cardiovascular system in lymphatic vessels; and (4) action potential flow, or nerve impulses, away from as well as toward the central nervous system in separate efferent and afferent nerve pathways. All four of these structural types collectively represent what would have been seen in the unfallen somatic

---

173 *Histology* is "microscopic anatomy." The adjective for *histology* is "histologic" or "histological."

identity of original Man as a circuitous network of conduits for pulsating spiritual energy ebbing and flowing throughout one's entire substantive being (that is, one's *astral gelatinous*™ somatic identity). Thus, it is important to imagine and to declare these channels all functioning perfectly in the metaphysical treatment of many different cardiovascular, neurologic, and lymphatic ailments.

The metaphysical treatment of ailments is not meant to involve word associations unless a clearly relevant and applicable higher concept is involved. *For example,* the heart has four chambers. Students of the Bible might know that there are four courts in the Second Jerusalem Temple — namely, the Gentiles' Court, the Women's Court, the Israelites' Court, and the Priests' Court. Restrictions were associated with each of the four courts relative to movement and flow of people from one court to another. From a spiritual standpoint, a figurative use of the four courts might help to illustrate the progressive process of sanctification for a person or for a group of people but would not be useful as a representation of the four chambers of the heart. Just because there are four chambers of the heart and there are four courts of the Second Jerusalem Temple does not automatically mean that there is an implicit metaphysical connection between the two. Please be aware that some of the most ineffective metaphysical practitioners will use a form of clanging[174] in an oversimplified analysis of unhealthy conditions as they try to get their patients to strain out gnats and swallow camels.

In the most efficacious metaphysical treatment of cardiovascular system ailments, it would be good for the practitioner: (1) to recognize the central energy vortex of each individual as the spiritual heart that controls the pulsing ebb and flow of life energy throughout the entire body (in this case, the etheric body double); and (2) to apply the recognition of that truth to relevant cardiovascular ailments in the physical body. Often, but not always, the physical body will respond to such a treatment. If the physical body does not respond favorably, then one should

---

174 *Clanging* is a psychiatric/neurological condition that is based on word association through word sounds rather than word meanings. The word *clanging* is used in a figurative sense here and not meant to imply that the ineffective metaphysical practitioners have psychological disorders.

grasp even more tightly the general metaphysical truth that God is the source of all life, spiritual light, and metaphysical energy while he/she seeks out and employs alternate methods of treatment. To be sure, we should never be disappointed if an unhealthy physical condition fails to respond to prayer and metaphysical treatment. We live in a multivariate universe, or multiverse,[175] that includes many variables, some known and some unknown. In that we are the created and not the Creator, we are not privy — nor should we be privy — to all knowledge concerning the variables for each unhealthy physical condition affecting individual human beings. That is why trusting God is so important to every healing and to all forms of healing.

Let us now take two representative and common diseases, (1) coronary artery disease and (2) type II diabetes, to create a mental check list to see if we are doing everything possible physically, psychologically, and spiritually to ameliorate their harmful effects.

Coronary Artery Disease (CAD)

Coronary artery disease is a leading cause of death worldwide. Coronary artery disease results in reduced blood flow to an area or areas in cardiac muscle because of a narrowing or complete blockage of a passageway (i.e., its *lumen*[176] or opening) within at least one coronary artery. CAD may be due to: (1) the presence of one or more atheromas (i.e., atherosclerotic plaques) that have built up in the wall of one or more coronary arteries as a result of long term atherosclerosis; (2) a sustained or periodic spasm of the muscle layer of the vascular wall (i.e., *tunica media*[177]) of one or more coronary arteries; or (3) an occlusion (i.e., blockage) due to a blood clot (i.e., *thrombus*) that has either formed *in situ* (i.e., at a

---

175 The word *multiverse* is used here in reference to a "multivariate universe" and not in reference to "multiple universes within the physical universe."
176 The Latin plural for the word *lumen* is *lumina*.
177 Three layers, or tunics, are clearly distinguishable in most arteries: the tunica intima (innermost layer), the tunica media (middle layer), and the tunica externa or adventitia (outermost layer). The tunica media of most arteries is composed of smooth muscle and elastic fibers.

particular site in the heart) or has dislodged in another blood vessel elsewhere in the body, traveling to a coronary artery as an *embolus,* and becoming relodged there (forming an *embolism*).

Coronary artery disease and the causes of it need to be properly diagnosed by a medical specialist through extensive diagnostic testing. Always leave the diagnosis of coronary artery disease solely to a medical specialist. However, as a practitioner of divine metaphysics, one should try to learn as much as possible about the disease as well as all the facets of the treatment plan proposed by the medical specialist.

In divine metaphysics, one is taught correctly not to be afraid of coronary artery disease or its possible consequences, including death. However, being fearless does not mean that one should not pay attention to a panic attack because of chest pains or shortness of breath. Responding to a panic attack just might help one to survive in the short term if an ambulance is called or if one is brought to the emergency room of a hospital to receive appropriate treatment in time. This, of course, presupposes that one wants to survive with minimal effects from such an attack. (If you do not want to survive or want nature to take its course, that is your right.) A student of divine metaphysics with CAD should not be embarrassed or feel like a failure spiritually if he or she has a panic attack. Panic attacks can be helpful alarms for us to seek immediate medical attention to avoid permanent damage or an untimely death.

Effective prayer does not require an accurate diagnosis of CAD, but the best metaphysical treatments will be aided by accurate diagnoses. *For example,* if someone's coronary artery disease is due to recurring emboli (singular *embolus*) from phlebitis, or an inflammation of the veins of the legs, then the metaphysical treatment should not only focus on the effects of an embolism in the heart but also on the disease condition of the veins in the legs. In the case of an embolism in a coronary artery, because dissolution of the embolism is desired, the metaphysical treatment would include declaring that God's truth dissolves all error just as His light causes all darkness to disappear, and that God opens passageways that nothing and no one can close or keep closed.[178] Concerning the condition of phlebitis in the legs, metaphysical treatment might include affirming that, because the Creator does not know physical irritation and inflammation,[179] neither do we know physical irritation and inflammation, especially since we have been remade in His complete image and perfect likeness through the shed blood of His only-begotten Son. It might also include these declarations: (1) that we walk unimpeded by faith; (2) that, as children of God, we stand firmly on the principles of God; and (3) that we thank God as the source of all healing virtue.

If a patient's coronary artery disease is due to atherosclerosis rather than thrombi, emboli, and embolisms from phlebitis, then other factors would be investigated by the medical specialist, such as diet as well as intestinal and liver functions. Again, just because the impact of a disease process is in one location — in this case, the heart — does not mean that the primary origin or source of the problem or recurring condition is not related to structures and functions in the human body other than the heart. To be sure, as a practitioner of divine metaphysics, one should not get bogged down in all the medical intricacies of an unhealthy physical condition. And one should remember that the specific causes of unhealthy physical conditions need not always be sought to treat them with success metaphysically. However, one should also want to be as intelligent as possible in the application of metaphysical principles and truths. For this reason, we should learn as much as we can concerning specific unhealthy physical conditions when we are treating them metaphysically. (Christian metaphysicians come to recognize which knowledge is

---

178 King James Version of Isaiah 22:22 and Revelation 3:8

179 Although God does not know *physical* irritation and inflammation, He does know *spiritual* irritation and inflammation that result in His justified Anger, or Wrath. However, God's Wrath forms in response to global evil, the worship of false gods, and/or the shedding of innocent blood, none of which applies here. It should also be noted that God has Wrath until it is dissipated in the form of earthly plagues, pestilences, or *woes*. When God's Wrath is dissipated, it is because His Justice and Judgment have been dispensed.

practical and which is impractical as they learn.)

Early practitioners of divine metaphysics were cautioned not to name a disease or ailment because it was thought that naming an illness granted power to the disorder. However, we need to move past that, reassuring practitioners of divine metaphysics that they should not be afraid of mere names. Indeed, Jesus Christ is the "name above every name."[180] His name is above the name of every unhealthy physical, mental, emotional, and spiritual condition. To be sure, the name of Jesus Christ is above the name of *coronary artery disease*; and the power of Jesus Christ is greater than the power of every disease process.

Type II Diabetes

Type II diabetes is associated with elevated blood glucose levels that impact most cells, tissues, organs, and organ systems in a diabetic person. It is an excellent disease to use as an example because elevated blood sugar levels are only one symptom of a very complex disease process that could be due to any number or combination of factors, including: (1) genetic inheritance patterns, (2) decreased insulin production by the pancreas, (3) decreased number of insulin-specific receptors on cell membranes throughout the body, (4) decreased sensitivity of insulin-specific receptors on cell membranes, (5) excess dietary intake of complex carbohydrates as well as simple sugars, and/or (6) obesity. And, not only are there many possible contributing factors to type II diabetes, there are many symptoms and effects that go well beyond just elevated blood sugar levels — including, but not limited to: elevated blood pressure, poor circulation, damaged and leaky blood vessels, neuropathy, poor wound healing, decubitus ulcers, gangrene, glucose in the urine (glucosuria), excessive urination (polyuria), excessive thirst (polydipsia), excessive hunger (polyphagia/hyperphagia), and obesity.

Medical practitioners will most certainly diagnose the causes and effects of type II diabetes in a patient before they devise a

---

180   King James Version of Ephesians 1:21 and Philippians 2:9

specific treatment plan. As mentioned earlier, spiritual intercessors who are praying for healing do not need to know the specifics about what they are praying for. But spiritual intercessors who use divine metaphysics will want to *consider* the possible causes[181] as well as various symptoms and effects of type II diabetes as they devise their own treatment plan.

Table One provides examples of contributing factors to type II diabetes and correlated methods of treatment. Table Two lists examples of causes and correlated metaphysical methods of treatment.

---

[181] I was once told by a heavenly messenger that "the cause for every condition need not be sought."

Type II Diabetes
Possible Causes and Methods of Treatment

Category	Examples of Contributing Factors	Correlated Treatment Methods
Mental/Emotional	Uneducated, miseducated, or undereducated about requirements for a regular healthy diet and routine exercise	Education Behavior modification Exercise
	Fear of lack, resulting in compulsive overeating	Education Behavior modification Exercise Psychological counseling Pharmaceuticals Prayer Divine metaphysics
	Fear of loss of control, resulting in binge eating	
	Pleasure-seeking to relieve stress and tension	
	Addictive personality	
Spiritual	Gluttony	Prayer to resist and overcome temptation Behavior modification
	Laziness	
	Carnality	
Physical	Diet too high in complex carbohydrates and/or simple sugars	Diet Behavior modification Exercise Pharmaceuticals Prayer Divine metaphysics *Obesity may also require psychological counseling
	Insulin insufficiency	
	Negative impact of obesity* on cellular insulin receptors as well as cellular metabolism/cellular respiration	
	Failure of body cells to utilize glucose consistent with rate at which it is consumed in the diet	
	Failure of body cells to utilize glucose consistent with rate at which it is stored and released by liver and muscle cells (glycogenesis/glycogenolysis)	
	Failure of body cells to utilize glucose consistent with rate at which it is made by liver cells (gluconeogenesis)	
	Disorders associated with the hunger and/or satiety centers in the hypothalamus	

TABLE ONE

Type II Diabetes Possible Causes and Correlated Metaphysical Treatments	
Cause	Metaphysical Treatment*
Fear of lack	1. Affirming that there can be no lack or loss in God
	2. Acknowledging that the children of God will never want because God is their Provider
Fear of loss	
	3. Declaring that perfect love casts out all fear
Excessive pleasure-seeking	1. Affirming that we can do all things through Christ who strengthens us
	2. Acknowledging that we were created to please God and not ourselves
Addiction	
	3. Declaring that we now have the mind of Christ
Obesity	1. Affirming that God's love is the same for each one of us regardless of appearance
	2. Acknowledging that we always have our eternal security in God through Jesus Christ
	3. Declaring that we have our emotional and physical stability in God through Jesus Christ
Insulin insufficiency	1. Affirming that we have sufficiency in all things through Jesus Christ
Decrease in number of cell membrane insulin receptors	2. Acknowledging that God opens doors that nothing and no one can shut
Decreased sensitivity of cell membrane insulin receptors	3. Declaring that we are renewed through the shed blood of Jesus Christ
Unbalanced cellular metabolism/cellular respiration	1. Affirming that the spiritual fire of God burns continually within us to keep us pure
	2. Acknowledging that we possess complete equilibrium and perfect equipoise in God through Jesus Christ
Decreased capacity of body cells to utilize glucose	3. Declaring that we are restored spiritually, emotionally, mentally, and physically through Jesus Christ
Decreased efficiency of liver cell functions	
Disorders of the hypothalamus	1. Affirming that God is always in complete control
	2. Acknowledging that Jesus is the one true and only real Head of the Body of Christ
	3. Declaring that there has never been a time when God did not sit upon His throne

*Metaphysical treatment always includes thanking God in advance for His healing.

TABLE TWO

Our Security in God

God not only wants us to be secure in our salvation (which means that He wants us to not doubt about our returning to Him after our life on Earth is over), God also wants us to be secure in who we are in Him while we are still on Earth. Our security in God is the sole basis for metaphysical treatment of unhealthy conditions. We need to know and proclaim within our inner core that, despite all circumstances and appearances to the contrary, we are still whole, complete, and perfect in God through Christ Jesus. God does not want us to be tossed about by being double-minded (i.e., sometimes believing and trusting, sometimes not). Instead, God wants us to know who we are in Him, acknowledge who we are in Him, affirm who we are in Him, and proclaim who we are in Him. That is why metaphysical treatment includes contradicting what appearances, circumstances, and situations might lead us to believe is true. Even if a leg has been amputated with our consent because it was gangrenous, God wants us to know that we are still whole, complete, and perfect in Him and that we have not disappointed Him because the healing of an unhealthy physical condition did not take place. What occurs in physicality should never shake our faith in God.

That there is such a thing as "metaphysical equipoise" does not mean that such a state of mind is so lofty that it is unobtainable or that it requires magical thinking or arrogance. Metaphysical equipoise includes resting in the knowledge that, although we may not know all the answers, God knows all the answers. It includes resting in the knowledge that we might get our spiritual legs through our right-standing with God in Christ Jesus at the same time that we lose our physical legs through amputation. An abiding gratitude to God for all that He has done, is doing, and will do for us is part of metaphysical equipoise. An abiding humility toward God — in the recognition that He is our sole Sovereign and that we are His beloved subjects — is also part of metaphysical equipoise. Metaphysical equipoise is attainable through gratitude, humility, and earnest study as well as practical application of the metaphysical principles contained within the Holy Bible.

Table Two in this chapter gives possible metaphysical methods for treating various causes of, and contributing factors to, type II diabetes. Does this mean that we cannot, or should not, treat a disease or ailment metaphysically unless we have a precise physical diagnosis for the condition? Not at all! Even without a precise physical diagnosis, we should be so secure in our knowledge of who God is and who we are in Him that we are able to see ourselves already well and healthy and whole. Even if we do not know the intricacies of our physical diagnosis, we will still be able to detect that something seems to be wrong here or there in our body or with this function or that. We might not know that we have coronary artery disease, but we will know that we have pain in our chest or referred pain in our left shoulder, arm, neck, or jaw. In response to this general knowledge, our metaphysical equipoise includes affirming that we live and move and have our being in God through Christ Jesus as well as boldly proclaiming that our heart (or shoulder or arm or neck or jaw) belongs to God and is used for His purposes and His purposes alone. We might not know the specific cause of our type II diabetes, but we do know that our ultimate causality originates and remains in God and that our one true and only real equilibrium is in Him as well.

If our country were at war, we would depend on security forces to help protect us by countering all strikes, insurgencies, and attacks. Similarly, if our body is at war physically, emotionally, mentally, and/or spiritually, we would depend on metaphysical equipoise in the form of proclaiming spiritual truths and affirming statements of *being*. My own beloved spiritual mentor and metaphysical coach had to take morphine while she dealt with excruciating pain from a kidney stone. She did this to regain composure so that she could more effectively treat the condition metaphysically. Her taking morphine was not a sell-out to the medical profession; rather, she combined medical and metaphysical treatments because it was circumspect, judicious, practical, prudent, and intelligent to do so.

God wants our security to include thinking metaphysically and intelligently at the same time. Granted, there are times when we need to rely unfailingly on God without the help of a medical practitioner or a psychological practitioner. But relying unfailingly on God should not begin for us at a point of seeming hopelessness or on our deathbed or in the throes of physical or psychological decompensation. Rather, relying unfalteringly on God should begin right now and continue unfalteringly for the remainder of our life here on Earth. It is not trite to say that today is the first day of the rest of our life or that every moment is the first moment of the rest of our being in God.

Recognizing the metaphysical truth that our physical, emotional, mental, and spiritual security rests in God is not only worth noting but also worth employing. Let us begin this very moment, undeterred that we have not been successful in the past concerning this challenge or that problem and recognizing that living in the here and now means exactly that. To be sure, the here and now is the place and time of our ever-beginning as well as our eternal surety.

Our eternal security rests in God.[182] Our spiritual security rests in God. Our mental and emotional security rests in God. And our physical security rests in God.[183]

God wants us to feel secure. He wants us to feel secure: (1) because we really are secure, (2) because we are His children, and (3) because He wants us to always take comfort in the spiritual truth of our being in Him.

---

[182] The phrase "eternal security" is used by some Christians to indicate that, once we are saved, we are always saved. For the sake of clarification, although Satan cannot pluck us out of God's hand and we cannot, in this way, lose our salvation, the gift of free will does permit us to throw our salvation away. (See Hebrews 6:4-6.)

[183] The present author advises that you not pray for your financial security but that you pray for your daily needs. Praying for your financial security is too limiting and confining and may unconsciously (i.e., subconsciously) include fear, greed, and/or an unhealthy dependency on money as a worldly solution to spiritual problems. In contrast, praying for your daily needs implies that you recognize that God can provide for your particular needs without using money and, also, in unimaginable and unexpected ways.

Chapter Questions

This section is intended to facilitate learning by providing relevant activities, exercises, and experiences to aid students of divine metaphysics in their quest for grasping spiritual concepts, integrating them into their own belief systems, holding them more assuredly, and making them more practical in daily life.

The following questions should be answered after reading each titled section. To answer a few of the questions, students may need to consult outside resources or external references. Students are also encouraged to answer these questions with others during group discussions.

Metaphysical Matters of the Heart

1. Compare and contrast purity and impurity relative to motives and intents.

2. How important spiritually is it for us to seek to do the Will of God?

3. In what ways does our heart express itself?

4. Is the human heart the actual seat of human emotions? Why or why not?

5. How can we know or discern the hearts of others?

6. What are the differences between human reasoning and spiritual reasoning?

7. How does one receive the ability to reason spiritually?

8. What is the true heart of an individual?

9. How important to spiritual reasoning is concern for others?

10. What importance does God place on shed or spilled blood in the Holy Bible?

11. What is the difference between inquiring of the Lord and asking Him to explain Himself?

12. What does oxygen represent metaphysically?

Treating Cardiovascular Ailments Metaphysically

13. In what ways are the anatomy and physiology of the cardiovascular system simple, straightforward, and relatively easy to understand and remember?

14. Discuss directions of flow in the cardiovascular system, lymphatic system, and nervous system.

15. Briefly discuss word associations as they relate to metaphysical treatment.

16. Should we ever be disappointed if an unhealthy physical condition fails to respond to prayer and metaphysical treatment?

17. Discuss the medical, psychological, and spiritual treatment of coronary artery disease.

18. Give examples of metaphysical affirmations, declarations, and proclamations that might be useful in the treatment of coronary artery disease.

19. List examples of how you can be more successful as a practitioner of divine metaphysics.

20. Should practitioners of divine metaphysics avoid using the names of diagnosed disabilities, diseases, and disorders? Why or why not?

21. Using Table One, discuss causes and treatment methods that may be useful for type II diabetes.

22. Using Table Two, discuss physical causes and metaphysical treatments of type II diabetes.

Written Exercise

As noted in the chapter on divine metaphysics of the cardiovascular system, God wants us to be secure. Security is a huge issue for human beings. Customarily, we are *not* taught how we might inculcate and nurture security in ourselves and others. Insecurities feed addictive behaviors related to gambling, substance abuse, overeating, promiscuity, manipulation and exploitation of others, poor self-esteem, thievery, and greed. God wants us to recognize that we are already secure, regardless of the specific unhealthy conditions that we each might have, because He provides for our security — emotionally, mentally, physically, and spiritually.

Humility and gratitude are important parts of our security. Therefore, this written exercise is designed to help you recognize and affirm that, regardless of circumstances, there are: (1) reasons why one should be humble; and (2) things for which one should be grateful:

1. Make a list containing reasons why you should be humble and discuss the list with friends and/or fellow students of divine metaphysics.

2. Make a list of things for which you are grateful and discuss the list with friends and/or fellow students of divine metaphysics.

3. Make a list of metaphysical statements that acknowledge and affirm your security — emotionally, mentally, physically, and spiritually. Share the list with like-minded friends and fellow students of divine metaphysics during small and large group focused discussions.

Chapter Six
Divine Metaphysics of the Lymphatic System and Immunity

O LORD my God, I cried out to You, and You healed me.

PSALM 30:2 KJV (PARAPHRASE)

One or Two Organ Systems?

The lymphatic, or lymphoid, and immune systems are generally discussed together in textbooks of human anatomy and physiology. In fact, the two systems are so closely allied that they are sometimes referred to as one system. Human anatomy and physiology textbooks often have a chapter on the lymphatic system in which a discussion about immunity is also presented. To be sure, one can't discuss lymphoid tissue without discussing immunity and one can't discuss immunity without discussing lymphoid tissue.

Just as the lymphatic and cardiovascular systems can be subsumed together under the rubric of "the circulatory system," so can the lymphatic and immune systems be subsumed together under the rubric of "the lymphatic system." Although the majority of the body's organ systems demonstrate a physical continuity between and among their respective organs, not all organ systems do. *For example,* the endocrine system is composed of various hormone-producing endocrine glands that are not all connected physically; yet its organs constitute a true organ system: They all produce hormones and are, thus, linked together from a functional standpoint. Similarly, although some of the organs associated with immunity are not physically continuous or contiguous with lymphatic vasculature, there is a degree of cellular continuity and functional connectivity among most organs of the lymphatic and immune systems. From this perspective, the immune and lymphatic systems are united.

To be sure, the immune system is just as much its own system as the endocrine system. However, for the purposes of this book, I will treat the lymphatic and immune systems as one organ system — namely, the lymphatic system. Paradoxically (but not surprisingly), there are some anatomists and physiologists who might advocate that the lymphatic system be subsumed under the rubric of "the immune system." Whichever categorization you choose, just make sure that your choice is defensible.

The Anatomy of the Lymphatic System

The lymphatic system *primarily* consists of: lymphatic vasculature, the fluid known as lymph, lymphocytes, and lymph nodes — as well as smaller lymphoid masses and cellular aggregates referred to as nodules, follicles, and patches.

Lymphatic vasculature includes lymphatic capillaries, lymphatic vessels sometimes referred to as "veins," and large lymphatic ducts that: (1) drain interstitial fluid (i.e., tissue fluid) from the body; (2) drain certain fats primarily from the small intestine; and (3) interconnect chains of lymph nodes that are found in various strategic areas of the body.

Chains of lymph nodes are found in the cervical, axillary, mediastinal, pelvic, and inguinal regions as well as in areas adjacent to the small and large intestines. (See Figure Eighteen for a depiction of the relationship between lymphatic vasculature and various lymph nodes.)

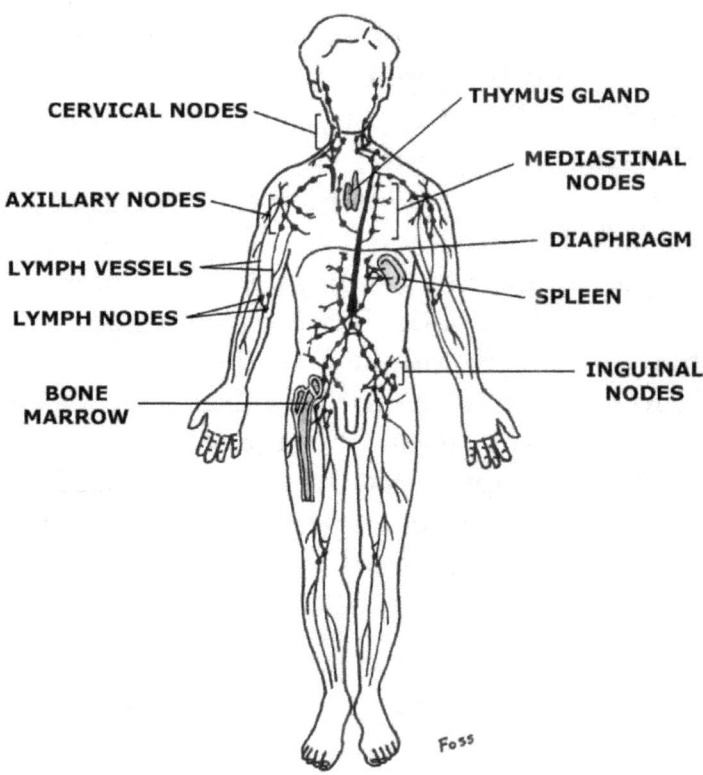

Organs of the Lymphatic System
Figure Eighteen

Although lymph nodes contain other cell types, they especially contain an abundance of: (1) T-lymphocytes that differentiate from thymocytes in the thymus gland and migrate to colonize lymph nodes; and (2) B-lymphocytes that differentiate from precursor cells in hematopoietic tissue (i.e., blood-producing red bone marrow or myeloid tissue) that migrate from red bone marrow to colonize lymph nodes. There is a bit of irony that lymphocytes are named T-lymphocytes ("T" for thymus) and B-lymphocytes ("B" for bone marrow) since the precursors of thymocytes (i.e., the cells in the thymus that produce T-lymhocytes) migrate to the thymus from red bone marrow after parturition (i.e., childbirth) all the way through senescence (i.e., old age with its accompanying deterioration).[184]

Lymphatic vasculature transports T-lymphocytes and B-lymphocytes as well as: (1) fat and fatty acids (i.e., *chyle* from the intestinal tract); (2) antigen[185]-presenting cells; and (3) white blood cells other than T- and B-lymphocytes (some of which, like *plasma cells,* are derived from lymphocytes).

Lymphoid tissue is not only found in the thymus, spleen, and red bone marrow, all of which are pictured in Figure Eighteen, but also in areas not pictured, such as those associated with the digestive system, including: (1) lingual and palatine tonsils; (2) follicular patches in the duodenum (i.e., lymphoid follicles known as Peyer's patches are found in this first segment of the small intestine); (3) follicular patches in the ileum (i.e., the third segment of the small intestine); and (4) throughout the large intestine as well as in its attached appendix. In addition, close to the lingual and palatine tonsils are the pharyngeal tonsils, or adenoids, that are also associated with the respiratory system.

Immunity and the Godhead

Of the topics in this book, the topic of immunity is one of the most crucial for students of divine metaphysics to understand both physiologically and metaphysically.

---

184 During *in utero* development, the fetal liver produces stem cells that migrate to the thymus and produce the earliest T-lymphocytes. This role of producing T-lymphocyte stem cells gradually shifts to red bone marrow by the time of parturition (childbirth).

185 In its simplest definition, an *antigen* is "a substance that stimulates the formation of antibodies." Because immunologists make a distinction between partial antigens and complete antigens, definitions for *antigen* by such specialists will be more elaborate than what is used in this textbook.

The Creator is responsible for imparting both biological immunity and spiritual immunity to His people. Despite the Adamic Fall, the Creator imparted physical immunity to His fallen children through nonspecific and specific biological defense mechanisms at work in their human bodies, just as He imparts spiritual immunity to His restored children through the shed blood of His only-begotten Son, Jesus Christ. Indeed, the redeemed in Christ have spiritual immunity from God's Judgment and Wrath because their sins are remitted, or cancelled, through their accepting a spiritual transfusion of the shed blood of Jesus Christ.

Metaphysically speaking, our spiritual immunity through Christ Jesus is eternal immunity. Whatever biological immunity we may already have, or will acquire, is not eternal immunity because it is transient and temporal. Not only does biological immunity end when our lives on Earth are over, biological immunity usually wanes as we age or when we encounter disease-producing organisms that our human bodies are not able to combat easily or at all. Indeed, there are substantive differences between spiritual immunity and physical immunity.

Regardless of their substantive differences, there is more of a connection between physical immunity and spiritual immunity than meets the eye. There are physical and metaphysical connections between these two types of immunity through blood and lymph as well as through red bone marrow and the thymus gland. Physically, red bone marrow and the thymus gland contribute cellular elements to both blood and lymph. Metaphysically, red bone marrow and the thymus represent the blood and water that continue to flow from Christ Jesus to fallen, corporeal man through God's grace and mercy.

In the first chapter of this textbook, I shared how original mankind fell from an *astral gelatinous*™ condition of being to a *protoplasmic* condition of being. It is not that fallen mankind became monstrous and no longer possessed any resemblance to the Creator; it is that the somatic identity of mankind became twisted and corrupted from its original shape, form, substance, and appearance because of iniquity and sin. However, despite falling from a spiritual, or *astral gelatinous*™, condition of being to a fleshly condition of existence, the Adamic Fall of original mankind did not annihilate the Creator's original intelligent design although that design was definitely altered.

To be sure, because the Creator knew that original mankind would eventually fall, He encoded and preprogrammed a human design (i.e., a flesh-body or corporeal design) as a default into unfallen mankind, which design included natural safeguards and biological measures that would help to maintain, preserve, and protect the newly acquired somatic identity of fallen mankind (though only for the specified period of one's lifetime). In other words, such safeguards and measures were designed to last for the appointed periods of time that individuals were *scheduled* to be here on Earth "to work out their own salvation with fear and trembling."[186]

As recorded in the Holy Bible, the Antediluvians (i.e., the human beings who lived before the Biblical flood) had much longer lifespans than human beings do now. Although their bodies were corrupted and corruptible from the Adamic Fall (just like our bodies are today), the Antediluvians' bodies were closer in time to original and unfallen mankind and, therefore, retained substantially more of the essence and life force from that condition of being than we do today. Indeed, their biological defense mechanisms were more robust. *For example,* (1) the telomeres, or end portions, of their chromosomes were more stable and fragmented less easily;[187] (2) the number of generations that their individual cell types could reproduce, or undergo cell division, was greater; and (3) their mechanisms for biological defense were stronger and, therefore, more resilient in maintaining and mounting nonspecific and specific responses to life-altering and potentially life-threatening physical changes.

Although our souls are now trapped, as it were, in human bodies that belong to the Animal Kingdom, we do not have to act like

---

186 Philippians 2:12, King James Version (Paraphrase)
187 Bull, Caroline and Michael Fenech. "Genome-health nutrigenomics and nutrigenetics: nutritional requirements or 'nutriomes' for chromosomal stability and telomere maintenance at the individual level." *Proceedings of the Nutrition Society* (2008), 67, 146–156.

animals. While on Earth, our bodies are in a fallen condition regardless of whether we are saved or unsaved. For that reason, we must learn to discipline and tame the animal bodies in which we now find ourselves. Although acceptance of salvation through Christ Jesus is the only step we need to take to get into Heaven, we must take additional steps daily if we are to be successful, or victorious, in taming our corporeal bodies by continually sanctifying them unto the Lord.

Without endorsing or denying the authenticity of her claimed spiritual communications, the portrait of Christ Jesus painted according to the specifications of Christian mystic, Sister Maria Faustina Kowalska, very much relates to both biological immunity and spiritual immunity.

In the portrait of Faustina's Christ (Figure Nineteen), the red ray[188] to the left symbolizes blood and the white ray to the right symbolizes water, both of which flowed from Jesus' side[189] after he was pierced in death on the cross by a Roman soldier's spear. Fluid (or "water") accumulated during Jesus' passion on the cross since it was not being drained and recirculated properly through blood vessels and lymphatic vessels.

---

188 Although not in color, Figure Nineteen illustrates the red ray on its left as darker.

189 "Side" is translated from the Greek *pleura* [G4125 in Appendix Table B] in John 19:34.

***Representation of Portrait Inspired by Saint Faustina*[190]**
Figure Nineteen

Blood plasma, tissue fluid (or interstitial fluid), and lymph are body fluids that are all essentially the same because they are transferred (that is, recirculated) from one body fluid compartment to another (i.e., from blood to tissue fluid to lymph and, then, back to blood) over and over again. The red and white rays in the portrait not only symbolize spiritual immunity; they also represent biological, or physical, immunity. The red ray represents salvation through the shed blood of Jesus; and the red ray also represents the biological defense mechanisms we carry in our blood. The white ray represents sanctification through the "water" of God's Holy Spirit; and the white ray also represents the biological defense mechanisms we carry in our lymphatic fluid.

---

190 The Polish signature below the feet of Christ is often translated as "Jesus, I trust in you."

Both rays are processing (i.e., proceeding) from the mediastinal area of the chest where the heart and bilobed thymus gland are located. The heart pumps and recirculates blood and the thymus gland produces T-lymphocytes that (1) colonize various lymph nodes and glands as well as (2) circulate in lymph and blood. Blood and lymph contribute to our biological resistance.

It is no coincidence that "water" (i.e., representative of the Holy Spirit) and blood (i.e., representative of the shed blood of God's only-begotten Son) are related to *spiritual immunity* and that "water" (i.e., also representative of lymphatic fluid) and blood (i.e., the elements of biological defense found in blood) are related to *biological immunity.*

It is also no coincidence that not a bone of Jesus' body was broken in order to fulfill prophecy[191] as well as to signal the importance of red bone marrow, or hematopoietic tissue, as a source of blood, which God identifies as "life."[192] Keep in mind that hematopoietic tissue is the site of the production of B-lymphocytes, which (like T-lymphocytes) colonize various lymph nodes and glands as well as circulate in both blood and lymph.

Blood represents life spiritually because blood is the source of our spiritual immunity through Jesus Christ. The shed blood of Jesus Christ metaphysically represents God's sacrifice of His own life for our iniquity and sin. (Yes, God gave his own Life to save our lives.) Blood also represents life physically because it not only is responsible for circulating nutrients to the living cells of the body, it is the major source of our biological defense mechanisms. It is no accident that God chose (1) blood to represent life and (2) water to represent renewal and sanctification. (Blood is also discussed in the section entitled *The Pulse of Life's Ebb and Flow* in the previous chapter on the *Divine Metaphysics of the Cardiovascular System.*)

Blood is a fluid compartment carrying biological defenders that mount nonspecific and specific responses to foreign organisms and

---

[191] John 19:36; Exodus 12:46; Numbers 9:12; Psalm 34:20
[192] Genesis 9:4; Leviticus 17:10-12 and 19:26; Deuteronomy 12:16, 23, 25 and 15:23

toxic substances. As the Holy Spirit, "water" represents the sanctification and dedication (or rededication) of our lives to God as well as the protection of our spirits and souls from invasion by unholy thoughts and demonic emotions: Sanctification, dedication, and protection affirm and confirm our spiritual immunity. As lymph, "water" also represents the cleansing of our physical bodies from biological foreign invaders, which cleansing affirms and confirms our biological immunity. Like blood, lymph is a fluid compartment that carries biological defenders to mount nonspecific and specific responses to foreign organisms and toxic substances.

The area of the mediastinal cavity that contains both the heart and the thymus gland corresponds to the Heart Chakra of tantric and yogic traditions in Hinduism and Buddhism as well as Sephirah 6 in Jewish Kabbalism (Cabalism). (Sephirah 6 is depicted in Figure Sixteen.) It is no coincidence that, in Tibetan Buddhism, the Heart Chakra contains the "white and red drop" (i.e., the life-bearing force or "wind") and that, in Jewish Kabbalism (Cabalism), Sephirah 6 contains the indestructible life force found first and foremost in the Godhead and identified by the Name of Yahweh, "the Self-Existent One."

In closing this section, I would like to add one more thing about Faustina Kowalska. Although the present author does not endorse praying to "saints" in Heaven (it is not their business to listen to our prayers), I find it more than fitting that the primary healing used to support Faustina's formal beatification by the Vatican was a healing of lymphedema.[193] (Lymphedema is an excessive accumulation of fluid, partly due to poor lymphatic circulation.)

Lifespan

God told Adam that, if he did not obey His command to not eat from the Tree of Knowledge of Good and Evil, he would surely die

---

193 Odell, Catherine M. *Faustina: The Apostle of Divine Mercy.* Huntington: Our Sunday Visitor Publishing Division, 1998, pages 159-160.

(Genesis 2:16). Subsumed within God's command was both a blessing and a curse. God's blessing of fellowship with Him would continue as long as Adam obeyed God's command, but that blessing would cease if Adam disobeyed and, synchronously, God's curse of death would take effect. *Death* here means two things: (1) "separation from God" as well as (2) "corruption, deterioration, senescence, and expiration, or termination, of one's somatic identity." In other words, that mankind now has a lifespan is part of God's curse upon mankind for its iniquity and sin. (Iniquity is the predisposition to sin and sin is action based on that predisposition.)

Often, people who understand that God is divine Love[194] resist the notion that God would curse anyone or anything. However, such is the nature of the Supreme Deity, who is altogether Just at the same time that He remains perfect Love. *For example,* the Lord God Almighty clearly stated in Scripture that He would bless those who bless Israel and that He would curse those who curse Israel.[195] He also clearly stated to the children of Israel that He set before them both blessings and curses: (1) blessings if they would follow Him and do His Will; and (2) curses if they followed false gods and, by doing so, go against His Will:

> *{26} Behold, I set before you this day a blessing and a curse; {27} A blessing, if you obey the commandments of the LORD your God, which I command you this day: {28} And a curse, if you will not obey the commandments of the LORD your God, but turn aside from the way that I command you this day to go after other gods which ye have not known.*
>
> DEUTERONOMY 11:26-28 KJV (PARAPHRASE)

Satan contradicted God (Satan always contradicts God) by telling Eve that Adam and she would not die if they ate from the

---

194 1 John 4:8 & 16, King James Version
195 Genesis 12:3, King James Version

Tree of Knowledge of Good and Evil (Genesis 3:2-4). Satan ended up deceiving not only Eve but also Adam through Eve. And once they ate the apple, they both did die by having their *astral gelatinous*™ substance change to *protoplasmic* substance at the same time that they no longer experienced spiritual intimacy (i.e., unhindered fellowship) with their Creator. Later, they would both eventually die in an additional way by experiencing the physical death of their corporeal bodies. Before the Adamic Fall, original mankind was created to be immortal — spirit, soul, and body. But mankind's immortality was forfeited when mankind fell and God's curse of death fell upon them. Metaphysically speaking, Man's spirit, soul, and body wasted away and died.

God cursed Adam and Eve by restricting their movements to the Earth for a predetermined period of time both in terms of individual lifespan and in terms of total millennia that the present Earth would be in existence. And God also cursed them so that their physical bodies would return to the basic elements from which they were made (i.e., from which they were materialized as *protoplasmic* in nature).[196]

It is important for people who are maturing spiritually to understand that God is the author of divine curses just as much as He is the author of divine blessings. As God set natural laws into motion and, therefore, does not need to "think" about them anymore, so did God set supernatural laws into motion and, therefore, does not need to "think" about them anymore either. In nature, the Laws of Thermodynamics were set into motion by God and they "rule" the material universe in accordance with the original direction God gave them. Likewise, supernatural laws were set into motion by God and they rule spiritual matters in accordance with God's original direction. To be sure, God can alter the Laws of Thermodynamics at any point in time. And God can alter supernatural laws, provided that their alteration does not negate or contradict His Nature, which is good, righteous, pure, holy, and just. *For example,* God's innate, immutable, and absolute Goodness has altered mankind's path toward spiritual annihilation

---

196   Genesis 3:17-19

and supernatural extinction by His Grace and Mercy for all who accept His Plan of Salvation through the shed blood of His only-begotten Son, Jesus Christ. (It is very important for the present author to keep repeating this spiritual truth for those who have become hardened or indifferent to it.)

Adam and Eve did not each have a life expectancy or lifespan until they fell from their original state of immortality. However, their immediate descendants had extremely long life expectancies and lifespans in comparison to human beings today. (This last statement, of course, is not true if you are reading this during the Millennium of Christ Jesus' rule on Earth because life expectancies and lifespans will be much longer then.)

It is recorded in the Fifth Chapter of Genesis that Adam lived for 930 years, Seth lived for 912 years, Enosh lived for 905 years, Kenan lived for 910 years, Mehalalel lived for 895 years, Jared lived for 962 years, Methuselah lived for 969 years, and Lamech lived for 777 years. The years lived for these Antediluvians are not fictitious, fraudulent, or figurative. They were accurately recorded in the Holy Bible. How could they have lived so long? The immediate descendants of Adam and Eve still felt the residual power of God's life energy within their *protoplasmic* flesh because of their proximity in time to His unfallen creation and the life force found in mankind's original *astral gelatinous*™ substance. However, as God Himself observed, the great power of His life energy would not always reside in mankind to the same degree or extent and, therefore, mankind's average life expectancy would dwindle to one hundred and twenty years. (Read Genesis 6:1-3.) Of course, the value that God gave in Genesis 6:1-3 proved to be true: Sarah died at the age of one hundred and twenty-seven (Genesis 23:1), Aaron died at the age of one hundred and twenty-three (Number 33:39), and Moses died at the age of one hundred and twenty (Deuteronomy 31:2; 34:7). And, by the time the Psalmist wrote Psalm 90:10, the maximum life expectancy had decreased further by another forty to fifty years:

> *The span of our years is seventy — or eighty if we have the strength; yet their span includes labor and sorrow,*

for our life is quickly cut off, and we fly away.

PSALM 90:10 KJV (PARAPHRASE)

In 2022, the life expectancy for someone living in the United States of America (U.S.A.) is approximately seventy-eight years of age. (By the time many of you will be reading this, the U.S.A. will have already ceased to exist — primarily, because of terrorism, bankruptcy, and anarchy; and, secondarily, because of natural and man-made disasters.)

The life expectancy of fallen, corporeal man is not only dependent on biological response mechanisms but also on genetics, exercise, sanitation, disease, deterioration, accident, trauma, availability of food and water, and nutrition. Speaking of nutrition, it is important to note that the Biblical Antediluvians were vegetarians since God had not yet given His permission for mankind to eat meat, which permission was given to Noah and his descendants after the Flood (Genesis 1:30; 2:16; 3:18; 9:3). It is also noteworthy that God's permission to eat meat was not unconditional since He forbad mankind to eat the blood within meat because the blood constituted the animal's "life."[197] (Blood is the *essence* of biological life.)

That mankind has a limited lifespan is a result of God's curse of death upon us. Certainly, God's curses have fallen upon mankind in other ways — *for example,* in the Flood during Noah's time and in the ten plagues of Egypt. And, to be sure, God's curses will be enacted as woes upon mankind during the Great Tribulation before Christ Jesus returns to Earth.

One day, when God the Son delivers the world up to God the Father (1 Corinthians 15:24), the curse of death will be removed completely (Revelation 22:3) and "death shall be no more."[198] To be sure, "the last enemy that shall be destroyed is death."[199] That day will come when there will be "a new heaven and a new

---

[197] Genesis 9:4; Leviticus 17:10-12 and 19:26; Deuteronomy 12:16, 23, 25 and 15:23
[198] Revelation 21:4, King James Version
[199] 1 Corinthians 15:26, King James Version

earth" (Revelation 21:1 KJV) at the end of the Millennial rule of Christ Jesus on Earth and after World War IV. (It should be noted here that the removal of "death" not only includes ending expiration of the human body but also includes the final dissolution of all corporeality as well.)

During that Millennium, or final 1,000-year period of time, the Holy Spirit teaches us through the Prophet Isaiah that human lifespans will be extended:

> *[During the Millennium] there will no longer be an infant who lives only a few days or someone who does not live out his or her full lifespan; [in fact,] someone who dies at the age of one hundred will still be a child and anyone who dies earlier than one hundred will be thought to be under a curse.*
>
> ISAIAH 65:20 KJV (PARAPHRASE)

In summary, relative to human lifespan: (1) mankind's bodies (i.e., somatic identities) were immortal before the Adamic Fall; (2) mankind's bodies lived, on average, between 700 to 900 years immediately after the Adamic Fall and before the Flood; (3) mankind's bodies lived approximately 120 years after the Flood (at least through the time of Moses); (4) mankind's bodies lived (and will still live) on average between 70 to 80 years from the time of Moses until the beginning of *the Millennium;* and (5) mankind's bodies will live hundreds of years during the 1,000 years of *the Millennium*. (Each year of *the Millennium* will be a cycle of repeating pleasantness except for the time of Satan's release from the Abyss, or Pit, toward the end of *the Millennium* and his precipitation of World War IV.)

You may remember from earlier chapters that: (1) the somatic identities of Christians are restored — that is, "redeemed" via rapture or resurrection — to immortality (i.e., an *astral gelatinous*™ condition) at the time of Christ's return; and (2) the somatic identities of the remaining children of God (identified as such during *the Millennium*) are restored, or redeemed, to immortality at the end of that 1,000-year period.

The end of *the Millennium* (Revelation 20:3), the end of World War IV (Revelation 20:8-9), and the relegation of Satan, death, and hell to the Lake of Fire (Revelation 20:10 & 14) immediately precede the creation of "a new heaven and a new earth" (Revelation 21:1) — at which time the somatic identities of all saved will again be immortal, eternal, and *astral gelatinous*™. Like their souls, the somatic identities of all saved people will be, by then, redeemed, too.

The metaphysical reason that the naked human body was ever considered shameful in the first place is not that someone might see someone else's genitals but that it was denuded of God's glory at the time of the Adamic Fall. However, when death is finally expunged, such shame will be completely removed as well.

Renewal

Renewal includes both *natural renewal* and *supernatural renewal:*

Natural Renewal

Although our somatic identities fell at the exact moment that our souls yielded to Satan's temptation, they "fell" into the default human body form that was preprogrammed into them when they were originally created in God's complete image and perfect likeness. Also preprogrammed into them were both general and specific means for renewal vis-à-vis: (1) growth, repair, and replacement of various elements of the human body *(for example*, in the regeneration of specific cells, tissues, and organs) as well as (2) biological defense mechanisms against pathogens (disease-producing organisms), toxins, and foreign tissues. In other words, God provided for the natural renewal and protection of the somatic identities we acquired from the Adamic Fall even before they existed.

Although souls are saved when they accept Jesus Christ as their Lord and Savior, somatic identities are not changed back to their original *astral gelatinous*™ condition: (1) until the return of Christ Jesus on Earth for those identified *before the Millennium* as belonging to God; and (2) until the end of *the Millennium* for the rest of those identified *during the Millennium* as belonging to God. And, although saved souls are saved before their somatic identities are redeemed (i.e., restored through resurrection, rapture, or translation), human bodies are still iniquitous and, therefore, prone to sin and prone to the effects of sin. For that reason, living in a human body contributes to our errant ways of thinking and feeling as well as deteriorating health even after our souls are saved. Indeed, it is dangerous to live in a human body because of the challenges and limitations corporeality imposes.

Because the human body is a by-product of spiritual death, it was never meant to be, or meant to become, immortal and eternal. To be sure, Christ Jesus raised his physical body three days after his crucifixion. However, he did not ascend into Heaven with an unchanged physical body but, instead, with a glorified, incorruptible body.

Regarding the transient and temporal nature of the human body and its preprogrammed eventual death, the story of Lazarus provides us with a solid understanding of the ultimate fate of the human body. Even though Lazarus was raised from the dead by Jesus Christ four days after his death (John 11:17 & 39), Lazarus was still destined to die again physically. Ironically, Lazarus emerged from the tomb not only still wrapped in his burial shroud but also with his soul still encumbered by a human body. To be sure, the ancient Greeks were not so far afield when they declared "Soma sema!" — which is to say, "The body [is] a tomb [for the soul]!"

The lifespan for human bodies that run their full course from parturition to natural death due to old age includes: (1) growth, (2) maturation, and (3) senescence (i.e., old age with deterioration). Aging is preprogrammed into the human body just as growth, repair, and replacement are preprogrammed into the human body. When physical growth stops, and the rate of regeneration is slower than the rate of degeneration, the human body ages and deteriorates. No degree of trusting God prevents the eventual shedding of our human form. Despite their efficacy, prayer and divine metaphysics do not stop physical death.

Senescence includes — but is not limited to — the following degenerative changes associated with aging, most of which are interdependent processes:

1. No regeneration of highly specialized cells of the body *(for example,* multipolar neurons in the brain) and decreased regeneration of other cell types.

2. A decrease in the size, number, and lifespan of the various cells of the body.

3. A decrease in the rate of cellular protein synthesis and an increase in cross-linking, misfolding, and tangling of both extracellular and intracellular proteins.

4. A diminished efficiency in cellular metabolism and cellular respiration.

5. A decrease in the capabilities and capacities of all body cells.

6. An increase in the presence of free radicals; a decrease in the absorption and cellular availability of antioxidants; and a diminished capacity for natural chelation.

7. A diminished efficiency in gene operation, activation, promotion, repression, modulation, interaction, and replication.

8. An increase in fragmentation, mutation, and translocation of chromosomal DNA.

9. A decrease in secretory functions of all glandular tissue, including exocrine glands (i.e., glandular tissue that secretes its products into ducts for distribution) and endocrine glands (i.e., glandular tissue that secretes its products into the bloodstream for distribution).

10. An increase in deleterious permeability changes of blood capillaries and lymph capillaries.

11. A decrease in the tensile strength and elasticity of muscle fibers and connective tissue fibers.

12. A decrease in the strength of muscle contractions in all three muscle types (i.e., cardiac, skeletal, and smooth muscle).

13. Harmful changes in blood pressure as well as diminished blood and lymph flow.

14. Diminished pulmonary air volumes and capacities as well as harmful changes in pulmonary compliance.

15. A decrease in the availability of oxygen at the cellular level (i.e., hypoxia).

16. An increase in tissue dehydration and tissue fluid accumulation (i.e., edema).

17. Harmful changes in digestive tract absorption, waste elimination, and bowel control.

18. Harmful changes in urinary excretion and bladder control.

19. A decrease in the efficiency of the immune system and an increase in the incidence of autoimmune disorders.

20. Diminished capacities of the senses (i.e., vision, audition, gustation, olfaction, and touch).

21. An increase in the demineralization of bone and in the loss of cartilage matrix organic components.

22. An increase in bone fractures (including microfractures) and a decrease in normal bone repair.

23. An increase in inflammation of supporting connective tissues (i.e., rheumatism) and in arthritic changes due to rheumatism of the joints.

24. Integumentary system changes that result in an aged and weathered appearance as well as in a diminished capacity of the skin to serve as an effective barrier to infectious microorganisms and toxic substances.

25. Diminished cognitive abilities and a decrease in brain functioning.

26. A decrease in the ability to engage in physical activities.

27. Harmful changes in body fat concentration and distribution.

28. An overall increase in the susceptibility to diseases and disorders.

To be sure, the previous list of degenerative changes varies from individual to individual based on inheritance factors, the external environment, the internal environment, nutrition, and age-appropriate physical activity. Regardless of the desire for these degenerative changes to be solely controlled by the mind and spirituality, these degenerative changes will continue to exist because they are programmed into the human body. However, they can be impacted upon favorably by supernatural renewal, causing them to be both reversed and healed in response to prayer and metaphysical treatment. And, to be sure, they will be favorably changed for human beings who live during the time of *the Millennium*. However, all *protoplasmic* forms will cease to exist at the end of *the Millennium* with the formation of "a new heaven and a new earth" (Revelation 21:1).

Supernatural Renewal

Supernatural renewal includes *spiritual*, or *metaphysical*, *renewal*.

Spiritual renewal is a process that requires daily self-examination and self-inventory through retrospection and introspection. First, human beings receive salvation after they accept the Lord Jesus Christ as their personal Savior. Then, for the rest of their earthly lives, human beings are required to "work out their own salvation with fear and trembling" (Philippians 2:12 KJV). In other words, after the salvation of their souls, people are (1) to realize that there are various areas in their lives that need to be surrendered to Christ Jesus and (2) to learn to consciously submit those areas to him one by one. (At the age of seventy-five in 2022, the present author is still identifying areas in his life that need to be surrendered to Christ Jesus.)

The only way that saved human beings can surrender themselves to Christ Jesus is to live in a state of contrition for each and every weakness, vulnerability, and infirmity that they have. However, it is very easy for saved human beings to get sidetracked.

For example, it might be easy for those who are submitting their unhealthy sexual appetites (i.e., sexual lusts) to Christ Jesus to conclude, since this is such a huge area of temptation and challenge in their individual lives, that they are doing all they need to do by living in a state of contrition (LSC) concerning purity and holiness as it relates to sexuality. To be sure, it is definitely "work" to keep custody of one's eyes and ears, to quickly dismiss unhealthy sexual thoughts and unholy feelings, and to turn "off" sexual thinking once that switch has been turned "on." However, regardless of how honoring to God that their contrition in this one area might be or become, and regardless of how much work that it might take daily, an honest person will eventually admit that, like an onion, there are many layers to one's carnal self (or, in the language of the King James Version of the Bible, one's "old man" or, by extension, "old woman"). Thus, after learning to live in contrition concerning unhealthy sexuality, and bringing that sexuality under subjection to Christ Jesus, they must admit to themselves that there are other areas in their lives about which they also need to live daily in contrition — areas like fearfulness, selfish pride, egotism, superiority, inferiority, unprincipled transactions, substance abuse, extreme risk-taking, gluttony, materialism, ingratitude, covetousness, thievery, exploitation of others, controlling attitudes and behaviors, and manipulation of others through cunning, conning, and conniving gambits and ploys. And, even if they can surrender all these things to Christ Jesus, they still have a final pitfall — the one of arrogance in thinking that they are better than others because they are daily living in a state of contrition (LSC). (Arrogance always surrenders the progress that one makes.)

We are given a choice daily either to indulge the carnal mind that is the driving force of our old nature or to demonstrate the mind of Christ Jesus that is the directing force of the new nature we now have in and through his shed blood. It is a daily choice. Really, it is a choice moment by moment. And it is *always* a choice. Indeed, it is *work* to pick up our cross daily and follow Jesus, doing only those things which we know will please him. However, this type of work is what is required for us to be in a constant state of spiritual renewal.

A constant state of spiritual renewal requires *living in a perpetual state of contrition* (LPSC). LPSC requires: (1) raising a banner of victory over each area of personal weakness, vulnerability, and infirmity and, once raised, to never let it down; and, then, (2) moving on to each new area of weakness, vulnerability, and infirmity to raise additional banners as we take captive every thought and feeling in the name of Christ Jesus. Thus, a constant state of spiritual renewal is also methodical and systematic.

It is important to remember that saved human beings never accomplish spiritual renewal through their own will power but through the power of Christ Jesus that resides in them through the Holy Spirit of God. Just as our physical renewal is inherited from our biological parents, so is our spiritual renewal inherited from our eternal father,[200] Christ Jesus, with whom we are metaphysically consanguineous through the blood that he shed for us individually, collectively, and corporately. This, of course, is predicated upon the supernatural transfusion of his blood and our subsequent spiritual renewal as a willing recipient of his life. (Remember, blood equals life.) All spiritually-sick patients (i.e., sinners) must accept such a transfusion for themselves: Salvation is never forced and, thus, can never be done on behalf of another person.

Satan has always hated the people of God (i.e., Jews and Christians) because he knows that we are destined to become co-heirs with Christ Jesus. Satan hates (1) that we will inherit all[201] that Christ has and (2) that he is not destined to inherit anything at all. This enrages Satan so much that he and his minions pursue the chosen of God relentlessly. Satan's rage is the basis for all battles in the world, including the three world wars before *the Millennium* (World Wars I, II, and III) as well as for World War IV, which occurs at the end of *the Millennium* (Revelation 20:7-9).

Where do Christians get their power? From their spiritual inheritance through the shed blood of Jesus Christ — the only

---

200 King James Version of Isaiah 9:6 and Galatians 4:7
201 Revelation 21:7

source of all real power. Either one accepts that blood and has real power or one rejects that blood and has no real power.

> *Wherefore you are no longer a servant but a son; and if a son, then an heir of God through Christ.*
>
> GALATIANS 3:7 KJV (PARAPHRASE)

Although there are feminists who might object to the use of "son" in the previously quoted verse, "son" is important to use historically because, at one time, only "sons" and not daughters received an inheritance. In contemporary language, the more accurate phrase for "sons of God" would be "heirs of God" because the latter expression captures the truer meaning, or real essence, of what was originally intended.

Having power in Christ Jesus does not mean that we will be healed of all physical maladies or that we will not suffer while we are on Earth:

> *And if we are children, then we are heirs: heirs of God, and joint-heirs with Christ; if so be that we suffer with Christ, that we may be also glorified together.*
>
> ROMANS 8:17 KJV (PARAPHRASE)

Metaphysical renewal expands spiritual renewal to include: (1) our declaration of wholeness in Christ Jesus, (2) our affirmation of regeneration in him through his shed blood, and (3) our declaration of his goodness in our lives — regardless of *all* appearances, diagnoses, and prognoses that might speak to the contrary, and regardless of *all* physical, emotional, and mental changes that may or may not take place in response to supernatural renewal.

The topic of living in a state of contrition (LSC) is discussed further in Chapters Seven and Eight of this book.

The Biological Response

Students of divine metaphysics need to be knowledgeable about human anatomy and physiology, microbiology, and immunology. Why? (1) They need to understand that there are biological response mechanisms already built into the human body to combat physical illnesses, diseases, and disorders. (2) They should not relegate biological response mechanisms to a realm of ignorance, false supposition, and superstition. (3) They should not be afraid of "granting power" to abnormal biological processes just by understanding and/or accurately naming illnesses, diseases, and disorders. (4) They should understand and assess all options available to them for their own care as well as for those whose care has been entrusted to them. (5) They need to know how to interpret normal and abnormal events in the human body and in what ways those events might be beneficial and/or harmful. And (6) they should have a biological foundation in truth, in addition to a spiritual foundation in truth, to metaphysically treat physical illnesses, diseases, and disorders more effectively.

(1) Students of divine metaphysics need to understand that there are biological response mechanisms already built into the human body to combat physical illnesses, diseases, and disorders.

Students of divine metaphysics need to understand that there are nonspecific defense mechanisms as well as specific defense mechanisms already built into the human body. They need to understand that elements of both categories help to impart normal and natural resistance against many physical illnesses, diseases, and disorders. Using divine metaphysics intelligently includes recognizing that the human bodies of even unsaved people have these defenses built into them to help protect them. Although God's just punishment of us fits mankind's original sin of not living in accordance with the Will of God, God did not leave us without a *physical comforter* in the form of an immune system — just as He did not leave us without a *spiritual comforter* in the Person of His Holy Spirit.

Nonspecific defense mechanisms to disease include vomiting, diarrhea, fever, increased lacrimation, increased salivation, rapid eye blinking, coughing, sneezing, expectoration, inflammation, and swelling as well as increased sensitivity to touch, pressure, pain, and temperature. Nonspecific defense mechanisms also include secretions of chemical agents that: (1) combat generic categories of pathogens and toxins; (2) coat exposed surfaces of the body; (3) line internal passageways of the body; and (4) circulate throughout the body in blood and lymph.

Specific defense mechanisms to disease include cell-mediated responses and antibody-mediated responses. These mechanisms are called "specific" because they mount a response to a specific (1) foreign protein, (2) foreign protein-based molecule, or (3) foreign polysaccharide that may be in association with a pathogen, a toxin, or a foreign tissue (including donor tissue that is mismatched to a recipient).

Nonspecific response mechanisms are sometimes collectively referred to as *innate immunity* and specific response mechanisms are sometimes collectively referred to as *adaptive immunity*.

(2) Students of divine metaphysics should not relegate biological response mechanisms to a realm of ignorance, false supposition, and superstition.

First and foremost, all healing power is in Christ Jesus. It proceeds and processes from his heavenly throne. Second, the name of Christ Jesus is above the name of every illness, disease, and disorder. Therefore, students of the Holy Bible should not fear scientific pursuits that have practical value. People who are uneducated, undereducated or miseducated about biological response mechanisms to foreign invaders, toxic substances, and foreign tissues — including transplantation and transfusion — end up fearing what they don't know or understand. It is ignorance that engenders false supposition and superstition. To be sure, we should not attribute to malice what belongs to ignorance, but we should still be aware of the various negative ramifications of ignorance.

(3) Students of divine metaphysics should not be afraid of "granting power" to abnormal biological processes just by understanding and/or accurately naming illnesses, diseases, and disorders.

If anything "grants power" to illness, disease, and disorder, it is medical ignorance and not medical education. Sometimes, Christians who use intercessory prayer and metaphysical intervention carry their concerns about understanding anatomy, physiology, microbiology, and immunology to an unhealthy extreme. Moreover, they stubbornly reject medical procedures that can save their own lives as well as the lives of those they love. This includes people who take "speaking things into existence" (i.e., so-called prophetic decrees) to a humorless conclusion and allow themselves to be bested by their own false egos. Unfortunately, because they are spiritually blind, they often lead other spiritually blind people to destruction. In Proverbs, we are directed by God to "get wisdom: and with all our *getting* to get understanding" (Proverbs 4:7b KJV Paraphrase).

(4) Students of divine metaphysics should understand and assess all options available to them for their own care as well as for those whose care has been entrusted to them.

Sometimes, Christians committed to spiritual healing are unwilling to learn and use simple things that will help keep them alive one more day to more effectively use prayer and metaphysical treatment on the following day. To be sure, there is a place for radical reliance on God for supernatural healing to the exclusion of all physical remedies. However, radical reliance should not include deciding that a child should not have a blood transfusion or a vaccination. To be sure, having a surgeon straighten out an entangled small intestine or twisted bowel is not in competition with intercessory prayer, metaphysical treatment, and trusting God.

(5) Students of divine metaphysics should know how to interpret normal and abnormal events in the human body and in what ways those events might be beneficial and/or harmful.

Students of divine metaphysics should be able to interpret correctly what is occurring within a sick human body without relegating what is happening to the realm of unknowable mystery. *For example,* it is important to know that diarrhea and vomiting can be beneficial to a sick human body if those reactions are helping to rid that body of harmful pathogens and/or toxic substances. Of course, it is equally important to know that prolonged diarrhea and vomiting can be harmful to a sick human body by causing dehydration or an unnecessary double exposure to a caustic agent from vomiting up what has been swallowed. To guard against dehydration from diarrhea and vomiting, it is important to know that pushing fluids either by mouth or intravenous injection is often helpful; it is also important to know what kinds of fluids to push. Why take any chances with infants or the elderly, whose smaller and weaker frames more easily succumb to dehydration in life-threatening ways?

Students of divine metaphysics should be able to utilize simple practical truths at the same time they are praying to God and declaring, affirming, and proclaiming spiritual truths of being in Him. Treating a condition with prayer and divine metaphysics does not mean throwing common sense out the window. And treating a condition using prayer and divine metaphysics certainly should not include embarrassment about not being omniscient — that is, about not knowing everything that could be done or should be done to completely eradicate a condition or mitigate its deleterious effects. Yes, we can use the power that God gives us through Christ Jesus and His Holy Spirit, but we are not omnipotent nor will we ever be omnipotent. There should be no embarrassment in that recognition and understanding.

(6) Students of divine metaphysics should have a biological foundation in truth — in addition to a spiritual foundation in truth — to metaphysically treat physical illnesses, diseases, and disorders more effectively.

Remember, intercessory prayer for healing a specific condition does not require the person praying to know anything about the illness, disease, or disorder other than that it exists within the individual in need of healing. God does not require us to have a medical diagnosis, prognosis, or treatment plan before we can approach Him prayerfully for healing. However, using divine metaphysical treatment in tandem with prayer does require at least a rudimentary understanding of what is occurring within the human body when it is in disequilibrium. Divine metaphysical treatments augment and enhance the human body's own biological response mechanisms to illness, disease, and disorder by declaring, affirming, and proclaiming what is rightfully ours in and through the shed blood and water of Jesus Christ. ("Water" is being used here to figuratively represent God's Holy Spirit and is not being used to distort the requirements for salvation.)

Although having an optimistic outlook on life impacts favorably on our physical, mental, and emotional well-being, understanding who we are metaphysically in and through the shed blood of Jesus Christ transcends mere emotionality. *For example,* a patient using divine metaphysics might be pessimistic about an outcome at the same time that the same patient declares, affirms, and proclaims who he or she is in Christ Jesus. Such a patient might state: (1) *"I know that I have life even though I also know that I am dying."* (2) *"I know that my life is eternal regardless of all appearances to the contrary."* Or (3) *"I have lost my legs through accident and amputation but I continue to stand in Christ Jesus."* Of such is the true nature, or essence, of divine metaphysics.

Self versus Nonself

Except for autoimmune disorders and removal of the body's own dying and deteriorating cellular debris, the human body does not attack itself. To be sure, healthy immune response mechanisms include recognizing differences between "self" and "nonself."

Metaphysically speaking, the family of God is also able to recognize the difference between "self" and "nonself." The family of God increases by decreasing, includes by excluding, and often varies yet never changes. John the Baptist[202] alludes to the metaphysical difference between "self" and "nonself" when he declares concerning Jesus Christ: "He must increase but I must decrease."[203] As a child, the present author remembers regularly hearing the great evangelist Kathryn Kuhlman pray: "Let there be less of me and more of Thee until there is none of me and all of Thee." In other words, our false identity is lost and our true identity is found in Christ Jesus. He alone is our *Self.* (This is not meant to imply that we are God or that we can ever expect to be God.)

Chapter Questions

This section is intended to facilitate learning by providing relevant activities, exercises, and experiences to aid students of divine metaphysics in their quest for grasping spiritual concepts, integrating them into their own belief systems, holding them more assuredly, and making them more practical in daily life.

The following questions should be answered after reading each

---

[202] *Iochanan the Baptizer* or *Yochanan the Immerser*
[203] John 3:30, King James Version

titled section. To answer a few of the questions, students may need to consult outside resources or external references. Students are also encouraged to answer these questions with others during group discussions.

One or Two Organ Systems?

1. In what ways are the endocrine and lymphatic systems similar?

The Anatomy of the Lymphatic System

2. Why are some cells called *T-lymphocytes* and others called *B-lymphocytes*?

Immunity and the Godhead

3. In what way do Christians possess spiritual immunity?

4. Briefly discuss how corporeality is different from mankind's original condition of being?

5. (a) What does the term *Antediluvian* mean? (b) Why did the Biblical Antediluvians have longer lifespans than people who lived after the Flood?

6. In what ways are human beings *animals with souls?*

7. Why should Christians not pray to saints in Heaven?

8. What do the red and white rays represent in the portrait painted according to Faustina Kowalska's instructions?

9. Discuss at length why God views blood and life as equivalent?

Lifespan

10. What originally caused the souls of human beings to reside in corruptible bodies?

11. How can you reconcile that a loving God is responsible for curses, wrath, and woe?

12. When will the curse of death be removed from mankind as a whole?

13. Explain how *death* can mean all of the following at the same time: (a) separation from God; (b) expiration of a human life; and (c) corporeality. (Hint: People often fail to recognize that most words have multiple meanings.)

14. Construct a simple graphic organizer (i.e., flow chart) or table that shows expected lifespans of mankind before the Adamic Fall, before the Flood, from the Flood to the time of Moses, from the time of Moses through the beginning of *the Millennium*, during *the Millennium,* and after *the Millennium*.

Renewal

15. (a) When did mankind's somatic identities *fall?* (b) What did the souls of original mankind fall into?

16. Why is it dangerous to live in a human body?

17. Choose any five of the twenty-eight degenerative changes associated with aging and discuss them physically as well as metaphysically.

18. Briefly discuss why degenerative changes vary from individual to individual.

19. Discuss at length the role that contrition has relative to "holiness living" by including examples from your own life.

20. What does a constant state of spiritual renewal require?

21. Who is the source of all power for Christians?

The Biological Response

22. Comment on each of the six reasons why students of divine metaphysics should be knowledgeable about anatomy, physiology, microbiology, and immunology.

Chapter Seven
Divine Metaphysics of the Urinary System

And all of the churches shall know that I am he who searches the kidneys and hearts ...

REVELATION 2:23b (TRANSLATED FROM THE GREEK)

Eliminating Impure Thoughts and Unholy Feelings

Living in a state of contrition (LSC) requires that you go way beyond just simple remorse for your own iniquity and sin. Although remorse may be a step in the right direction, remorse alone will not bring you to the point in your life where you can discipline your own flesh or have authority over evil. Remorse includes experiencing guilt, embarrassment, and even self-recrimination for your sins. You may have remorse: (1) because you have been caught doing something that is not reflective of God's highest honor; (2) because you have experienced a negative ramification for having done something of which you cannot be proud; or (3) because, regardless of what you say, you really don't believe in God's substitutionary atonement for your sins through the shed blood of Jesus Christ (if you did, you would not doubt that you have been forgiven for your sins by God after confessing them to Him).

Concerning the last point, it is possible to intellectually believe in the remission of your own sins, but it is also possible to not internalize that belief emotionally so that you are truly free from guilt and self-condemnation when you should be. Clinging to guilt and/or self-condemnation — because of past sinful thinking, feeling, and activity — can become a way of life for some people. They are unwilling to free themselves from self-loathing and end up feeling comfortable with living in guilt and self-condemnation simply because such living is familiar to them. This is where getting rid of impure thoughts and unholy feelings comes into play — thoughts and feelings that are a waste of time, effort, and energy as well as harmful to our physical, emotional, mental, and spiritual well-being.

In an earlier chapter, I told you that it is more beneficial to affirm who you really are rather than refute what you are actually experiencing. *For example,* it is dysfunctional to say that you are not in pain when you *are* in pain or that you are not experiencing insomnia when you *cannot* sleep. People who are healthy spiritually, emotionally, mentally, and physically do not refute *experiencing* a disease process or a debilitating condition when they *are* experiencing it. People living with pain can affirm, declare, and proclaim the spiritual truth that there is no pain in God, but the affirmation, declaration, or proclamation may not in itself be sufficient to rid them of their chronic condition. Insomniacs can affirm, declare, and proclaim the spiritual truth that God rests in action, but the affirmation, declaration, or proclamation may not in itself be sufficient to rid them of their inability to sleep. So, at this juncture, I am formalizing these three concepts for you to use in the metaphysical treatment of an illness, disease, or disorder for your own unhealthy conditions or the unhealthy conditions of others you are trying to help:

1. Affirm, declare, and proclaim who you really are in God through the shed blood of His only-begotten Son, Jesus Christ.

2. Admit to experiencing difficulty or having been diagnosed with a specific illness, disease, or debilitating condition and be willing to seek help from a healing arts practitioner — including, but not limited to, those educated and trained in medicine, psychology, and/or spiritual intercession.[204]

3. Identify and acknowledge all thoughts and feelings you have about yourself that are harmful or potentially harmful to you and eliminate them — which is to say, get rid of them.

Metaphysically speaking, excretion is getting rid of thoughts and feelings that are harmful, or potentially harmful, regardless of whether they have been originally self-generated or accepted from others and internalized as one's own thoughts and feelings. Such thoughts and feelings are counterproductive to healing and living victoriously. This really involves examining every one of our own thoughts and feelings to see if it is harmful or potentially harmful to us or others and taking it captive by putting it under our feet. In this case, *our feet* metaphysically serve as the earthly representation of Christ's feet, whose spiritual truth tramples all erroneous thinking and feeling to neutralize their power and poison. Here, the word *erroneous* (1) does not just mean "false" but also "harmful and poisonous" and (2) refers to those thoughts and feelings that do not fit within the framework of a spiritual being

---

[204] The phrase "but not limited to" is included because some healing arts practices do not fit easily or clearly into the categories of medicine, psychology, and spiritual intercession nor do they come to mind when one thinks of those three categories. *Hypnotherapy* is one such practice that would be debated by many medical, psychological, and spiritual practitioners. However, *hypnotherapy* can play a credible role in mitigating chronic pain. *Hypnotherapy* is different from optimism, positivism, and divine metaphysics; it fits into its own compartment although there is some overlap with other compartments in the categories of medicine, psychology, and divine metaphysics. Hypnotherapy should neither be trivialized nor denigrated.

who has been remade in the complete image and perfect likeness of God.

From a physical standpoint, excretion is getting rid of harmful and poisonous substances through their detoxification and passage from inside to outside of one's body. From a metaphysical standpoint, excretion is getting rid of harmful and poisonous thoughts, feelings, ideas, concepts, constructs, and paradigms through their neutralization and passage from within to without — that is, from inside to outside of — one's being. Erroneous thoughts and feelings should be extruded into the nothingness of their reality.

There comes a point in time for all spiritually-mature people to make a firm decision to no longer entertain and indulge thoughts and feelings or commit deeds that are harmful or potentially harmful because retaining such impurities causes them to be out of step with the Creator's Will.

Being human often involves the self-justification of carnal thinking, carnal feeling, and carnal behavior. A carnally-minded attitude is represented by such statements as:

1. "I am just a human being."

2. "A man (or woman) has to do what a man (or woman) has to do."

3. "I couldn't help myself."

4. "I just could not overcome that thought or feeling."

5. "That thought or feeling was too powerful for me."

6. "God created me this way."

7. "I needed the release."

8. "I was celebrating."

9. "I was depressed and needed to pamper myself."

10. "I was worried and needed to take my mind off of my desperate situation."

As stated earlier, just because our souls and spirits are in the bodies of animals does not mean that we must act like animals. We should resist animal instincts either by refraining from acting on them altogether or by using God-given principles related to acting on them. *For example,* in the Holy Bible, God asks for us to refrain from sex outside of a holy union, covenant, or marriage. God knows that acting on sexual instincts without constraint can lead us to a depraved and unclean state of being through unholy living. Instead, God wants us to take the highest road to purity that is available to us. That is why God wants us to refrain from sex until we are in a lifelong and covenant-based spousal commitment, which commitment is honoring to His ideals, principles, commands, and requests.

God understands that the adrenaline secreted within human bodies "on the prowl" produces a "rush" and that the neurotransmitters released within our brains during and after orgasm are opiate-like and, therefore, can be physically and emotionally addicting. God understands that such chemical messengers reinforce addictive thoughts, feelings, and behaviors. God wants us to avoid thoughts, feelings, and behaviors that are harmful to ourselves and others.

That we should examine what thoughts and feelings we may need to eliminate is certainly in keeping with the declaration by God that He "searches the heart and tries the reins" of every person.[205] *Reins* is an Early Modern English word that is derived from the Latin *renes,* which literally means "kidneys" and is appropriately used in the King James Version of the Old and New Testaments because it correctly translates *kil-yoth'* [plural of H3629 in Appendix Table A] from the Hebrew in the Old Testament and *ne-phros'* [G3510 in Appendix Table B] from the Greek in the New Testament, both words referring to "kidneys."

The phrase "heart and kidneys" in the original languages of the Old and New Testaments is also correctly translated as "heart and mind" because the two kidneys figuratively represented the innermost parts of one's being, which parts include one's motives

---

205 King James Version of Psalm 7:9, 26:2; Jeremiah 11:20, 17:10, 20:12; and Revelation 2:23

and intentions. God "searches our heart" to find out the primary object of our love and desire; and God "tries our reins" to test the purity of our motives, intentions, and resolve. Because the expression "heart and kidneys" is idiomatic, it is permissible to translate it as "heart and mind" without doing an injustice to God's written Word.

The two primary organs of urinary excretion are the kidneys. They purify the blood by removing harmful and potentially harmful substances as well as by altering the composition of blood to help create the most ideal liquid milieu for the living cells of the body. Not only must our blood be filtered for us to be clean physically, our blood (in this case, our *life force)* must be filtered for us to be clean metaphysically. In other words, we must cleanse all impure motives and unclean intentions from the life force that pulses through our being. (God's life force cannot contain impurities for beings who live in an unfallen state, but it can contain impurities destined for elimination from beings who live in a fallen state.)

We must eliminate every thought and feeling that has an impure motive or unholy intention behind it. We should retain all thoughts and feelings that are generated out of the highest motives and purest intentions, but we should actively eliminate (i.e., excrete) those that contaminate the purity of our being. The blood, or life force, of saved people must not become tainted nor remain tainted. If tainted by impure thoughts and unholy feelings, our life force must be purified through actively transporting such thoughts and feelings out of our consciousness and away from our being. Of such is the role of the metaphysical *kidney*.

If we need to examine every thought that we think and every feeling that we feel, how do we avoid becoming automatons — which is to say, robotic, rigid, and uncreative? Taking captive every thought and feeling is only something that a spiritually mature person can do. And spiritually mature people choose to do this because of their love for the Creator and their desire to please Him in all that they think, feel, say, and do. We expect such self-monitoring not by spiritual infants and toddlers but by true spiritual adults and elders. And, by the time that you have accepted your adulthood and eldership in the Body of Christ, the filtering of your thoughts and feelings is not robotic but exciting because such filtering liberates you to more fully and more completely do the work of God as well as more intimately communicate with God through His Holy Spirit.

Filtering out impure thoughts and unholy feelings is responsible for the purification of our thinking and feeling, which purification is requisite for our spiritual progress. Metaphysically speaking, the kidneys correspond to the prehominid conscience of original mankind. (For the sake of clarification, in this textbook these prehominid beings are the *unfallen spiritual ancestors* of *Homo sapiens* and not the prehominids thought to be our physical ancestors from an evolutionary or anthropological standpoint.)

When Adam and Eve were tempted, they possessed the capability of filtering their own thoughts and feelings through the conscience that God had given to them. The conscience is that part of our mind and spirit-being that knows right from wrong. Unfortunately, Adam and Eve permitted their thoughts and feelings about the possibility of knowing both good and evil to overpower them. Rather than quickly eliminate such thoughts and feelings, they permitted them to run rampant throughout their life force (i.e., their "blood" from a metaphysical standpoint), tainting it with an unclean, infectious load that caused them to change from an *astral gelatinous*™ condition of being to a *protoplasmic* condition of being. At the precise moment of their Fall, the spiritual substance of their individual consciences then coalesced into the kidneys, or primary organs that make up the urinary excretory system in fallen, corporeal man.

Migrating from the absolute space-time of the spiritual universe to the relative space-time of the physical universe, the consciences of Adam and Eve concretionized within their newly-formed physical bodies and moved retroperitoneally[206] to their loins. Physically speaking, "loins" are those areas on either side of the vertebral

---

206 The parietal peritoneum lines much of the abdominal cavity. Organs such as the aorta, inferior vena cava, and kidneys are technically not inside the abdominal cavity because they are behind that peritoneum and, hence, *retroperitoneal*.

column between the ribs and hipbones where the kidneys and certain back muscles are located (among other structures). Metaphysically speaking, "loins" are some of the most vulnerable places of one's spiritual being just as they are some of the most vulnerable places on one's physical being (because they are not protected by bone). To be sure, Adam and Eve proved that the conscience is the most vulnerable part of the spiritual being since it can be overridden by self-will. For both saved and unsaved people, the conscience is most vulnerable because it is the seat of judgment. That is why unsaved people are able to justify their own impure motives and unholy intentions. In contrast, despite the temptation to do otherwise, saved people are able to purify themselves even as God is pure because they have God's Holy Spirit residing in them:

> *{2} Beloved, now are we the heirs of God, and it does not yet appear what we shall look like: but we know that, when Christ Jesus shall appear, we shall look like him; for we shall see him as he is. {3} And all people that have this hope in themselves purify themselves, even as Christ Jesus is pure.*
>
> 1 JOHN 3:2-3 KJV (PARAPHRASE)

In anticipation of our transformation from a *protoplasmic* somatic identity back to an *astral gelatinous*™ one, we purify our own thoughts and feelings by filtering out everything that is not in agreement with — and, therefore, contradictory to — the Will of God. So, even as Christ Jesus is pure, one day we will be as pure as he is, not only in spirit and soul but also in body.

Please reread the sections entitled *Conscience Matters* and *The Role of Trust in Matters of Conscience* in Chapter Four of this book to correlate what was previously written about the conscience to what has just been written. Also, take the time now to read the disclaimer that follows.

Disclaimer

It is important to emphasize as well as regularly reiterate to the readers of this book that the modern human anatomic structures themselves are no longer what they represent metaphysically. For example, the human kidneys do not constitute the conscience. All human structures simply represent a supernatural reality that existed within original, unfallen man as well as exists within the etheric body double of every restored soul (i.e., saved human being).

The invisible and etheric body double for each saved person is a shadow or type of electromagnetic impression — more specifically, a spiritual *alto relief* (or high definition image) — of immortal man's original somatic identity. (This is in contrast to the spiritual *bas relief* — or low definition image — found in unsaved persons.)

Just as the photograph of a person only represents the person, so do modern human anatomic structures merely represent higher spiritual verities. Just as the photograph of a person is not the actual person, so are modern human anatomic structures *not* the verities-in-themselves.

The Water of Life ("Living Water")

The Holy Spirit is the Water of Life, where the word *Life* is synonymous with the word *God*, for "God is Life."[207] Indeed, the Water of Life is *the* "living water" that Jesus offered to the Samaritan woman at Jacob's well. Jesus said:

> *"Whoever drinks of the water that I shall give them shall never thirst because the water that I shall give shall be in them a well of water springing up unto everlasting life.*
>
> JOHN 4:14 KJV (PARAPHRASE)

---

[207] Deuteronomy 30:20, King James Version

God's Holy Spirit is also the self-generated or self-ignited fire of God that self-propagates by birthing new believers. How? It impregnates them with the knowledge of salvation through Jesus Christ. At the precise moment we accept for ourselves that Jesus Christ is the only-begotten Son of God and Savior of the world, we are born again.

The question "Why does God exist?" is flawed because it implies causality with regard to the existence of God. Although God provides the causality for what He creates, there is nothing that caused God to come into Being because God is Self-Existent and, therefore, without beginning and without ending.

Asking the question "Why does God exist?" is a product of the rational mind, which expects that there is a cause for everything and that every individual thing is an effect of some particular cause or causes. However, neither *cause-and-effect* thinking nor *if-then* thinking is sufficient for us to comprehend the Self-Existence of God. We might be able to work backwards (i.e., regress) from the current state of God's creation and, using pure reason, derive suppositions about God's existence, but we would never be able to answer the exact question "Why does God exist?" In fact, that question does not have an answer. However — if the question "Why does God exist?" is meant to ask "What role does God have within the whole universe?" — then there is an answer to that question: God's role within *the whole universe* (consisting of both spiritual universe and physical universe) is that of Sole Sovereign, Only Creator, and Single Redeemer.

That God's Holy Spirit is the Water of Life answers the question "What role does the Holy Spirit have within the Universe of God?" As the liquid medium for blood within every living human body, physical water carries electrolytes, nutrients, cellular elements, and waste products. As the fluidic medium of God's life force, the Holy Spirit carries: (1) spiritual energy as foundational bundles of Life; (2) spiritual truth as nourishment for the soul; and (3) in the case of saved people who are still in earthly flesh, rejected thoughts and feelings as impurities destined for elimination. (The purity of God's Holy Spirit is not to be questioned here. That the Holy Spirit carries impurities out of our spiritual beings does not make the

Holy Spirit impure.)

When Adam and Eve fell, original mankind suffered distortion of its spiritual being. Since the conscience is a part of one's spiritual being, the conscience of each individual also suffered distortion. The fallen conscience was no longer capable of perfectly knowing the difference between right and wrong or good and evil. Just as the spirit-being, or soul, of the individual was warped from the Adamic Fall, so was the spirit-being's conscience warped. That is why an unsaved human being's conscience is capable of justifying almost any thinking, feeling, and action that is wrong, harmful, and evil. Even if the conscience has been correctly taught by other human beings, or if a human being has concluded on its own what is right and wrong or good and evil, the conscience as a moral compass is still imperfect and incomplete without guidance from God's Holy Spirit. The warped conscience still has issues with integrity in its own self-justification of wrong thinking, wrong feeling, and wrong acting. ("Wrong" here means "evil," "erroneous," and "not in compliance with God's Will.")

Unless people have God's Holy Spirit residing within them because their souls are "saved" (through accepting God's one and only Plan of Salvation), the conscience of each individual person remains distorted and warped and may eventually become seared (i.e., impenetrable by spiritual truth). It is only through God's Holy Spirit that the conscience of each saved person is renewed to its original state because the Holy Spirit actually becomes each saved soul's renewed conscience. In salvation, the Holy Spirit replaces our damaged conscience with God's own elevated sense of (1) right and wrong as well as (2) good and evil.

So, God's Holy Spirit not only woos us to salvation and resides within our saved souls, God's Holy Spirit replaces our damaged consciences and, therefore, serves as the medium for the influent, or infilling, thoughts of God and the effluent, or out-going, thoughts of Evil. Of course, after their souls make the final transition from a corporeal condition of existence to a spiritual condition of being, saved people will no longer be subjected to bombardment by impure thoughts and unholy feelings, which originate from the source of all evil, Satan's mortal mind.

The three processes involved in urine formation by the kidneys include: (1) filtration, (2) reabsorption, and (3) secretion-excretion.[208] Metaphysically speaking, these three processes are reflected in the actions of the Holy Spirit (as each saved person's conscience) in: (1) sifting, (2) retaining, and (3) eliminating various thoughts and feelings.

1. *Sifting* involves examining each thought, feeling, idea, concept, construct, and paradigm within the saved person.

2. *Retaining* involves holding, or keeping, within the saved person all that is in agreement with absolute truth and God's Will.

3. *Eliminating* involves removing everything that is in disagreement with absolute truth and out of step with God's Will. As a result, all that is harmful or poisonous to one's being is gradually, painstakingly, and tediously removed from the life force of the soul under the direction of the Holy Spirit. Eventually, only the pure thoughts and holy feelings of God remain within each saved person.

After our salvation through the shed blood of God's only-begotten Son, the Holy Spirit is responsible for the sanctification of the saved individual — which is to say, making the person perfectly holy and completely pure. In this capacity, the Holy Spirit is responsible for actively transporting spiritual truth into one's life force (and, therefore, into one's being) and for actively transporting spiritual error out of one's life force (and, therefore, out of one's being). It is in this way that we are made perfectly holy and completely pure. (Please do not make the mistake of thinking that

---

208 Generally speaking, "secretion" is the production of beneficial substances that are used elsewhere in the human body; and "excretion" is the production of useless or harmful substances destined for elimination by the human body. Because of the unique role of the kidneys in the regulation of various ions and molecules through countercurrent mechanisms, there is an overlap between the processes of secretion and excretion as they relate to kidney nephron function.

your sanctification is finished in advance of your physical death: That is not possible.)

Examples of impurities that are transported out of one's being by the Holy Spirit include:

1. Vulgarities

2. Cruelties

3. Lusts (selfish, willful, and wasteful desires)

4. Negative thoughts and feelings about oneself and others

5. Self-righteousness, arrogance, and feelings of superiority

6. Self-pity and feelings of inferiority

7. Anxieties

8. Doubts (faithlessness)

9. Incapacitating fears

Examples of spiritual elements that are transported by the Holy Spirit into one's being (and retained by that being) include those addressed by the following verse from the Holy Bible:

> *Finally, brothers and sisters, whatsoever things are true, whatsoever things are honest, whatsoever things are just, whatsoever things are pure, whatsoever things are lovely, whatsoever things are of good report; if there be any virtue, and if there be any praise, think on these things.*
>
> PHILIPPIANS 4:8 KJV (PARAPHRASE)

The Metaphysical Treatment of Urinary Problems

Using divine metaphysics to treat spiritual, emotional, mental, and physical health problems not only entails looking at life and its specific challenges and difficulties in a special way, it is a singular way of consistently living in and through Christ Jesus daily. Because prayer includes communication and communion with God, divine metaphysics could be described as a specialized form of prayer that uses affirmation, declaration, and proclamation of the absolute realities of God as they relate to solution and resolution of earthborn problems. Divine metaphysics is a way of making those absolute realities tangible through one's healing or restoration to well-being. It is in this way that divine metaphysics is both practical and scientific. (Although I have previously separated out prayer from metaphysical treatment for the purpose of discussion, it is important to note that there is overlap in these two methods of spiritual intercession and intervention.)

Except for specificities concerning various aspects of the urinary system, treating urinary problems metaphysically is no different than treating health problems for any other organ system. Here are some general questions to ask as you seek to develop an intelligent treatment plan for urinary problems:

1. Is the problem primarily mechanical in nature?

2. Is the problem primarily psychological in nature?

3. Is the problem primarily microbial in nature?

4. Is the problem primarily physiologic in nature?

5. Is the problem primarily age-related in nature?

1. Is the problem primarily mechanical in nature?

Examples of mechanical problems for the urinary system include: (1) urethral stricture (i.e., constriction of a portion of the urethral passageway); (2) obstruction of any part of the pathway of urine flow from renal papillae through minor and major calyces to ureters to urinary bladder and urethra (see Figures Twenty and Twenty-One); and (3) herniation, or rupture, of the urinary bladder wall.

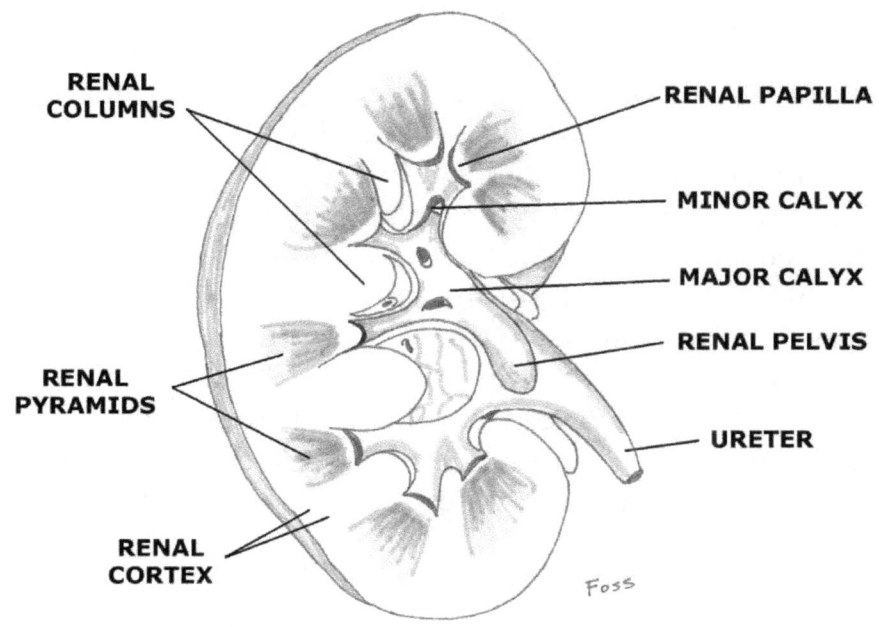

Structures of the Kidney
Figure Twenty

Although a metaphysical way of looking at life should be employed in treating the urinary problems just mentioned, as well as treating their potential recurrence, it is important to know that the primary treatment for mechanical problems should be, quite simply, mechanical.

Mechanically widening a constricted part of the urethra by using a balloon catheter or by inserting a ureteral (i.e., ureteric) stent makes practical sense. Removing an obstruction, such as a kidney stone, in the pathway of urine flow by pushing intravenous fluids or by using lithotripsy, basket retrieval, or a more invasive surgical procedure makes practical sense. And the repair of a hernia in the urinary bladder wall through surgically sewing, patching, and/or installing mesh network to strengthen the bladder wall makes practical sense, too. Just because we depend on God as our sole Provider and as the source of infinite supply does not mean that we throw reason and common sense out the window. To be sure, reason is sometimes unreasonable and common sense is all too uncommon, but they must be recognized as important in devising a treatment plan. People who choose divine metaphysics as a way of life should not be embarrassed or feel like failures if they use mechanical modalities and laws of physics to treat problems that are primarily mechanical in nature.

To be sure, there can be metaphysical causes and treatments for the conditions mentioned. Metaphysical causes of mechanical problems might relate to our failure to eliminate impurities in our own patterns of thinking and feeling (examples are listed in the nine categories in the section entitled *The Water of Life*). Metaphysical treatment would then follow suit, depending on the identified cause and what it is that we need to specifically eliminate from our individual lives.

2. Is the problem primarily psychological in nature?

Examples of psychological problems related to the urinary system might include bed-wetting (i.e., enuresis), other forms of urinary incontinence (i.e., involuntary urination), or retention of urine in the bladder for an inordinately long period of time. The word "might" is used in the previous sentence because any of the problems mentioned could be due to causes that are not primarily psychological in nature (i.e., their cause might be mechanical, microbial, physiologic, age-related, and/or metaphysical in nature).

If emotional stress is playing a role in the contraction and relaxation of the detrusor muscle in the wall of the urinary bladder body or of circular muscle fibers in the external urethral sphincter (Figure Twenty-One), then the cause of the emotional stress needs to be identified and alleviated and/or the patient needs to be taught how to better handle that stress.

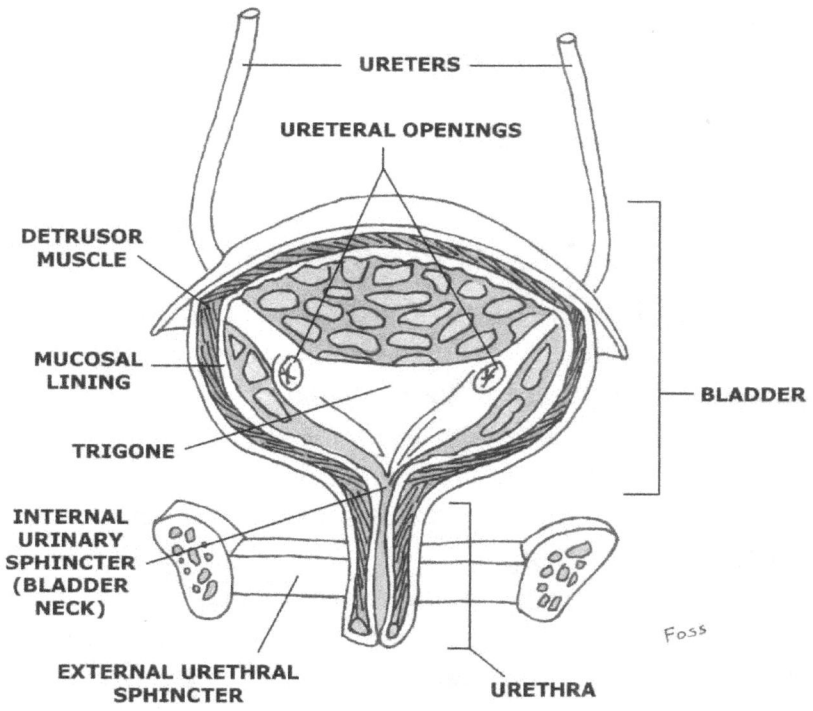

Ureters, Urinary Bladder,[209] and Urethra
Figure Twenty-One

Metaphysical intervention should be used to help the patient understand his or her wholeness in God through Christ Jesus, but metaphysical intervention might not be the primary treatment here. People who choose divine metaphysics as a way of life should not be embarrassed or feel like failures if they use psychological counseling to treat problems that are primarily psychological in nature.

To be sure, there can be solely metaphysical causes and treatments for such conditions as well. Metaphysical causes of uncontrolled bladder function, uncontrolled urination, or blocked passages might relate to the inability to restrain or discipline

---

[209] For the sake of clarification, the *trigone* of the urinary bladder is a triangular area whose apex is determined by the bladder opening to the urethra and whose posterior border is marked by the openings into the bladder from the two ureters (i.e., the ureteral openings).

oneself relative to addictive behaviors or to holding onto or harboring (i.e., retaining) harmful thoughts and poisonous feelings. Metaphysical treatment would then follow suit, depending on the identified cause and in what way the patient's thinking needs to be adjusted.

3. Is the problem primarily microbial in nature?

Examples of problems that are primarily microbial in nature include kidney, ureteral, bladder, and urethral infections from fungi, bacteria, mycoplasms,[210] and viruses.

As mentioned in the chapter on *Divine Metaphysics of the Lymphatic System and Immunity*, there are nonspecific as well as specific biological responses to infection already built into the human body. Thus, letting nature take its course allows for those responses to rid the human body of infection. To be sure, one can state that God has healed someone of a urinary infection in a generic sense in that God has appointed (i.e., preprogrammed) biological responses to take care of such problems naturally for human beings. Just as God's sunshine and rain fall on the unrighteous as well as the righteous (Matthew 5:45), so are God's preprogrammed biological responses at work in the unsaved as well as the saved human being.

The problem becomes a much larger problem when the body's own defense mechanisms are insufficient to mount a successful response. In such cases, we can turn to various chemical agents, antibiotics, antivirals, and fungicides to treat a persistent infection, especially if the causative agent has been identified. To be sure, one can state in a generic sense that God has healed someone of a urinary infection using such antimicrobial agents in that God has supplied human beings with the intelligence to determine medical remedies for microbial causes of infection. People who choose divine metaphysics as a way of life should not be embarrassed or feel like failures if they use antimicrobial agents to treat problems that are primarily microbial in nature.

---

210 Mycoplasms were once referred to as Pleuropneumonia-Like Organisms (PPLO).

To be sure, there can be solely metaphysical causes and treatments for these conditions, too. Metaphysical causes of infection might relate to the inability to restrain or discipline oneself relative to addictive behaviors or to holding onto or harboring (i.e., retaining) unholy thoughts and feelings whose harmful effects spread like wildfire within oneself and/or to other susceptible human beings. Metaphysical treatment would then follow suit, depending on the identified cause and the contagious nature of the spiritual infection.

Certainly, metaphysical treatment can always be used to augment (1) the body's own natural defense mechanisms as well as (2) medical remedies.

4. Is the problem primarily physiologic in nature?

Examples of problems that are primarily physiologic in nature include problems in electrolyte balance or problems in molecular exchanges related to countercurrent mechanisms involved in urine filtration, reabsorption, and secretion-excretion.

Although a metaphysical way of looking at life should be employed in treating all such problems, as well as treating their potential recurrence, it is important to know that the primary treatment for physiologic problems can be related to nutrition, fluid intake, physical activity, pharmaceuticals, genetics (i.e., inheritance factors), or old age (geriatric conditions are discussed in the following section). People who choose divine metaphysics as a way of life should not be embarrassed or feel like failures by altering their lifestyles to accommodate the use of diuretics or hemodialysis to treat problems that are primarily physiologic in nature.

To be sure, there can be solely metaphysical causes and treatments for the identified conditions as well. Metaphysical causes of physiologic problems might relate to: (1) our failure to eliminate impurities of unholy living (nine categories of impurities are listed in the section of this chapter entitled *The Water of Life*); and (2) the inability to restrain or discipline oneself relative to addictive behaviors or to holding onto or harboring (i.e., retaining) harmful thoughts and feelings. Metaphysical treatment would then follow suit and depend on the identified cause.

If the underlying cause for the physiologic problem is due to inheritance factors, those seeking healing metaphysically would declare that, although they have biological parents, their heavenly Father's Will supersedes all forces of nature.

5. Is the problem primarily age-related in nature?

Examples of problems that are primarily age-related in nature include: (1) enuresis in children who are not yet old enough to voluntarily control micturition (i.e., urination) through the conscious regulation of their external urethral sphincter (see Figure Twenty-One); and (2) gradual deterioration of urinary functions due to one's geriatric status.

Although a metaphysical way of looking at life should be employed in treating all such problems, it is important to understand the normal age-related changes that take place in the human body, especially regarding early childhood and old age. An understanding of developmental anatomy[211] and ever-changing geriatric physiology is definitely relevant.

Concerning old age, although our souls were created to be eternal, our human bodies were designed to be temporal. Therefore, people who choose divine metaphysics as a way of life should not be embarrassed or feel like failures because their bodies are deteriorating due to old age.

To be sure, there can be metaphysical causes and treatments for deterioration associated with aging. Metaphysical causes of such problems might relate to: (1) erroneously viewing ourselves as incapacitated and feeling that we have no purpose and are, therefore, useless; and/or (2) the failure to identify areas of productivity for geriatric adults, including ourselves or others. Metaphysical treatment would then follow suit, depending on the identified cause — possibly along with appropriate treatments that are mechanical (such as occupational therapy), psychological (such

---

[211] Developmental anatomy includes embryology, fetology, and postnatal development up to adulthood. Complete ossification of the epiphyseal plates in long bones during early adulthood is one way to mark a formal end to developmental anatomy.

as counseling for self-worth and self-esteem), antimicrobial (such as vaccination for infection control), and/or physiologic (such as diet, hydration, pharmaceuticals, and/or hemodialysis to help ensure fluid and electrolyte balance).

People who use divine metaphysics as a way of life may choose spiritual treatment as the sole modality in their treatment plan. This choice is between the individual and their Creator. Regardless of level of success or failure, no one should be exalted, judged, or condemned because they have elected spiritual treatment — including intercessory prayer and metaphysical intervention — as their sole means for treating one or more of their own unhealthy conditions. (Remember, we do not have the right to choose spiritual treatment as the sole or primary modality for other people, including those over whom we have legal guardianship.)

To be comprehensive in our thinking, we also must not neglect the possibility that a specific disease, illness, or disorder is appointed or allowed by God because of the therapeutic nature of suffering for stubborn people who are learning: (1) that "God's grace is sufficient for them" and (2) that "God's strength is made perfect in weakness."[212] Suffering is a great teacher for people who are stubborn, impatient, and overly self-reliant because, sometimes, only suffering can teach them to be more flexible, patient, and dependent on God. Suffering is also a great teacher for caregivers who are stubborn, impatient, and overly self-reliant as well as controlling. Relative to caregivers who are controlling, they eventually learn to not be afraid of having no control. Indeed, there is no greater teacher of obedience to God's Will than suffering. In this spiritual truth, then, we should take great comfort and rejoice:

> *Although Jesus Christ was the Son of God, yet he learned obedience by the things that he suffered.*
>
> HEBREWS 5:8 KJV (PARAPHRASE)

---

[212] 2 Corinthians 12:9, King James Version

Chapter Questions

This section is intended to facilitate learning by providing relevant activities, exercises, and experiences to aid students of divine metaphysics in their quest for grasping spiritual concepts, integrating them into their own belief systems, holding them more assuredly, and making them more practical in daily life.

The following questions should be answered after reading each titled section. To answer a few of the questions, students may need to consult outside resources or external references. Students are also encouraged to answer these questions with others during group discussions.

Eliminating Impure Thoughts and Unholy Feelings

1. Briefly discuss remorse as it relates to living in a state of contrition (LSC).

2. Is self-loathing a desired state for saved people?

3. Restate in your own words the three concepts recommended for use in the metaphysical treatment of an illness, disease, or disorder.

4. Metaphysically speaking, what does excretion represent?

5. Reshape the ten statements representative of a carnally-minded attitude into those representative of a spiritually-minded attitude. *For example,* statement number one, "I am just a human being," might be transformed into the affirmation "I am more than a human being, for I am one with Christ Jesus."

6. Is the present author implying that the physical kidneys constitute the actual seat of the conscience? Please explain why or why not.

7. How is our life force purified from impure thoughts and unholy feelings?

8. According to the present author, what is the most vulnerable part of the spiritual being? Please explain.

The Water of Life

9. What is the major flaw in the question "Why does God exist?"

10. What role does God's Holy Spirit have within the whole universe?

11. Compare and contrast the three physical processes involved in urine formation with the three metaphysical processes involved in eliminating impure thoughts and unholy feelings.

12. Give examples of impurities that are eliminated from us by God's Holy Spirit.

The Metaphysical Treatment of Urinary Problems

13. Why is it important to ask the five questions given in this section?

14. Using an external resource or outside reference, give at least one additional example of an unhealthy condition that is primarily mechanical in nature. Please explain your choice.

15. Using an external resource or outside reference, give at least one additional example of an unhealthy condition that is primarily psychological in nature. Please explain your choice.

16. Using an external resource or outside reference, give at least one additional example of an unhealthy condition that is primarily microbial in nature. Please explain your choice.

17. Using an external resource or outside reference, give at least one example of an unhealthy condition that is primarily physiologic in nature. Please explain your choice.

18. Using an external resource or outside reference, give at least one additional example of an unhealthy condition that is primarily age-related in nature. Please explain your choice.

19. Briefly explain how we may learn obedience to the Will of God through suffering.

Chapter Eight
Divine Metaphysics of the Digestive System

Now may God, Who gives seed to the sower, both give bread for your food and multiply your sown seed and increase the fruits of your righteousness.

2 CORINTHIANS 9:10 KJV (PARAPHRASE)

As the deer pants after a water stream, so pants my soul after You, O God.

ISAIAH 36:12 KJV (PARAPHRASE)

Hunger and Thirst for the Deepest Meaning of Life

Relieving hunger and quenching thirst as well as seeking satiety are primal and primary instinctual drives. They are instinctual drives because they do not need to be taught or learned. They are primal because they are common to all human beings. And they are primary because, unlike sex and aggression, they are independent of extrauterine maturation and development. In other words, human beings are born with an innate drive to eat and drink as well as to feel satisfied physically from eating and drinking. This contrasts with sexual and aggressive urges that are dependent on: (1) hormones secreted in significantly higher concentrations at the onset of puberty; (2) the proportionality of those hormones; (3) hormone-driven temperaments and responses; and (4) individual interpretations of one's environment as it relates to well-being, intimacy, safety, and perceived threats to safety.

To be sure, there are those who would debate the use of the word "instinctual" for hunger, thirst, and satiety because these drives can be consciously overridden. However, they can be overridden only after one has *learned* how to consciously override them and only after one has experienced what it is like to be fed, hydrated, and satiated. (Human beings don't really elect to give up what they cannot have or have never had.)

Human beings do not need to learn to eat and drink. They may need to learn *how* to eat and drink or *how* to override the desire to eat and drink, but they do not need to learn that there is a need to eat and drink. Neither do human beings need to learn how to feel satiated or hydrated. Satiety is the sense of satisfaction that has its physiologic basis in: (1) gastric distention; (2) increasing blood concentrations of certain hormones (like gastrin, secretin, and cholecystokinin); and (3) increasing blood concentrations of specific simple sugars, fatty acids, and amino acids — the availability and usability of which are dependent on other hormones (like insulin). Lack of thirst is a physiologic state that normally comes from proper hydration, which has its basis in the concentration of water in various body fluid compartments (i.e., intracellular fluid, tissue fluid, blood, and lymph) and how those concentrations especially impact osmoreceptors[213] in the

---

213 *Osmoreceptors* are nerve cells (i.e., neurons) that are especially sensitive to fluid movements due to osmosis: When the concentration of dissolved substances is higher in extracellular fluid, the relatively lower concentration of water in the extracellular fluid compartment causes water from inside of cells to move outside so that osmotic pressures in the two locations are equalized. The flow of water from inside to outside of

hypothalamus, the location of the thirst center.

Human beings may need to learn: (1) *how* to distinguish various levels of satiety (for example, short term versus long term); (2) *how* to compensate for lack of satiety with various activities and behaviors; and (3) *how* to override the need for physiologic satiety; but human beings do not need to learn how to feel "full" when stretch receptors in the stomach are stimulated or when certain hormones and nutrients reach levels necessary to stimulate the satiety center and/or inhibit the hunger center.[214] (Along with the thirst center, the hunger and satiety centers are also located in the hypothalamus.)

Responses to hunger and thirst and lack of satiety and hydration are reflexive behaviors that occur because of: (1) insufficient nutrient supply, (2) dehydration, and (3) inhibition and/or excitation of various regulatory neurons in the brain. Unfortunately, later in life we may learn to try to compensate for what is missing emotionally in our lives (or what we perceive to be missing) with compulsive eating and/or excessive drinking to try to approximate emotional satiety or mimic an overall sense of well-being. However, such misdirected activity is partly due to the brain's inability to sort out and distinguish various causes of stress from one another as well as various effects of stress from one another. (Of course, hormone and neurotransmitter imbalances can contribute to compulsive, excessive, and addictive behaviors as well.)

Individuals and entire societies that experience starvation and dehydration due to lack of edible food and drinkable water especially know what deprivation is. Without sufficient food and water, there can be no leisure time or time for emotional, mental, physical, and spiritual growth because all of one's time is consumed by the instinctive drives of hunger and thirst as well as

---

the osmoreceptors stimulates the thirst center in the hypothalamus and, therefore, the desire to drink. A parched oral cavity and throat also add to this desire.

214 This assumes that cells of the hypothalamus are exposed to normal levels of hormones, especially insulin, and that cell membrane receptors for these hormones are present and functioning normally.

poor health from physically wasting away due to their lack. To be sure, satiety and continuous hydration may not even be an option for individuals in certain geographic locations or in certain economic situations. That is why some people never grow to their full potential physically, emotionally, mentally, and spiritually. This is one way that God entrusts others to our care: It is our individual and collective responsibility to ease the suffering of others and to help ensure that others live up to their full potential. This is the basis for real altruism, or demonstrable love. It is what God wants from us for others.

In the twenty-first century, obesity is especially rampant in some individuals and in certain societies because: (1) food and drink are plentiful; (2) ignorance abounds regarding nutrition as it relates to physical health and well-being; (3) people are less active physically; and (4) people try to compensate for lack or perceived lack in one or more areas of their lives with feelings of satiety experienced from eating and drinking.

In certain geographic locations and during certain periods of history, being over one's normal weight was equated with health, wealth, and success — all three of which usually resulted in personal leisure as well as in entire leisure classes of society. The increased availability of, and accessibility to, ample food and potable water have enabled people to flourish in multiple ways at different historical periods and in different places throughout the world. Of course, this often comes at an expense to others who serve as indentured servants or slaves or for whom food and water are neither available nor accessible.

When a person is referred to as "fat" in the Holy Bible, the reference is not synonymous with being corpulent in a decadent, materialistic society:

> *The soul that blesses others shall be made fat: and the person that provides water shall be watered also.*
>
> PROVERBS 11:25 KJV (PARAPHRASE)

> *The person that is of a proud heart stirs up strife: but*

the person that puts his trust in the LORD shall be made fat.

PROVERBS 28:25 KJV (PARAPHRASE)

Metaphysically speaking, to be "fat" means to be "blessed by God" and, therefore, "prosperous." When God promises people "the fat of the land," He is promising them the richness of the land itself as well as His blessings upon that land to cause it to be abundant as a "land of plenty." To be sure, God blesses His people with an increase in healthy crop production and domesticated animal reproduction despite harmful changes in climate, temperature, weather, and barometric pressure. Such blessings include concomitant interactions between and among our own individual and group electromagnetic fields and the Earth's electromagnetic field, all of which can favorably impact the environment, too.

That the people of the Old Testament were to offer God the "fat of the flock" means that they were to sacrifice the choicest and best animals to Him in gratitude. During Old Testament times, blood was offered to God in sprinkling by the priest as a sacrifice for sins, but fat was also offered to God in burning by the priest as an acknowledgement that God alone gives increase and abundance to His people. The offerings of fat were intended to signify that the people were offering Him the choicest and best as well:

> *{3} And the priest shall offer of the sacrifice of the peace offering, an offering made by fire unto the LORD: the fat that covers the abdominal organs, and all the fat that is upon the abdominal organs[215]... {16} And the priest shall burn them upon the altar: it is the food of the offering made by fire for a sweet savor: all the fat is the LORD's. {17} It shall be a perpetual*

---

[215] Anatomically, this refers to the greater omentum, lesser omentum and all adipose dispersed throughout the mesenteric connective tissue within the abdomen.

> *statute for your generations wherever you live, that you eat neither fat nor blood.*
>
> LEVITICUS 3:3 & 16-17 KJV (PARAPHRASE)

Like the people of God in the Old Testament, the people of God today are to offer God their very best. Only our very best is acceptable to Him. Like Abel, and not like Cain, we are to offer God what He requires of us and not what we decide to give to Him. We are to give to God of our *fat* — in other words, we are to give to God from the increase and abundance that He Himself has given to us. Such offerings bless God. They are a sign of peace between us and God; and they themselves engender peace. The burning of fat is called a peace offering in the Holy Bible, but it is also an offering of thanksgiving for health and prosperity as well as for safety and satiety.

It does not matter what our lot in life is, it is from that lot that we are to give to God. If we are responsible for lavatory sanitation, then we are to present to God the cleanest and most hygienic bowl or pit toilets that we possibly can. If we are responsible for literary works, then we are to present to God the most accurate and correct writing that we possibly can. We should be thrilled to please the Lord God as well as excited concerning the possibility of pleasing Him. Whatever we do, let us do it to please God. And, whatever we do for God, let it be our best. Just as Christ Jesus gave God the Father his very best, so are we to give Him our very best. (To be sure, Christ Jesus also gave *us* his very best, too.)

As mentioned earlier in this book, it was not until the time of Noah that descendants of Adam and Eve were given permission from God to eat meat. Before that time, they were to depend on seeds, nuts, vegetables, and fruit for nutrition. Perhaps God gave His permission to eat meat to Noah and his descendants because He knew that there would be mass migrations of people and that they would not be able to wait on planted crops to grow and produce food annually. Regardless, the Antediluvians proved that human beings can flourish without eating meat.

God has always cared about what we eat and drink. If you read through the various dietary laws within the Book of Leviticus, you will find great practical requirements for the Old Testament people of God. *For example,* people were told not to eat pork or fish without scales because, of all animals, these creatures especially eat garbage and detritus,[216] increasing the likelihood of our ingesting their parasites, toxic substances, and other agents of disease. Of course, New Testament Christians are no longer subject to the dietary restrictions in Leviticus. Nonetheless, it pays to learn from general education about nutrition what to eat and what not to eat as well as how to farm the healthiest animals, how to cultivate sea creatures in clean waters, and how to prepare foods using the most sanitary and hygienic methods.

Regardless of what we choose to eat or not eat, today we are taught through God's written Word that, metaphysically speaking, Christ Jesus is our true food and real drink:

> *{33} Jesus said, "For the bread of God is he which comes down from heaven and gives life to the world." {34} His followers then responded to him: "Lord, give us this bread from now on." {35} Jesus replied: "I am the bread of life: the person that comes to me shall never hunger; and the person that believes on me shall never thirst."*
>
> JOHN 6: 33-35 KJV (PARAPHRASE)

> *{53} Then Jesus said to them: "Truly, truly, I say to you, 'Except you eat the flesh of the Son of man, and drink his blood, you have no life in you. {54} Whoever eats my flesh, and drinks my blood, has eternal life; and I will raise that person up at the last day. {55} For my flesh is meat indeed, and my blood is drink*

---

[216] In this sense, *detritus* refers to "undissolved potentially-harmful substances from decomposing organic remains."

indeed.'"

JOHN 6:53-55 KJV (PARAPHRASE)

When Jesus heard those to whom he was delivering his sermon in the synagogue murmur in disgust that they would be required to eat his flesh, Jesus corrected their thinking because he was speaking metaphysically, not literally:

"It is the spirit that quickens [or makes alive]; the flesh profits nothing: the words that I speak unto you, they are spirit, and they are life."

JOHN 6:63 KJV (PARAPHRASE)

In other words, eating the flesh of Jesus and drinking his blood means feeding on his spiritual truth. It has nothing to do with transubstantiation, Eucharistic adoration, or the prohibition of intinction.[217] (The first is a fable, the second is an idolatrous practice, and the third is a product of extreme literalism.)

If we hunger and thirst after God's spiritual truth (there really is none other), then we shall be satiated and slaked by experiencing God's love for us through the sacrifice of His only-begotten Son, Jesus Christ. Such sacrifice is represented metaphysically in communion bread plus the "fruit of the vine" (i.e., communion wine or grape juice). However, regardless of its metaphysics, the communion meal always represents and commemorates the physical crucifixion of Jesus Christ. People who say that Jesus Christ did not come to die in the flesh for humankind have

---

217 Some Christian denominations prohibit the dipping of bread into wine or grape juice for the communicant because they believe that such *intinction* (i.e., dipping) would not honor the words of Christ to "eat" (i.e., chew) his body and "drink" his blood. This is just one example of how some religious people "strain out gnats and swallow camels." Both processes require swallowing; *that* is their commonality. Drinking from a shared cup today also demonstrates an extreme ignorance of microbiology and communicable diseases; such a practice is inexcusable in this day and age.

absolutely no understanding of God's spiritual truth.

People are so hungry and thirsty today for the deepest meaning of life that they often will accept anything for truth without measuring it against the written Word of God. They accept perfidious lies about who God is and what He has done. They accept anti-Christian doctrines as well as ecclesiastically-devised errors[218] and fanciful tales; and they are glad to do so. They do so because they are unwilling to learn and apply spiritual truths as principles from the Holy Bible. The Holy Bible is an embarrassment to them because it talks of God as a Father who kindles love from within and dispenses judgment as wrath in woes to those who reject the physical sacrifice of Jesus Christ for their iniquity and sin. By the way, without the physical sacrifice of Jesus Christ, there can be no metaphysical understanding. Metaphysics laughs at itself without Christ Jesus. Without the shed blood of Christ Jesus, metaphysics cannot be divine; it can only be mundane.

Today, the human heart pants for what it does not have. Yet it will not accept what it has been given. Human beings look for explanations for the deepest meaning of life in what appears to them to be occult, mysterious, or esoteric. They fail to realize that the written Word of God has all the meaning that they will ever need while on Earth. Throughout the Holy Bible, there are (1) superficial (but not shallow) levels of meaning, (2) deeper levels of meaning, and (3) deepest (even profound) levels of meaning — enough meaning for them to feed on, drink from, and be satiated with for the entirety of their lives.

Certain Jewish children of the Babylonian Captivity — namely, Daniel (Belteshazzar), Hananiah (Shadrach), Mishael (Meshach), and Azariah (Abednego) — refused to eat and drink the Babylonian King Nebuchadnezzar's rich food and beverage (i.e., his "meat and wine"). Instead, they asked for, and received,

---

218 There is a difference in nuance between the English word *perfidy* (and parts of speech derived from it) and the Latin word *perfidium*. The English *perfidy* is the quality or state of being faithless and deceitful. The Latin *perfidium* is treacherous apostasy that has its origin in cunningly-devised and ecclesiastically-based systematic theology.

vegetables and water. They not only survived, they thrived. They even fared better than those who daily ate the king's meat and drank his wine. As recorded in Daniel 1:15 (KJV): "their countenances appeared fairer and fatter in flesh than all the children who ate the portion of the king's meat."

Some people are starved for affection because they have been deprived of it during their formative years. However, the knowledge of why we seek recognition from others, or the knowledge that we are trying to make up for our lack of healthy nurturance through self-promotion, is insufficient in itself to make us stop seeking recognition or promoting ourselves. Rather, coming to understand that God knows our name and recognizes who we are and our efforts on His behalf brings us to a healthier emotional state. In that state, we are less needy and, therefore, desire less to vainly draw attention to ourselves.

It is important to point out that there is an emotional hunger not only in people who have been deprived of healthy nurturance but in those who have been abused, victimized, oppressed, and, for these reasons, disenfranchised. That is why some people hunger for control and thirst for power. Rejection creates this hunger and thirst — so much so that, when these people play church or politics (which are sometimes one and the same), they tend to not only mimic existing hierarchies to lend credibility to what they do but also seek positions of leadership and titles to feed their huge emotional hunger and thirst for validation through recognition. However, we all need to be reminded that, first and foremost, it is most important what God thinks of us. To be sure, it is also important what we think of ourselves by understanding ourselves in the context of God's divine metaphysics.

Both self-promotion and seeking recognition from others try to plug a hole in the heart that, really, only Christ Jesus can fill. People are often willing to accept the counterfeit because they don't know or have never experienced (i.e., tasted) the original. Often, emotionally-deprived and disenfranchised people who play church and/or politics have never experienced validation in educational, home, or work settings. So, they tend to lord it over people in any setting that might give them an opportunity to do so.

(This might explain their hunger for control and thirst for power, but this explanation does not justify such unhealthy drives.) Existing social groups may provide them with that setting. However, if an existing group does not provide them with such a setting, then they might begin their own group to meet that need. (It is important to acknowledge that some healthy motivations can be mixed with some unhealthy motivations.)

Concerning the local church, this is not to say that positions of leadership or titles should never be granted. This is to acknowledge that some positions are created and some titles are given for wrong reasons. To be sure, there exists a real dilemma that the people of God need to recognize and acknowledge. Not everyone is equipped to minister to others. And it can be devastating for a congregation to lead itself when there is no one person or group of people in church leadership with extensive knowledge of the Holy Bible. For example, the Religious Society of Friends (i.e., Quakerism) was truly a Christian denomination at the time of its formation in the mid-17th century; the group elected to form without an ordained leadership at a time in history when people read, studied, comprehended, and valued the Holy Bible. Unfortunately, because of the lack of systematic Scriptural teaching and understanding that developed over the years since that time, Quakers no longer belong to a true Christian church. In the name of progressivism and inclusiveness, they now accept all religions (not just all Christian denominations) as equivalent. Quakerism fell to error — like the denomination known as "The Church of Christ, Scientist" — because of the failure to recognize the need for an ongoing fivefold (or fourfold) ministry.[219]

Concerning the use of titles in local church leadership, Elijah and Daniel never introduced themselves with titles. So, an educated discussion needs to include answering the questions: "What are legitimate offices of ministry within a local church?" and

---

[219] Ephesians 4:11 indicates that God gave ministries to people as apostles, prophets, evangelists, pastors, and teachers. Some Bible scholars interpret "pastors and teachers" to be one combined ministry and, therefore, refer to these ministries as *fourfold* rather than *fivefold*.

"To what extent should titles be used or not used." Jesus did permit himself to be called "Rabbi" and "Son of God." And Jesus used many titles to describe himself in the first three chapters of Revelation. I write this because the issue of positions and titles is complex and, therefore, worthy of further discussion and respectful debate in many circles. And I write this because it relates to hunger and thirst for the deepest meaning of life and errors related to those drives.

People who hunger and thirst for the deepest meaning of life need to take great care concerning whom they permit to feed them spiritually. Many people, including those who are counted as spiritual leaders, don't recognize the difference between spiritual truth and spiritual error. That is why all people need to depend solely on God's Holy Spirit as their Well for Living Water because it is from this well that the deepest meaning of life is drawn and poured.

Although Christians should focus on what is pure (Philippians 4:8), it is dysfunctional not to recognize impure motives in others. As Scripture teaches us, we should be harmless as doves but, at the same time, wise as serpents (Matthew 10:16). Ignoring impure motives and pretending they don't exist keep us from identifying serpents as well as warning others.

Beware of wolves in sheep's clothing (Matthew 7:15). And be willing, like the young boy in the tale of Hans Christian Andersen, to stop a farce from continuing. That young boy exclaimed: "The Emperor has no clothes!" We can exclaim: "That teaching has no spiritual substance!" or "That teaching is inconsistent with the entirety of God's written Word!"

Fasting in Prayer through Faith

When Christ Jesus was asked by the religious leaders of his day why his disciples did not wash their hands before they ate, he answered: "It is not what goes into the mouth that defiles a person [meaning, the dirt they might ingest] but what comes out of the mouth that defiles a person."[220]

Later, in private, when his disciples asked him to explain his remarks, Jesus replied:

> *{17} Don't you understand that whatever enters in at the mouth goes into the abdomen, and is eventually eliminated as waste? {18} But those things that come out of the mouth actually come from the heart. So, a person is defiled [or made spiritually unclean] only by his or her own spoken words, {19} since it is out of the heart that evil thoughts, murders, adulteries, fornications, thefts, false witnessing, and blasphemies proceed: {20} These are the things that defile a person. On the contrary, to eat with unwashed hands does not defile a person.*
>
> MATTHEW 15:17-20 KJV (PARAPHRASE)

In the previous quotation, Christ Jesus was not speaking about nutrition. He was not advocating eating anything, everything, or nothing. Instead, he was talking about what really makes us unclean, unholy, and "defiled." Our unclean desires, or sinful lusts, make us spiritually unclean, not the foods we eat or do not eat.

> *{14} But every person is tempted, when that person is drawn away of his or her own lust and enticed. {15} Then, when lust has conceived, it brings forth sin: and sin, when it is finished, brings forth death [i.e., separation from God].*
>
> JAMES 1:14-15 KJV (PARAPHRASE)

Regardless of whether we are saved or not, all human beings are still subjected to the thoughts, feelings, and ideas of a carnal mind. Satan preys upon us through that carnal mind. However, although

---

[220] Matthew 15:11, King James Version (Paraphrase)

we are subjected to the thoughts, feelings, and ideas of a carnal mind, saved people do not need to be subject to them nor subject to Satan's mortal mind (i.e., either ruled by them or ruled by Satan). We can ignore the machinations of the carnal mind, recognizing them for what they are, as well as resist Satan's mortal mind.

Living in a state of contrition (LSC) is important for us to be spiritually well-fed, slaked, and satisfied. LSC is a free will offering to God. It is the daily sacrifice of our carnal self that fulfills Jesus Christ's commandment to deny ourselves as we carry our own burdens to follow him:

> *And Jesus said to them all: "If any will come after me, let them deny themselves, and take up their cross daily, and follow me."*
>
> LUKE 9:23 KJV (PARAPHRASE)

Conceptualize a state of contrition as a place or location within a circle. The circle *does not* represent a prison. A state of contrition has neither a wall nor a fence around it. Imagine the circumference of the circle as a two-dimensional line that can be crossed at any time in either direction. To enter a state of contrition, we need only to step across the circumference and enter into the circle consciously and willingly.

In this book and elsewhere in my writings, I state that our sole eternal purpose for being is to bless the Name of the Lord God Almighty. I would like to add that the sole reason for our being here on Earth in corruptible bodies is to learn not to yield to temptation at the same time that we learn to trust in God. LSC does not protect us from being tempted, but it does keep us from acting on temptation. In fact, LSC is the only way that we can successfully overcome the world. LSC provides a necessary checkpoint because, to cross over the line to yield to temptation, we must ask ourselves: "Do I really want to leave my state of contrition?" "Am I willing to sacrifice my special intimacy with God to yield to temptation?" "Am I willing to cross my self-imposed boundary to give in to temptation?" "Do I really want to act on this temptation?" "Am I willing to leave my protected state to embark on the journey of a prodigal son or daughter?" These are the questions that Adam and Eve should have asked themselves but did not. Nevertheless, we can and should ask them and other questions like them.

There comes a point in one's life journey with Christ Jesus that LSC becomes LSPC, which stands for "living in a state of *perpetual* contrition." LSPC comes only after one has made a lasting commitment or vow not to wander or leave one's self-chosen state of contrition for any reason — not for the comfort or compulsion of any addiction, not for the purpose of entertaining any thought or indulging any feeling unworthy of Christ Jesus, and not for a moment of carnal pleasure.

There is a point in our life journey that LSPC becomes our only option — our only choice *if* we want to continually please our Creator. Of course, there are other options or choices, including choosing to please ourselves, others, and/or Satan. (1) Binding ourselves to self-gratification, (2) subjugating our wills to the will of any other being or entity (human or otherwise), and (3) blaspheming God's Holy Spirit by voluntarily choosing to serve Satan when we consciously know that there is an alternative — all represent actively choosing to displease the Creator. This is not choosing to displease the Creator in ignorance but displeasing Him by consciously choosing to do what we know will displease Him. There comes a point in our lives when we must accept the responsibility that we have to choose either to serve God or not to serve Him. Either we give our lives completely to Him or not. However, this does not mean that giving our lives completely to Him is instantaneous. In fact, giving our lives completely to God is usually taken just one step at a time.

LSPC is not so much a *tabula rasa* (i.e., "blank slate") as it is a *tabula pura* (i.e., "pure and clean slate") and a *tabula sine cera* (i.e., "writing tablet without wax"). When the mind is just a blank slate, anything or anyone from the world of the invisible can write on it. In contrast, when the mind has been wiped clean by the shed blood of Jesus Christ (i.e., *tabula pura)* and is unchangeable in its commitment to please God (i.e., *tabula sine cera)*, the hand of God can write on it through His Holy Spirit. This is how we become highly attuned to the thoughts, feelings, and desires of God. To be sure, God can speak to us in a hot thunderous voice that is audible to all, but He usually speaks to us in a still small voice from within us that is inaudible to others.

Living a life of purity is dependent on LSPC. It is only through LSPC that we can resist temptation by acknowledging that temptation is there at the same time that we consciously elect not to step outside of the state of perpetual contrition in which we have chosen to live. LSPC becomes a way of life that permits us, whether awake or asleep, to monitor every idea, thought, and feeling, take it captive by scrutinizing it in the light of God and, then: (1) reject it outright; (2) reject that part of it that is, or would be, displeasing to God; or (3) accept it by *accommodating and assimilating* it (or, using language associated with the digestive system, *digesting and absorbing* it).

LSPC *is not* rejecting God's forgiveness for our iniquity and sin. (Accepting the shed blood of Jesus Christ is all that we need for eternal forgiveness from God.) LSPC *is* acknowledging that while, still in a corruptible body, we are prone to sin because we are continually subjected to temptation. (That is why *perpetual* contrition is necessary.) LSPC involves our rejection moment by moment of any and all things that might displease God.

Periodic and regular fasting is just one facet of LSPC, but it is an important one. Fasting is a way of denying ourselves in supplication to the Lord God Almighty. King David fasted and prayed when his child by Bathsheba was ill (2 Samuel 12:16). King Jehoshaphat of Judah proclaimed a fast for the people when they were under siege (2 Chronicles 20:1-4). The Prophet Ezra proclaimed a fast for the people as a sign of humility that God might be asked earnestly by them for protection (Ezra 8:21, 23). Queen Esther asked the Jews to fast by refraining from both food and drink that she might find favor with the king as she attempted to intercede for them (Esther 4:16).

Through the Prophet Isaiah, God Himself broadens the definition of fasting to include ministering to those who are oppressed, victimized, and abused as well as ministering food, shelter, and clothing to those in need:

> *{6} Is this not the fast that I have chosen for you: to loosen the handcuffs of wickedness, to undo heavy burdens, and to let the oppressed go free, and that you break every yoke? {7} Is it not to give your bread to the hungry, and that you bring the poor who are cast out into your own home? And when you see the naked, that you cover them; and that you do not hide yourself from other human beings in need?*
>
> ISAIAH 58:6-7 KJV (PARAPHRASE)

In prayer and fasting, there is both singularity of purpose and heightened sensitivity to the thoughts, feelings, ideas, and desires of God. It is in prayer and fasting that we receive answers and understand them more clearly. It is in prayer and fasting that we can demonstrate the power of Christ over Satanic temptation, demonic possession in others, and carnal desires within ourselves. If we are not living in a state of contrition, God will not hear our prayers even though we are fasting. So, fasting in itself is insufficient for God to respond. God will not respond to those who regularly yield to temptation and, then, misconclude that they can get His attention in prayer and fasting. Real prayer and fasting require that we refrain from doing what is evil in the sight of the Lord (Jeremiah 14:12). When we are sincere (i.e., *tabula sine cera*), fasting is a sign of our repentance.

Adversity, pain, and suffering can also have the same effect as fasting in prayer through faith. However, adversity, pain, and suffering are imposed from without whereas fasting in prayer through faith is chosen from within (i.e., self-imposed). Ironically, if we do not discipline ourselves, God will do it for us. If we do not constrain ourselves, God will constrain us.

The one guideline that Jesus gave for fasting was that we fast in secret by telling no one what we are doing and by demonstrating cheerfulness throughout the fasting process. If we do this, Christ Jesus promises that God the Father will reward us with the desires of our heart that have been expressed in our prayers during the time of fasting (Matthew 6:16-18).

Jesus was mindful that fasting should not be for too long, especially when the fasting person must be involved in physical activity. Before Jesus multiplied the seven loaves of bread and the few fish that they had for the multitude who were with them, he told his disciples:

> *I have compassion on the multitude because they continue with me now three days and have nothing to eat: and I will not send them away fasting because they will faint along the way.*
>
> MATTHEW 15:32 KJV (PARAPHRASE)

When the disciples of Jesus asked him why they could not cast out a particular demon from a possessed child, Jesus replied that "this kind of demon cannot be cast out except through prayer and fasting."[221] He also indicated that their lack of sufficient faith played an important role in their inability to cast the demon out. Moving mountains and casting out demons require fasting in prayer through faith.

Food in an *Astral Gelatinous*™ Condition

Nutrients are often defined as "raw materials necessary for life." And *foods* are often defined as "specific nutrients that, when broken down within the cells of the body, provide the body with usable chemical energy." These simple definitions are commonly known to both teachers and students of human anatomy and physiology.

You will recall from the three premises stated in Chapter One of this book that God's original creation was *astral gelatinous*™

---

221 Mark 9:29, King James Version (Paraphrase)

before the Adamic Fall and not *protoplasmic*. (Souls in the Garden of Eden were clothed with a different kind of flesh than "souls in dust" are clothed.) You will also recall that *as* Christ Jesus returns to Earth, those on Earth who have accepted him as Savior of the world and personal Savior will be returned instantaneously *en masse* to an *astral gelatinous*™ condition from the *protoplasmic* condition in which their souls are now residing. And you will recall that, immediately preceding that instantaneous translation of somatic identities from a *protoplasmic* condition to an *astral gelatinous*™ condition, souls already in Heaven will have received their *astral gelatinous*™ bodies first (i.e., also *en masse* but only a split second before "souls in dust" receive theirs). Finally, all unsaved people who remain in a *protoplasmic* condition, and who are eventually identified as belonging to Christ Jesus (because they will have submitted to his Sovereignty), will not receive their *astral gelatinous*™ bodies until the end of the 1,000-year period (i.e., *the Millennium* of Peace), during which time Christ Jesus will reign on Earth. The change of those souls in dust from a *protoplasmic* to an *astral gelatinous*™ condition will also occur *en masse* but only at the end of *the Millennium,* when the current heaven and Earth pass away.

I will now consider the following five questions to answer the primary question: "Is there food in an *astral gelatinous*™ condition?"

1. What food was available to Adam and Eve before the Adamic Fall (when they were still *astral gelatinous*™)?

2. What was the spiritual and physical nature of *manna* given to the children of Israel as they wandered the desert for forty years?

3. When Jesus Christ was on Earth, what comments did he make to his disciples about eating and drinking after the restoration of the Kingdom of God?

4. After Jesus Christ ascended into Heaven, what did he reveal to the Apostle John — as recorded in the Book of Revelation — about food and drink in the Kingdom of God?

5. How do chemical energy requirements in a physical state (i.e., in a *protoplasmic* condition) help us to understand spiritual energy requirements in a spiritual state (i.e., in an *astral gelatinous*™ condition)?

1. What food was available to Adam and Eve before the Adamic Fall (when they were still *astral gelatinous*™)?

It is recorded in Chapters One and Two of the Book of Genesis that God made fruit-bearing trees in the Garden of Eden, including the Tree of Life and the Tree of Knowledge of Good and Evil, both of which were in the center of the Garden. Adam and Eve were given permission to eat fruit from every tree in the Garden of Eden, including the Tree of Life, but were commanded not to eat fruit from the Tree of Knowledge of Good and Evil.

It is recorded in Chapter Three of Genesis that, because Adam and Eve ate fruit from the Tree of Knowledge of Good and Evil, they were expelled from the Garden of Eden. It is also recorded that they could not reenter the Garden of Eden because cherubim (i.e., the Hebrew plural of *cherub*) were posted at its entrance to guard it along with "a flaming sword that turned in every direction [the reader should picture this as a spinning energy vortex] to keep the way of [or prevent access to] the Tree of Life."[222]

Metaphysically speaking, (1) the flaming sword represents closure to the rift through which Adam and Eve fell from the absolute space-time of the spiritual universe, (2) the trees in the Garden of Eden represent life-giving and life-maintaining spiritual substance, and (3) the fruit upon the trees represents the usable energy available to feed people in an *astral gelatinous*™ condition.

Thus, the usable energy for people before the Adamic Fall was not provided by elemental matter since the chemical elements did not first form until after the Luciferian Fall (which came before the Adamic Fall) — when a small portion of the pure, unbound energy in God's spiritual universe became bound as dark energy, dark matter, antimatter, and the subatomic particles of elemental matter. Concerning *elemental matter* (also known as *ordinary*

---

222 Genesis 3:24, King James Version (Paraphrase)

matter and *baryonic matter)*, the Apostle Peter tells us that its atoms will not release their currently-bound energy (in a reverse of their formation) until *the day of the Lord:*

> *{10} But the day of the Lord will come as a thief in the night; in which the heavens shall pass away with a thunderous noise, and the elements shall melt with fervent heat, the earth also and the works that are therein shall be burned up. {11} Seeing, then, that all these material things shall be dissolved, what manner of persons should you be in holy conversation and godliness, {12} expectantly and earnestly desiring the coming of that day of God, wherein the heavens being on fire shall be dissolved, and the elements shall melt with fervent heat?*
>
> 2 PETER 3:10-12 KJV (PARAPHRASE)

What the Apostle Peter described is consistent with what is described by the Apostle John in the Book of Revelation, which records that there will be "a new heaven and a new earth" after the current heaven and Earth pass away:

> *And I, the Apostle John, saw a new heaven and a new earth: for the first heaven and the first earth were passed away; and there was no more sea.*
>
> REVELATION 21:1 KJV (PARAPHRASE)

2. What was the spiritual and physical nature of *manna* given to the children of Israel as they wandered the desert for forty years?

While the children of Israel were wandering in the desert for forty years after their exodus from Egypt, God provided them with a food that in Hebrew is called *manna*. The children of Israel called it "manna" (which means "What is it?") because they literally did not know what it was. As described in the Bible, *manna* was "like coriander seed (i.e., furrowed and striped), white, and the taste of it was like wafers made with honey."²²³ *Manna* is also referred to in the Bible as "corn of heaven" (Psalm 78:24 KJV) and "bread from heaven" (Exodus 16:4 KJV). As dew physically fell (or condensed) at night, so did *manna* fall (or condense) from a spiritual state to a physical state. From Numbers 11:9 and Nehemiah 9:20, it seems that the *manna* absorbed some of the morning's dew and, in this way, also provided the children of Israel with water to quench their thirst in addition to providing them with food to satisfy their hunger.

Manna is called "angels' food" (or "angels' bread") in Psalm 78:25 either because the *manna* was dispensed by angels or the *manna* was the manifestation of food that angels eat (or, possibly, for both reasons).

What *manna* really looked like is pure conjecture. However, that the *manna* miraculously appeared from Heaven in condensation (through the coalescence of spiritual energy and concretioning of spiritual substance) is not conjecture.

3. When Jesus Christ was on Earth, what comments did he make to his disciples about eating and drinking after the restoration of the Kingdom of God?

In all three synoptic gospels (Matthew, Mark, and Luke), Jesus said that he would not drink wine again (i.e., "the fruit of the vine") until he drinks it *anew* (i.e., in a different form and new state) after the restoration of the Kingdom of God (which is an immortal state):

> *But I say unto you, I will not drink henceforth of this fruit of the vine until that day when I drink it new with you in my Father's kingdom.*
>
> MATTHEW 26:29 KJV

> *Verily I say unto you, I will drink no more of the fruit*

---

223 Exodus 16:31, King James Version (Paraphrase)

of the vine, until that day that I drink it new[224] in the Kingdom of God.

MARK 14:25 KJV

For I say unto you, I will not drink of the fruit of the vine, until the Kingdom of God shall come.

LUKE 22:18 KJV

To be sure, Jesus might have been speaking only figuratively. However, he also promised the following to his Apostles after the restoration of the Kingdom of God:

{29} And I appoint unto you a kingdom, as my Father has appointed unto me; {30} That you may eat and drink at my table in my kingdom and sit on thrones judging the twelve tribes of Israel.

LUKE 22:29-30 KJV (PARAPHRASE)

4. After Christ Jesus ascended into Heaven, what did he reveal to the Apostle John — as recorded in the Book of Revelation — about food and drink in the Kingdom of God?

Key words in the KJV translation of the Book of Revelation: *eat, manna, feed, tree, fruit, fruits, hunger, supper*

When speaking to the church in the city of Ephesus, Jesus said that those who overcome temptation in the world will "eat of the Tree of Life, which is in the center of the Paradise of God."[225] You will remember that the Tree of Life was described in Genesis as being in the center of the Garden of Eden. Thus, the nomenclature "Garden of Eden" is used figuratively to describe the Paradise of God in the Book of Genesis. It is God's Paradise — or His "Garden

---

224 Metaphysically, the phrase "drink it new" means that it will be drunk in a different form and in a new state.
225 Revelation 2:7, King James Version

of Eden" — to which saved souls are returned after they die. Because of the shed blood of God's only-begotten Son, we are no longer prohibited from entering (i.e., reentering) the Kingdom of God.[226]

To the church in the city of Pergamos (Pergamum), Jesus said that those who overcome will be given "hidden manna" to eat — which is to say, manna that is not now known or seen (Revelation 2:17 KJV).

It is recorded that the Tribulation saints shall be hungry no more (Revelation 7:16) because the Lamb, Christ Jesus himself, will feed them in Heaven:

> *For the Lamb, who is in the center of the throne, will feed them, and will lead them into living fountains of water...*
>
> REVELATION 7:17 KJV (PARAPHRASE)

An angel of the Lord announced to the Apostle John:

> *Blessed are they who are called to the marriage supper of the Lamb!*
>
> REVELATION 19:9 KJV (PARAPHRASE)

Later, the Apostle John described the city of New Jerusalem, which appeared to him just after he saw the new heaven and new earth that God made (Revelation 21:1 KJV). Within New Jerusalem

---

[226] Those who strain out gnats and swallow camels often try to make a distinction between and among the following terms and phrases, but these terms and phrases are all used interchangeably in the Bible: "Kingdom of God," "Kingdom of Heaven," "Heaven," "Garden of Eden," and "Paradise." As they split hairs in ignorance, there are even those who support erroneous notions and false doctrines with the argument that "Abraham's bosom" is an additional, separate location. (This spurious teaching is as erroneous as the teaching that has elaborated "limbo" and "purgatory.")

was a main conduit with a river of the water of life that ran through the city:

> *And the angel showed me a pure river of water of life, clear as crystal, proceeding out of the throne of God and of the Lamb. On each side of the river was a tree of life, which bore twelve kinds of fruit and which yielded fruit every month. And the leaves of the tree were for the healing of the nations.*
>
> REVELATION 22:2 KJV (PARAPHRASE)

Finally, concerning the Tree of Life, the last chapter of Revelation records the blessing that God bestows on those who belong to Him:

> *Blessed are they who obey His commandments [remember, Adam and Eve fell because they disobeyed His command not to eat from the Tree of Knowledge of Good and Evil], that they may [again] have the right to the Tree of Life and may enter in through the gates into the Heavenly city of New Jerusalem.*
>
> REVELATION 22:14 KJV (PARAPHRASE)

5. How do chemical energy requirements in a physical state (i.e., in a *protoplasmic* condition) help us to understand spiritual energy requirements in a spiritual state (i.e., in an *astral gelatinous*™ condition)?[227]

The Lord God Almighty, or God the Father, has a fiery nature because He is composed of unbound energy in its purest form. In their original *astral gelatinous*™ condition, souls reflected God's fiery nature without harm to themselves because they were without iniquity and sin. In short, souls in an *astral gelatinous*™ condition

---

227 The present author has inferred this understanding through the guidance of the Teacher of all truth, God's Holy Spirit.

were cast in God's complete image and perfect likeness. Therefore, the usable spiritual energy available to original, unfallen mankind as "food" was also unbound energy, or energy in its purest form. This unbound energy is best represented by the "E" in Einstein's reversible equation $E = mc^2$ (unbound energy is equal to the atomic mass of bound energy multiplied by the squared velocity of light).

At the time of the Luciferian Fall, a small amount of the energy in God's spiritual universe became bound to form elemental matter in the material, or physical, universe. God used the elemental matter formed — much as a potter molds clay or a spider spins thread — to elaborate the default mechanisms of anabolic and catabolic reactions[228] that: (1) were built into original mankind before the Adamic Fall, (2) were triggered into physical existence by the Adamic Fall, and (3) are now responsible for all chemical machinery and processes associated with *protoplasmic* life.

Although the Sun in our solar system is not God and definitely not to be worshiped, the Sun was put in place by God to represent Him and His fiery nature to souls in dust as well as to serve as the Earth's primary source of physical energy. The Sun, our solar system's only star, is the major source of physical energy within the Earth's solar system — just as God is the source of all spiritual energy within His spiritual universe. And, just as human beings cannot look at the face (or fiery appearance) of the Sun without having their vision destroyed, so human beings cannot look upon the face, or fiery appearance, of God without having their physical forms annihilated or expunged.

In many ways, hydrogen is the common denominator for understanding bound energy in the physical universe:

The majority (approximately 70%) of the Sun in our solar system is composed of hydrogen. This is roughly consistent with hydrogen's percentage of elemental matter in the entire material universe (75%). After hydrogen, the remainder (28%) of the Sun is

---

[228] Anabolism is constructive metabolism vis-à-vis synthetic chemical reactions that require energy, and catabolism is destructive metabolism vis-à-vis analytic chemical reactions that release energy.

mostly helium. Even the helium that exists in the Sun is derived from the nuclear fusion of hydrogen atoms.

Instead of making nuclear bombs, the tremendous power in hydrogen atoms could be harnessed to power all land, sea, and air vehicles in a safe way — not like the unsafe liquid hydrogen that has been used during the present author's lifetime for outer space flight. Outer space flight will not become safe until electromagnetism generated by modified Tesla coils is harnessed to power spacecraft. (See Author's Note that follows.)

....

Author's Note: In the relative spacetime of the physically-observable universe, because time only fills the space allotted, and space is compressed in intrauniverse wormholes, time is slenderized in those wormholes, permitting accessibility between disparate points of time, making time travel possible for propulsion systems that use electromagnetic technology to glide through space. Rocket propulsion systems that use jet fuel for space travel are too primitive to move through relative spacetime at the warp speeds required for time travel. Only electromagnetic propulsion systems that glide through relative spacetime permit travel through wormholes to the past, distant locations in the present, and/or future. Traversable intrauniverse wormholes are "eyes," or portals, to other times and distant locations in relative spacetime.

....

The most abundant form of hydrogen (i.e., its most common isotope) consists of one proton and one electron. When hydrogen's proton is denuded of its electron, the charged atom, or ion, that results is simply a solitary proton. The solitary proton (an atom of hydrogen without its electron) represents a common denominator for the subatomic structure of all elemental matter in the material universe.[229] The presence or absence of hydrogen's associated

---

[229] To be sure, all atoms other than the most common isotope of hydrogen also possess at least one neutron. A neutron is simply composed of a proton, an electron, and an electron antineutrino (all three of which are emitted when a neutron decays).

electron (an electron, by the way, has a negligible mass when compared to a proton or a neutron) represents uncharged energy when the electron is present and charged energy when the electron is absent. The uncharged and charged states of hydrogen are represented, respectively, by the common symbols: (1) H for one hydrogen atom (i.e., one proton and one electron) and (2) H^+ for one hydrogen ion (i.e., one proton).

The energy in God's spiritual universe that became bound to form elemental matter in the material universe is best represented by hydrogen in its uncharged state as a neutral hydrogen atom (H) as well as its charged state as a hydrogen ion (H^+).

In deep space as well as in solar flares, protons (hydrogen atoms denuded of their electrons) are the most abundant type of charged particle. So much radiation is emitted from them that astronauts on the moon in space suits would not survive without additional protection during solar flares.

Photosynthesis is the primary source for food — or main generator of usable chemical energy — on Earth. During the most common forms of photosynthesis, visible sunlight helps generate hydrogen ions, whose production is ultimately responsible for the synthesis of special hydrocarbons associated with living things (and known as *organic molecules).* The visible sunlight does this by utilizing various specific hydrogen carrier molecules.[230]

All fossil fuels, such as coal, natural gas, and petroleum oil (which are derivatives of the organic molecules produced by living things) are composed of special hydrocarbons. And all organic molecules in living things are composed of special hydrocarbons. To be sure, special hydrocarbons form the basis of carbohydrates, fats, and proteins. When the chemical bonds of carbohydrates, fats, and proteins are broken, they release energy. The more hydrogen atoms per carbon atom, the more energy is released: (1) in uncontrolled oxidation (for example, during the spontaneous

---

[230] In the living cells of all green plants and all mammals, common hydrogen-carrier molecules include nicotinamide adenine dinucleotide (NAD^+ and NADH), nicotinamide adenine dinucleotide phosphate ($NADP^+$ and NADPH), and flavin adenine dinucleotide (FAD^{2+} and $FADH_2$).

combustion of hydrocarbons in fossil fuels *by fire)* as well as (2) in controlled oxidation (for example, during the breakdown of hydrocarbons in living things *by enzymes* and their associated *coenzymes).*

Removing the element hydrogen from organic metabolites (intermediates of carbohydrate, fat, and protein metabolism) and passing it along to hydrogen-carrier molecules (and then, eventually, to oxygen) produces chemical energy that is usable by the cells of the human body. This process is best seen in (i.e., most efficiently shown by) aerobic cellular respiration, which occurs within the mitochondria of living cells. The process is represented by the following general equation:

$$MH_2 + \text{carrier} \rightarrow \text{H-carrier} + H^+ + M + E^0$$

(M represents the metabolite and E^0 represents emitted energy)

To be sure, oxygen is important to the overall process, but its primary role is as a final hydrogen acceptor to free hydrogen from the hydrogen carrier molecules and, thereby, release as much usable chemical energy as possible. Oxidation, or dehydrogenation, of various organic molecules occurs in living cells in the presence of various dehydrogenases (i.e., enzymes that remove hydrogen).

Although this is an oversimplification, the complex chemical machinery that God elaborated in both plants and animals was made by Him to safely utilize energy associated with hydrogen atoms and their electrons. Thus, the physical food that God provided to souls in a *protoplasmic* condition is bound chemical energy that greatly depends on the transference of this energy: (1) from hydrogen to hydrogen carriers, (2) from hydrogen carriers to hydrogen acceptors, and (3) by electrons associated with hydrogen.

In contrast to energy bound in the form of atoms and subatomic particles, the energy of the spiritual universe is found in the spiritual light of the Lord God Almighty, which is energy unbound and in its purest state. Thus, the spiritual food that God provided (and still provides) to living beings in an *astral gelatinous*™

condition is pure, unbound energy.

If, for some reason, you have concluded that I am trying to say that God is composed of hydrogen atoms and that when we are in Heaven we will be consuming protons and electrons derived from hydrogen atoms, then you have misunderstood my answer to question number five. (To be sure, one of the reasons for that misunderstanding may have come from my comparing physical apples to metaphysical oranges.)

In summary, the answers to questions one through five help us to conclude that *astral gelatinous*™ beings — including saved souls who will one day have restored somatic identities — eat spiritual substance and derive spiritual energy from heavenly food and drink. Thus, in Heaven, saved souls with restored somatic identities will experience, ingest, accommodate, and assimilate substance and energy, just not the same type of substance and energy we taste, swallow, digest, and absorb on Earth. *Here and now,* it is bound chemical energy. *There and then,* it will be unbound spiritual energy. As it once was before the Adamic Fall, so shall it again be.

Many of you will be pleased to know that calories will not be counted in Heaven. And, because people in Heaven — all with restored somatic identities — will possess a spiritualized metabolism, there will be no waste and, therefore, no process of elimination.

Chapter Questions

This section is intended to facilitate learning by providing relevant activities, exercises, and experiences to aid students of divine metaphysics in their quest for grasping spiritual concepts, integrating them into their own belief systems, holding them more assuredly, and making them more practical in daily life.

The following questions should be answered after reading each titled section. To answer a few of the questions, students may need to consult outside resources or external references. Students are also encouraged to answer these questions with others during group discussions.

Hunger and Thirst for the Deepest Meaning of Life

1. In your own words, how are hunger and satiety different from sexual and aggressive urges?

2. Where are the hunger center, the satiety center, and the thirst center located within the human body?

3. From a physiologic standpoint, why is compulsive overeating easy to understand?

4. What responsibilities do we have for meeting the nutritional needs of others?

5. Metaphysically speaking, what does *fat* represent?

6. Can human beings be physically healthy without eating meat (i.e., muscle)? In your answer, refer both to the Antediluvians as well as to the Prophet Daniel and his childhood friends.

7. Find at least five dietary restrictions in the Book of Leviticus and explain their practicality from a physiologic and/or hygienic standpoint.

8. Discuss hunger and thirst as they relate to the body and blood of Jesus Christ.

9. Discuss levels of meaning within the Holy Bible and how their existence can be twisted to fuel both denominationalism and cultism.

10. Discuss leadership and the use of titles in local churches.

Fasting in Prayer through Faith

11. What makes a person spiritually unclean? Explain.

12. Explain why saved human beings are still subjected to the thoughts of a carnal mind.

13. How does living in a state of contrition (LSC) relate to resisting the Devil's mortal mind and resisting the temptations of the human carnal mind?

14. At what point in one's life journey does living in a state of contrition (LSC) become living in a state of perpetual contrition (LSPC)?

15. How does LSPC relate to a life of purity?

16. What is real fasting and how does it relate to LSPC?

Food in an *Astral Gelatinous*™ Condition

17. Discuss when souls who belong to Christ Jesus receive their *astral gelatinous*™ bodies. (There should be three divisions or categories explained here.)

18. What food was available to Adam and Eve before the Adamic Fall (when they were still *astral gelatinous*™)?

19. What was the spiritual and physical nature of *manna* given to the children of Israel as they wandered the desert for forty years?

20. When Jesus Christ was on Earth, what comments did he make to his disciples about eating and drinking after the restoration of the Kingdom of God?

21. After Jesus Christ ascended into Heaven, what did he reveal to the Apostle John — as recorded in the Book of Revelation — about food and drink in the Kingdom of God?

22. How do chemical energy requirements in a physical state (i.e., in a *protoplasmic* condition) help us to understand spiritual energy requirements in a spiritual state (i.e., in an *astral gelatinous*™ condition)?

Chapter Nine

Divine Metaphysics of the Respiratory System

The Spirit of God has made me, and the breath of the Almighty has given me life.

JOB 33:4 KJV (PARAPHRASE)

Our Only Breath of Life

The Lord God Almighty, as the one true and only real Creator, is our breath of life. God is our inspiration and our expiration.

As human beings, it is from God that we draw our first breath of air as newborns (when we transition from intrauterine to extrauterine life) and it is to God that our last breath of air is released when our time here on Earth has expired (when we transition from this plane of consciousness to the next). As spiritual beings, God is our Life through the blood that He has shed for us. We live spiritually by His breathing life into us through that blood. It is the shed blood of Jesus Christ that transports God's life into us as spiritual breath. This is how our souls are reborn and restored and how we have our breath in God metaphysically.

It is easy to understand why individual Hebrew and Greek words in the Holy Bible convey multiple meanings simultaneously, including: "breath," "spirit," "soul", "being," and "self." For example, the Hebrew word *neh'-fesh* [H5315 in Appendix Table A] — which is translated as "soul" in Genesis 2:7 — not only means "soul" as (1) the seat of life, (2) the seat of innermost being, and (3) the seat of thinking and feeling but also as (4) "the essence" of a person (i.e., one's "being-in-itself" or the "person-in-himself or -herself") as well as (5) "that which has breath and respires."

> *And the LORD God formed man from the dust of the ground and breathed into his nostrils the breath of life; and man became a living soul.*
>
> GENESIS 2:7 KJV (PARAPHRASE)

For human beings, respiration includes: (1) pulmonary ventilation (i.e., the process of moving air into and out of the lungs); (2) external respiration (i.e., the exchange of gases in the lungs between terminal air sacs, or alveoli, and surrounding capillaries); (3) internal respiration (i.e., the exchange of gases in body tissues between capillaries and the living cells of the tissues); and (4) cellular respiration (i.e., cellular metabolism). Of course, before the Adamic Fall, original mankind had no need of the physical apparatus and chemical machinery involved in each of the four processes just mentioned. In an *astral gelatinous*™ condition, respiration means something different.

In an *astral gelatinous*™ condition, respiration is symbolized by the pulsating ebb and flow of God's life as well as the *Atman*, defined in this book as "the higher — and highest — *Self*," "the true *Self*," "the supraself," and "our absolute identity in God." Even though *Atman* is a Sanskrit word used in Buddhism, Hinduism, Sikhism, and Jainism to represent the invisible or hidden "Self," it is an appropriate word to use by Jews and Christians for the unseen essence of an individual. The word *Atman* is derived from an Indo-European root that also forms the basis for the German words *Atem* (which means "breath") and *atmen* (which means "breathing" and "to breathe"). In the reality of God, it is impossible to discuss the soul, spirit, being, or self of an individual human person without discussing the breath of God and the spiritual breathing associated with *living* and *being* in Him.

It is easy to understand why the regulation of breathing through disciplined physical and mental exercises plays a large role in the meditative practices associated with various so-called Eastern religions and philosophies. Unfortunately, Jews and Christians usually reject all practices that have had pagan fables and mythologies built up around them. Indeed, Jews and Christians *should* reject all pagan fables as well as mythologies about false deities, but they should also scrutinize the meditative and healing practices that are used by different religions and philosophies to see if there is any value to them. There are some exceptions to such exploration, including Islam and Spiritism.

Why are Islam and Spiritism exceptions? Islam is inherently blasphemous of the God of the Holy Bible. Thus, Jews and Christians should never participate in practices associated with Islam or its offshoots — including Shia Islam, Sunni Islam, Wahhabi Islam, Sufism, and Chrislam. (Would you have a dialogue with the Devil?) And Spiritism has Satanic underpinnings and uses demonic invocations. Thus, Jews and Christians should never participate in practices associated with any form of Spiritism — including, but not limited to, Voodoo (Voodou or Voudon), *Candomblé,* and Spiritualism.[231] The various forms of Islam and Spiritism, however, may be investigated for: (1) purposes of academic and comparative study of religions, (2) associated scholarly debate and discussion, and (3) dispelling the myths and fables engendered by them. During the millennial rule of Jesus Christ on Earth, there will be no adherents of Islam and Spiritism.

As they should, most Jews and authentic Christians shy away from anything suggesting that human beings are ever going to be

---

[231] Spiritualism is borne of: (1) self-deception, (2) the unconscious (i.e., subconscious) desire to have oneself deceived, and/or (3) the very conscious desire to deceive others for personal gain.

gods or equal to God, which supposition got us into trouble in the first place (i.e., through Satan's original temptation for Adam and Eve to be "like God" or "as gods"). Yes, Jesus quoted Psalm 82:6, which refers to the people of God as "elohim" (or "gods").[232] But *el-o-heem'* [H430 in Appendix Table A] is used by Jesus only in the sense of elevated spiritual beings "to whom the word of God came" (John 10:34 KJV) and who are the "children of the Most High" (Psalm 82:6 KJV). The term *elohim* harkens back to our original state and condition of being, wherein we were made in the complete image and perfect likeness of "Elohim," which plural noun in Hebrew means (depending on context): "God," "gods," "divine ones," "immortal beings," and "immortals." (Thus, the term *elohim* also prefigures the future condition of being for saved people, when their somatic identities will be recast in God's complete image and perfect likeness.)

(1) Just because we are "divine ones" does not make us Deity. (2) Just because we are godlike does not make us God. (3) Just because God is our life does not make us the Source of Life. (4) Just because we are monarchs in Heaven does not make us the Monarch of monarchs (i.e., "the King of kings"). (5) Just because we will one day again become glorious spiritual beings does not make us the Supreme Being. (6) Just because we "live and move and have our being"[233] in God does not make us the Lord God Almighty. (7) And just because we have "the mind of Christ"[234] does not make us Jesus Christ. To be sure, there is a delicate balance of understanding in each one of the seven previous statements. That is why it is so easy for human beings to tilt their scales in the wrong direction.

Many authentic Christians want to proclaim: "We are no longer worms or wretches!" But as long as we are human beings with carnal desires, we are living in a wormlike and wretched condition of existence because we are still prone to influences from Satan's mortal mind as well as subjected daily to the thoughts of a carnal,

---

232   John 10:34-35, King James Version
233   Acts 17:28, King James Version
234   1 Corinthians 2:16, King James Version

or fleshly, mind. Yes, one day, we will no longer have a carnal nature, but as long as we continue to remain *souls in dust* (i.e., "souls in flesh") that day has not yet arrived. And, yes, we no longer need to obey our carnal natures, but that does not mean that we are not still tempted to yield to those natures.

Our spiritual identity is in God without our ever being, or becoming, God Himself. God is our only breath of Life. Although we can give God joy, we are not His breath of Life. We do not give Life to God. He gives Life to us.

The Self We Have in God

Breath serves as an excellent analogy for spirit, soul, being, and self (all four terms are synonymous here) because breath is invisible — just as spirit, soul, being, and self are invisible. Both Einstein's general theory of relativity and his special theory of relativity help us, in analogy, to understand the nature of the invisible world of spirit, soul, being, and self. What spirit, soul, being, and self actually are depends on where we are standing and if we are looking at them locally or globally (i.e., universally). Einstein's special theory of relativity elaborates an understanding of the local behavior of matter and its mass as if they were invariant but also as if they were perceived (or being measured) in a vacuum without major influencing factors such as gravitation. Einstein's general theory of relativity generalizes the understanding of special relativity to variable conditions, most notably multivariate conditions imposed on matter and its mass, as well as on light, by the curvature of relative space-time due to gravitation. Indeed, the momentum of energy is influenced by the mass of mass.

What the spirit, soul, being, and self are depends on where we are standing and if we are looking at them locally or globally (i.e., universally). If we are looking at them locally, then we see the many spirits, souls, beings, and selves that were originally created. If we are looking at them universally, then we see (1) the only real *Self*— or one true Identity — provided to us through our collective consciousness in Christ Jesus as well as (2) the unity for which he prayed before his death: "Father, I pray that they may be one in us even as we are one."[235]

Metaphysically speaking, being "one" goes much further than being united in purpose. Being "one" means that we are not really separate from one another in the world or universe of the invisible *Self*. To believe that we have our purpose and our identity in God does not deform our true individuality but, instead, grants it to us. Like the special theory of relativity, we can discuss how we behave individually as if we are separate from one another. But, like the general theory of relativity, in the reality of God we behave in relationship to one another because, in that reality, we are not really separate from one another. The individual trajectories of our lives weave, interweave, and intermittently collide to influence the direction of our future trajectories.

Regardless of whether the hypothesized *string theory* is entirely accurate or not as a *Theory of Everything* (ToE) in the physically observable universe, the cohesiveness that it provides for understanding the various forces and mechanics of physical nature represents that we also need unification for our various perspectives regarding spiritual matters. We can have two or more different perspectives at the same time, or two or more different opinions about the same thing, without requiring one of them to be wrong. Where we are standing determines our individual perspectives. And, metaphysically speaking, we can be standing in more than one place at the same time. That is why we may have multiple perspectives of the same truth — just as we may hold multiple positions on the same issue.

In the same chapter of John in which Jesus prayed for us, we also find the declaration that Jesus has already given to us the glory which he had, and still has, in the Father:

> *"And the glory that You gave to me, I have given to them; that they may be one, even as we are one."*
>
> JOHN 17:22 KJV (PARAPHRASE)

---

235 John 17:11 & 21-23, King James Version (Paraphrase)

How is it possible that Christ Jesus has already given the glory to us when we are not yet glorified spiritual beings? The answer is that he has already given the entitlements of glory to us that we may call upon him and metaphysically invoke his healing presence. *Invoke?* Yes, Jesus is at our beck and call but only when we are calling to him from a position of contrition through humility. Jesus does not and will not respond to arrogance of any kind. Although Jesus *is* the Servant of all, he is not subservient to any one of us. It is foreign to his nature and his *Self* (which is the same self and identity that saved people have in God) to serve arrogance. Although theoretical physicists have looked for "the Answer" and some expect that *the Answer* will soon be provided, *the Answer* has already been provided in and through Christ Jesus. Without Jesus as personal Savior, we cannot have Christ Consciousness. Christ without Jesus is just not possible. Jesus is *it* every bit and every bit of *it*. Jesus metaphysically fulfills the *Theory of Everything* (ToE) because *Jesus owns Everything* (JoE) — which is to say, everything has been placed under his authority (Matthew 28:18).

Jesus Christ saw us as glorified not only because he saw that we will become glorified spiritual beings but because he saw us as we already *are*. Similarly, that we are *selves* or have one *Self*, like Einstein's special and general theories of relativity, depends on where one is standing. Indeed, "denying ourselves" refers to denying the carnal natures that are still with us and does not refer to denying our highest *Self* — Christ Jesus himself, our one true higher self and only real supraself.

Can you hold the whole while simultaneously attending to the whole's various parts? If *yes*, then you are capable of abstract analytical thinking. If *no*, then you are not exercising the mind that God has given to you. What are the primary differences between an educated and experienced saved person and an under-educated and inexperienced saved person? The primary differences include a more refined understanding through deeper levels of abstract analytical thinking as well as a greater ability to discern motives, intents, and absolute truth. (Because people are untethered without Christ Jesus, education and experience for the unsaved can only result in more intricate meaningless information and knowledge as well as more blathering.)

In the final analysis, unity of multiple perspectives and multiple positions is simple when employing a metaphysical approach to being in two or more places at the same time and, thus, having two or more different legitimate perspectives at the same time. However, it is important to point out here (as well as reiterate later) that, although seemingly different truths are true at the same time, they are not true to the point of absurdity.

....

Author's Note: At the time that the present author was writing the first edition of this book in 2012, he recognized that it might be helpful to students of Christian metaphysics if he wrote a metaphysical primer to be read after *As I See It: The Nature of Reality by God* but, ideally, before *Divine Metaphysics of Human Anatomy*. As a result, in 2013, the present author wrote and published the book entitled *God, Our Universal Self: A Primer for Future Christian Metaphysics*.

....

Vocalization

For human beings, vocalization includes the use of musculature in controlled and uncontrolled inhalation and exhalation. Muscles involved include the diaphragm, external and internal intercostal muscles, various abdominal and thoracic wall muscles, laryngeal muscles, pharyngeal muscles, tongue muscles, and even some facial muscles. The production of sound is associated with coughing, sneezing, sighing, yawning, sobbing, crying, laughing, hiccupping, speaking, and singing. All of their associated sounds can be linked, although not always, to different kinds of thinking and/or feeling — *for example:* (1) coughing from anxiety and nervousness, (2) sneezing from surprise, (3) sighing from tedium, (4) yawning from physical or emotional fatigue, (5) sobbing from grief, (6) crying from sadness or gratitude and joy, (7) laughing from happiness, (8) hiccupping from pressure and stress, (9) speaking from the desire to communicate, and (10) singing from the desire to share emotion. (Of course, there can be overlap between and among the ten examples just cited.)

As indicated in the first prequel to this book,[236] Jesus himself — as the Logos — is the primordial Word or vocalization of God, spoken at the precise moment of creation. After creating us (and He created all souls at the same time), God spoke to original, unfallen mankind without hindrance, directly to us through His Holy Spirit. After the Adamic Fall, God spoke to fallen, corporeal mankind indirectly through His earthly prophets and heavenly messengers. Today, however, because of the spiritual redemption and restoration of people saved by Christ Jesus, God again speaks to us directly through His Holy Spirit. (This does not preclude His also using prophets, angels, and saved souls already in Paradise.)

Throughout the Bible, the people of God are compared to sheep. Although sheep are not highly functioning from a cognitive standpoint, sheep have a very well-developed temporal lobe, where the neurons for the primary auditory cortex are found (Areas 41 and 42 in human brains). Thus, sheep can easily determine if the tenor and timbre of human voices are familiar or unfamiliar to them. So, there is a biological basis for the figurative statement by Jesus that:

> *{4} "...my sheep follow me because they know [or recognize] my voice. {5} A stranger will they not follow, but will flee from that person: for they do not know [or recognize] the voice of strangers.*
>
> JOHN 10:4-5 KJV (PARAPHRASE)

From the Holy Bible, we know that the Lord God Almighty has a voice because it is recorded that He spoke His creation into existence. (Metaphysically speaking, Christ Jesus is the Voice of God.) We also know that the Lord God Almighty breathes because He "breathed into man the breath of life."[237] (We can also infer this

---

[236] *As I See It: The Nature of Reality by God* by Rev. Joseph Adam Pearson, Ph.D. Christ Evangelical Bible Institute, 2015. ISBN 978-0615590615

[237] Genesis 2:7, King James Version (Paraphrase)

because human beings must inspire before they speak.) To be sure, breathing for *astral gelatinous*™ beings is different from breathing for human beings, but the normal processes that occur in our human bodies mirror physically what occurs on a higher plane metaphysically. After all, we were originally created in the complete image and perfect likeness of God.

God speaks when He creates, blesses, rewards, comforts, grants mercies, and judges. God expires as He speaks. But, because God is eternal — without beginning and without ending, God never expires by ceasing to exist or ceasing to *be*. God *is,* and *was,* and *ever shall be*. God is the Eternal Self-Existent One. And, because our souls were created to be eternal, we have been jumped into eternity; therefore, we also will never cease to exist or *be*. Unfortunately, for those who steadfastly choose to reject Jesus Christ as their personal Savior and only Sovereign, their "never" includes eternal damnation.

As mentioned earlier, God's voice can be thunderous and booming or still and small. But God's voice is also the sound of many waters[238] by which our spirits are soothed and comforted. Moses even heard "the voice of God speaking out of the midst of the fire."[239] As the people of God, we, too, hear His voice in different ways. Regardless, hearing the voice of God requires obeying what He says because He is God. If we hear the voice of God and do not obey, then we will eventually cease hearing that voice. God told the children of Israel during their exodus from Egypt:

> *If you will diligently listen and obey the voice of the LORD your God, and will do what is right in His sight, and will give ear to His commandments, and keep all His statutes, I will put none of the diseases upon you, which I have brought upon the Egyptians, for I am the LORD that heals you.*
>
> EXODUS 15:26 KJV (PARAPHRASE)

---

238 King James Version of Revelation 1:15 and 14:2
239 Deuteronomy 4:33, King James Version (See also Exodus 19:19 and Deuteronomy 5:24.)

A voice within a vacuum cannot be heard, but God does not live in a vacuum. Likewise, those whose identity is found in God through Christ Jesus do not live in a vacuum. That is why God hears our voice when we pray, praise, and proclaim. Proclaim what? Proclaim His goodness. And proclaim our wholeness in Him. (Adoration of God includes the proclamation of His Goodness.)

Although we should proclaim the goodness of the Lord God Almighty and our wholeness in Him, we should never boast of our own abilities because we are not the source of those abilities. Which sin was common to both Moses and the Apostle Peter? Moses boasted of his own abilities when he said to the people of Israel during their exodus from Egypt: "I got you this water!"[240] And the Apostle Peter boasted of his own abilities when he said to Jesus: "I will never deny you!"[241] We are arrogant whenever we proclaim our own goodness, our own mercy, our own strength, our own wisdom, our own power, or our own special insight. Why is this arrogance? Because, in the final analysis, these proclamations are designed to control, manipulate, and influence others into believing: (1) that we are more gifted than they are, (2) that we have a more intimate relationship with God than they have or can have, or (3) that we possess special powers that they do not have.

If someone compliments us, how can we take credit: if God is the source of our life, if God has given to us gifts of the Spirit, if God blesses the operation of those gifts, if God has operated those gifts through His Holy Spirit in accordance with His Will and perfect timing, and if God brings all things together for good to serve His own purpose? No, we cannot and must not take credit or praise away from God; we must give all credit and praise to Him, to Whom all praise belongs and for which sole purpose we have been created. If someone compliments us, we are permitted to say: "Thank you, and praise the Lord!" A work of God is always God's

---

240 Moses took credit for bringing water out of a rock and did not give all credit to God for the water. Moses also did not follow God's instructions exactly as they were given to him. Read Numbers 20:8-12.
241 Matthew 26:35

work and not our own.

Our Deepest Inspiration

Physically, the deepest inspiration for human beings is the maximum volume of air that can be inhaled after a forced expiration. Metaphysically, the deepest inspiration for human beings comes from their: (1) knowing, (2) understanding, (3) accepting, and (4) doing what God has called them to do while they are still in the flesh. All four of the processes involved in this deepest inspiration come directly from God's Holy Spirit. We cannot "know" the truth without God's Holy Spirit residing within us. We cannot "understand" the truth without God's Holy Spirit imparting that understanding to us. We cannot "accept" the truth without God's Holy Spirit enabling us to yield to God's Will. And we cannot "do" anything of value or substance without the strength, guidance, counsel, encouragement, and blessing of God through His Holy Spirit.

To be sure, people can be inspired by things other than God's Holy Spirit, but such inspiration is neither pure nor true. (Something can be accurate without being true to God.) For example, when the Apostle Paul and his entourage were in the city of Philippi, there was a young girl who was "possessed with a spirit of divination" (Acts 16:16 KJV). This young girl was able to accurately proclaim their mission; however, her knowledge did not come from God's Holy Spirit but from a demonic source. The word *divination* in that verse of the King James Version comes from the Greek word *pu-thone'* [G4436 in Appendix Table B], which is the name of the serpent, or python, that was thought to guard the oracle of Delphi — who, at that time in history, represented those who discerned motives and predicted the future through unholy spiritual means.

Unfortunately, this accurate portrayal of the Philippian girl's devilish source of knowledge has been generalized by Christians to refer to all true psychics, sensitives, and susceptible channels who have an extrasensory gift that enables them to accurately perceive motives, discern intents, and/or foreknow probable future events. The word "probable" is used here because only God knows all future events that will occur. Only God does not see the future "through a glass darkly." Only God does not "see in part," "know in part," or "prophesy in part" (1 Corinthians 13:9 & 12 KJV).

Today, the majority of humankind still lives in the dark ages relative to misunderstanding the spiritually natural talents and gifts related to extrasensory perception. Indeed, the overwhelming majority of the people who sell such "abilities" for personal gain are not who they claim to be and do not possess what they claim to possess. Just as many people who are unable to figure out the motives of others misconclude that such an ability does not exist for anyone, so also do people who are unable to sense invisible things conclude that such an ability does not exist at all.

In contrast to the disbelieving, there are many gullible people who will believe almost anything and anyone if it bolsters their own prejudices and biases. Interestingly, some Christians are so desperate to prove that God's written Word is true that they will believe those who promote themselves as apostles, prophets, and mystics even when such people are perpetrating a hoax. To be sure, God does not need anyone's help to prove that His written Word is true. But few people are willing to courageously speak out. They are afraid of being accused of quenching God's Holy Spirit when they would actually bless His Holy Name by stating the truth.

In John 14:6 (KJV), Christ Jesus said: "I am the truth (or *truth-in-itself*)," Thus, our deepest inspiration is achieved only in and through him.

Respiratory Illness

Various forms of respiratory illness have always been common. Colds, influenzas, pneumonias, and cancers have plagued humankind throughout its recorded history. Although causative agents exist for such physical ailments — like viruses, bacteria, fungi, plasmodia, and carcinogens, individual susceptibility plays an important role in whether or not we contract a respiratory disease. Genetics, nutrition, and stress are all as important as the virulence of disease-producing microbes and the harmfulness of chemical agents.

Sometimes, mild forms of respiratory illness are helpful to an individual's emotional well-being, causing us to slow down and rest and forcing us to take necessary downtime for introspection and retrospection. Our human bodies were never meant by God to be perpetual motion machines. That is one of the reasons He scheduled a time for rest from our daily and weekly activities. When we fail to take sufficient time for rest, He has built within us various cause and effect relationships that help provide for that rest.

Response mechanisms of natural immunity, prayer to God, meditation on His written Word, and metaphysical proclamations of wholeness in God are all important to our recovery from respiratory illness. Knowing who we are in God at the same time that we rest periodically, eat properly, and take nutritional supplements are all helpful to our recuperation and full recovery.

If full recovery does not take place, then we are to assume that the appointed time for our recovery has not yet arrived and that we are to meet the challenges of the illness daily for as long as necessary, perhaps even until the day that we go home to be with our Lord.

If we smoke cigarettes and are diagnosed with Stage IV lung cancer, we should not be surprised by the diagnosis or angry with God. If we live next door to a nuclear plant at the time of its meltdown or a factory that daily spews tons of carcinogens from its smokestacks, then we should not be surprised or angry with God if we develop respiratory problems. Rather, we need to understand and accept them as effects traceable to specific ungodly causes. Such acceptance, however, does not preclude our praying for, meditating on, and proclaiming God's goodness or radically relying on His healing mercy for conditions that have traceable causes.

As long as I am emphasizing common sense in this section, it is also important for us to always remember that, if we are healed, we have not been healed because we deserve to be healed but because

God is full of grace and mercy. There is a fine line between affirming who we are in God and boasting that we have healed ourselves. We must never cross that line.

Chapter Questions

This section is intended to facilitate learning by providing relevant activities, exercises, and experiences to aid students of divine metaphysics in their quest for grasping spiritual concepts, integrating them into their own belief systems, holding them more assuredly, and making them more practical in daily life.

The following questions should be answered after reading each titled section. To answer a few of the questions, students may need to consult outside resources or external references. Students are also encouraged to answer these questions with others during group discussions.

Our Only Breath of Life

1. Using a biblical concordance with Hebrew and Greek lexicons, find at least three original words that have been translated into English as "breath." List the words and give their other meanings (i.e., other words to which they could be translated).

2. Why does respiration mean something different for *astral gelatinous*™ beings?

3. What is the *Atman?*

4. In your own words, why should all people avoid practices associated with Islam and Spiritism?

5. (a) Using a Hebrew lexicon, what are the various meanings of the word *Elohim/Elohim?* (b) Did Christ Jesus mean that human beings are destined to become gods when he referred to us as *Elohim?*

The Self We Have in God

6. How do Einstein's two theories of relativity give us an analogy to help understand the invisible world of spirit, soul, being, and self?

7. What is the meaning of Christ Jesus' prayer that we *become one?*

8. How can we hold two different opinions about the same thing and neither of the opinions be wrong?

9. The theoretical physicist John Archibald Wheeler (1911-2008) is often credited for the phrase "it from bit." How is Jesus Christ *it every bit* and *every bit of it?*

10. How can unity of multiple perspectives be simple?

Vocalization

11. (a) Where are the external and internal intercostal muscles? (b) With which aspects of respiration are the external intercostals and the internal intercostals associated? (c) What is the larynx and where is it in the human body? (d) What is the pharynx and where is it in the human body?

12. Read and compare Genesis 1:1-5 and John 1:1-5 before answering this question: In what way is Jesus the primordial Word, or first vocalization of God, spoken at the time of creation?

13. Using an outside resource, locate Areas 41 and 42 on the temporal lobe of the cerebrum and write those two numbers, each in a circle, on their respective locations in Figure Ten of this book.

14. How do we know that the Lord God Almighty has a voice?

15. Why should we obey the voice of God?

16. Briefly discuss humility as it relates to taking credit for our accomplishments.

Our Deepest Inspiration

17. Briefly discuss the role of God's Holy Spirit in spiritual inspiration.

18. (a) How are people "inspired" by demonic forces? (b) Are all psychics, sensitives, and susceptible channels possessed or influenced by demonic sources? Please explain your answer.

19. According to the present author, why are so many people gullible concerning their beliefs in self-appointed apostles, false prophets, and fake mystics? Are there other reasons, too?

Respiratory Illness

20. In what way or ways might a simple cold or influenza prove to be beneficial?

21. Do we ever heal ourselves or others? Please explain.

Chapter Ten
Divine Metaphysics of the Endocrine System

In case I should be exalted above measure through the abundance of the revelations given to me, there was also given to me a thorn in the flesh, a messenger of Satan to repeatedly strike me, in order that I not be exalted above measure.

2 CORINTHIANS 12:7 KJV (PARAPHRASE)

The Essence of the Endocrine System

The essence, or essential nature, of the endocrine system is to maintain equilibrium and resolve potential physiologic conflicts within the human body through specific chemical messengers that have excitatory and/or inhibitory effects on various body processes. These chemical messengers are known as *hormones*. The English word *hormone* comes from the Greek *hor-ma'-o* [G3729 in Appendix Table B], which means "to set in motion," "to effect a change," or "to precipitate a response." The meaning of this Greek word includes the connotation of *rushing* or *running* from an area of greater concentration toward an area of lesser concentration. This connotation also holds true for the word's use in the Greek New Testament.[242]

Hormones "rush" or "run" from their individual sites of production and secretion to all parts of the body through the bloodstream. Although hormones may be equally distributed throughout the body by the bloodstream, some hormones impact specific target cells, tissues, and organs to only, or mainly, effect changes in their activities and not at all, or very little, in other cells of the human body. In contrast, other hormones virtually impact all the living cells of the body although their effects may be different depending on the numbers of cellular receptors and kinds of biochemical machinery that exist in specific cell types.

Hormones are produced by specific endocrine cells that are usually grouped together into discrete organs called *endocrine glands*. Some endocrine cells are sparsely distributed in non-endocrine organs like the stomach or small intestine. Unlike *exocrine glands,* endocrine glands are dependent on the bloodstream for the distribution of their secretory products. In contrast, exocrine glands are usually dependent on ducts leading from them for the distribution of their secretory products.

It should be mentioned here that the thymus, pancreas, ovaries, and testes have exocrine as well as endocrine functions. Consequently, they are also included within the following organ systems: lymphatic system (thymus), digestive system (pancreas), and reproductive system (ovaries and testes). The pineal gland (epiphysis), hypothalamus, and neurohypophysis (posterior pituitary gland) in the brain, and even the medulla, or inner portion, of the adrenal gland can also be included within the nervous system because they are all derived from embryonic neural tissue known as neuroectoderm, or neural ectoderm.

The major endocrine glands are pictured in Figure Twenty-Two:

---

[242] King James Version of Matthew 8:32; Mark 5:13; and Luke 8:33

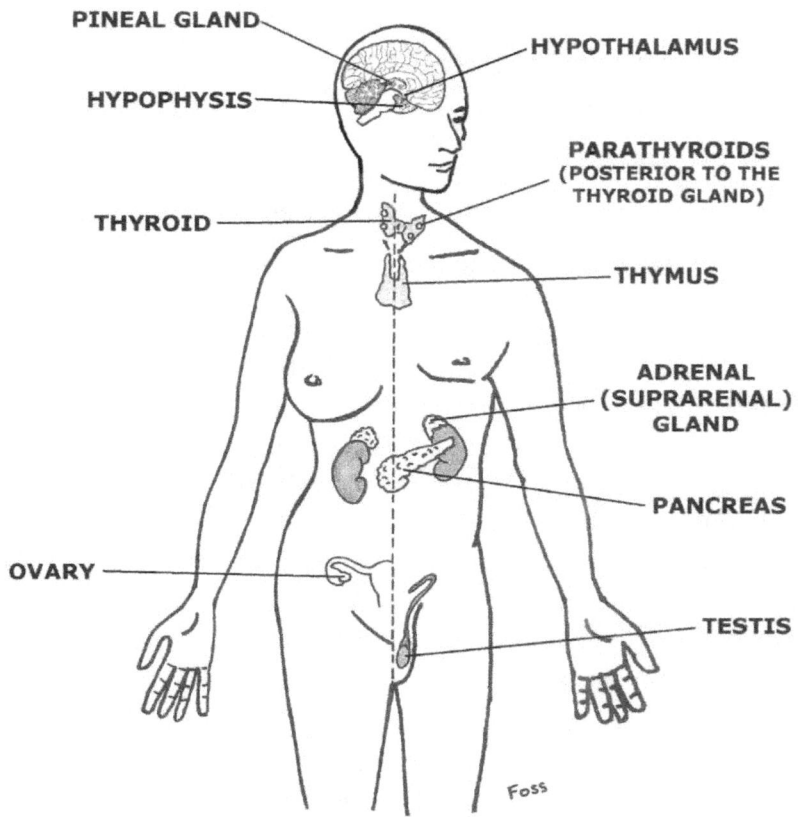

The Endocrine System
Figure Twenty-Two

Please note the relationship of the major endocrine glands to the central axis of the human body. Their general positions mirror placement of specific electromagnetic vortices: (1) that existed in our *astral gelatinous*™ bodies before the Adamic Fall, (2) that will again exist prominently after the restoration of our somatic identities in Christ Jesus, and (3) that currently exist in *bas relief* or *alto relief* in our electromagnetic body double (the so-called *subtle body*). These axis-related vortices roughly correspond to Sephiroth 1, 6, 9, and 10 shown in Figure Sixteen and to the following five of the seven commonly-recognized Chakras:[243]

---

[243] Although chakras are recognized in both Hinduism and Buddhism, the number and names of the chakras vary depending on the traditions from

1. Third Eye Chakra (Ajna), which includes the pineal gland, hypothalamus, and hypophysis;

2. Throat Chakra (Vishuddha), which includes the thyroid gland and parathyroid glands;

3. Heart Chakra (Anahata), which includes the thymus gland;

4. Solar Plexus Chakra (Manipura), which includes the pancreas and adrenal glands;

5. Sacral Chakra (Svadhisthana/Svadhishthana), which includes the generative organs (testes and ovaries).

It is through the changes they mediate that hormones maintain and reestablish equilibrium (i.e., homeostasis, "steady state," or physiologic stability) and avoid disequilibrium (i.e., physiologic imbalance, disharmony, and physiologic instability). Analogous to their endocrine counterparts, major electromagnetic vortices respond to and regulate changes in our electromagnetic body double by receiving and transmitting energies associated with maintaining as well as restoring spiritual well-being and metaphysical equipoise. Restoring spiritual well-being and metaphysical equipoise also impacts favorably on restoring homeostasis in the *diseased* human body. (This last statement does not disavow employing a medical model in tandem with a metaphysical model when treating disease.)

Physical and Metaphysical Conflicts

Like the nervous system, the endocrine system regulates and coordinates various activities of the human body. The nervous and endocrine systems overlap in regulating and coordinating many physiologic processes. In fact, some hormones are produced by neurons and function as both hormones and neurotransmitters:

---

which they have originated. (Although chakras are mentioned in this book, their mention is not meant to grant credence to pagan deities that are sometimes associated with them.)

These "neurohormones" include oxytocin (OT),[244] antidiuretic hormone (ADH),[245] and epinephrine (adrenaline) as well as hypothalamic regulating hormones, such as adrenocorticotropin-releasing hormone, gonadotropin-releasing hormone, and thyrotropin-releasing hormone.[246]

In general, hormones that function as neurotransmitters either belong to the category of *biogenic amines* or the category of *neuropeptides*. Examples of prominent biogenic amines that function as both hormones and neurotransmitters include: norepinephrine, epinephrine, corticotropin,[247] gastrin, glucagon, and secretin. Examples of prominent neuropeptides that function as both hormones and neurotransmitters include: hypothalamic regulating hormones, angiotensin II, cholecystokinin (CCK),[248] oxytocin (OT), and antidiuretic hormone (ADH). Finally, in a most general way, all neurotransmitters can be thought of as hormones whose target cells are just a synaptic cleft away.

Sex steroid hormones — including progesterone as well as various estrogens and androgens — are not considered neurotransmitters for multiple reasons. However, I would lobby for their inclusion as neurotransmitters or neuromodulators because of their major feedback and regulatory impacts on brain physiology that influence mood, affect, satiety, pleasure, addiction, anxiety, depression, rage, aggression, libido, and behaviors related to sexual affinity.

The Holy Bible is clear in helping us to conclude that, in the final analysis, we really do not battle with other people but with

---

244 *Oxytocin* is also known as *pitocin*.
245 *Antidiuretic hormone* is also known as *vasopressin*.
246 Individual hypothalamic regulating hormones were originally referred to as "releasing factors."
247 *Corticotropin* is also known as *adrenocorticotrophic* (or *adrenocorticotropic*) *hormone* (ACTH).
248 *Cholecystokinin* (CCK) was previously known as *cholecystokinin-pancreozymin* (CCK-PZ) to signal that what was originally thought to be two hormones — named "cholecystokinin" and "pancreozymin" — was, in fact, one hormone. Today, that one hormone is simply referred to as *cholecystokinin*.

unseen evil forces:

> *For we wrestle not against flesh and blood but against principalities, against powers, against the rulers of the darkness of this world, against spiritual wickedness in high places.*
>
> EPHESIANS 4:12 KJV

For the sake of clarification, the passage of Scripture just quoted is referring to external unseen evil forces and power struggles but not to internal conflicts from hormones and neurotransmitters. Indeed, human beings regularly fight the effects of hormones and neurotransmitters that: (1) induce and heighten fear, rage, addiction, and aggression; (2) stimulate the libido as well as various associated sexual behaviors; and (3) heighten abilities during predator-prey activities. Abilities heightened during predator-prey activities include vigilance (i.e., hypervigilance), stalking, and strategizing — all of which translate to an office environment just as well as they translate to a jungle or forest environment (in subtler ways, of course).

Both saved and unsaved human beings wrestle with the urges of their own personal flesh and blood. They wrestle with their own behaviors, attitudes, and activities that stem from the production of certain hormones and specific neurotransmitters. They wrestle with positive feedback mechanisms that stimulate behaviors, attitudes, and activities that are, at times, uncontrollable. They wrestle with various addictions, including those promoted by the biochemical rush induced from daredevil activities, sexual orgasms, predatory behaviors, and general risk-taking (such as from the anticipation of winning — as well as the actual winning — at sports and gambling). Not all of our conflicts are with unseen external forces; some of our conflicts are with our own personal physical natures and group biology. Thus, human beings wrestle with their own flesh and blood in addition to wrestling with unseen evil forces.

Although saved and unsaved human beings wrestle with their own flesh and blood, only saved human beings have God's Holy

Spirit residing within them. For this reason, only saved human beings can turn to God for spiritual, emotional, mental, and physical help in combating and overturning their own animal instincts and biologically-driven personality predispositions. But such victory is never easy. You can sense the Apostle Paul's frustration with his own carnal nature in his statement: "I do not do the good that I want to do, but I do the evil that I do not want to do" (Romans 7:19 KJV Paraphrase), which precipitated his following conclusion and accompanying question:

> *O wretched man that I am! Who will deliver me from this body of death?*[249]
>
> ROMANS 7:24 KJV

Victory over Animal Instincts and Personality Predispositions

Many religious people refuse to accept that our souls live in the bodies of human animals. They refuse to accept that human beings are part of the Animal Kingdom. They would rather not acknowledge that human beings are vertebrates, mammals, and primates. For them, the dichotomy between the spiritual and natural is contrived and insulting to God and/or to humankind. They don't want to know that individual biology shapes instincts, personality, gender identity, sexual orientation, and extrasensory abilities. They don't want to know that disorders like Tourette's syndrome, schizophrenia, and criminal insanity are determined by biology. Instead, they would rather demonize the causes of such diseases as well as the people who suffer from them. To be sure, some people with Tourette's syndrome, schizophrenia, or criminal insanity may be possessed by demons and their disorders can be exacerbated by their possession. But the disorders themselves are of biochemical, and not demonic,

---

[249] The Holy Bible also speaks of the human body as "the body of sin." See Romans 6:6, King James Version.

origin.

We must think spiritually — that is, prayerfully and metaphysically — if we are to have victory over our animal instincts and biologically-driven personality predispositions. Here are three examples of flesh and blood conflicts over which we can have victory through God's absolute truth:

First, epinephrine (or adrenaline), produced by the adrenal medulla, is responsible for our physiologic responses to stress caused by perceived threats from environmental stimuli. Produced in response to perceived threats, epinephrine enables us to have enough energy, oxygen, and blood flow (1) to stay and defend ourselves or (2) to turn and flee. That is why epinephrine is sometimes referred to as the "fight-or-flight" hormone. However, spiritually-minded people know that there is a third option other than fleeing or fighting. We can remain exactly where we are — not to fight but to love and forgive and trust in God. We *can* transcend our individual circumstances and biochemistry. *For example,* some martyrs who suffered (i.e., permitted) their own murder without resistance achieved victory over their fears and the physiologically-mandatory effects of epinephrine. But they were only able to do this through their faith in Christ Jesus. To be sure, they experienced fear as well as increased glucose availability, heart rate, blood flow, vasoconstriction, and respiratory capacities.[250] However, they had the presence of mind in Christ Jesus to stand by faith without yielding to their fear and epinephrine's physiologic imperatives.

Second, sometimes the combined effects of epinephrine and the brain's enkephalins, endorphins, and dynorphins (i.e., so-called *natural opioids)* trigger an addictive pleasurable "rush" from extreme sports, daredevil activities, and other forms of risk-taking like gambling and illicit activities. However, through Christ Jesus, spiritually-minded individuals can override their desires to re-experience this rush by refusing in Christ Jesus to put themselves

---

250 Although epinephrine causes contraction of smooth muscle in arteries and arterioles (and, thus, vasoconstriction), epinephrine also causes relaxation of smooth muscle in respiratory passageways (and, thus, bronchodilation).

in potentially harmful, dangerous, and unhealthy situations that are addictive in nature, tempting, and unwise.

Third, scientific research has demonstrated the inordinate amount of time that people — especially males during their sexual prime — devote to thinking about sexual intercourse and related imagery due to high concentrations of androgens.[251] Although some males may use these biological predispositions to justify their having sex with as many partners as possible or having extramarital affairs, such behaviors do not live up to God's ideal of faithfulness to one covenant-based, lifelong spousal partner. Hormones and neurotransmitters often make us victims of our animal instincts and not victors over them.

The only way that human beings can become victors over their own hormones and neurotransmitters is for them to understand who they are as animals at the same time that they understand who they are supposed to be as spiritual beings in Christ Jesus. Refocusing our attention away from biological imperatives and thoughts associated with addictive behaviors to absolute spiritual truth is requisite if we are to overcome temptations from our own corporeality and its associated carnality.

Victory through Absolute Truth

Satan has been, and still is, in relentless pursuit of those who belong to God. In the final analysis, Satan is not really concerned about what happens to human beings; instead, he is concerned about what he thinks is the collateral damage God sustains when he victimizes those human beings who have returned to God or who might return to God in the future.

Although Satan cannot present himself in pure spiritual light because he is not spiritually pure (i.e., his spirit is iniquitous,

---

251 Androgens contribute to libido and sexual behaviors in females as well as in males. Although sexual behaviors, like *presenting* in females and *mounting* in males, are more obvious in other primates and mammals, they also exist in the human primate but in less obvious ways.

soiled, and unclean), he can combine invisible spectral hues together to falsely present himself in an iridescence that, at times, appears to be white. This is how he "is transformed into an angel of light" (2 Corinthians 11:14 KJV). To be sure, Satan is not an angel of light: he is just able to present himself as one. However, he fools no one except those who have rejected Christ Jesus.

If you think that you are going to outrun or outwit Satan, you are sadly mistaken. Satan is in constant pursuit of those who belong to God. However, in this dispensation, which is the age before Christ Jesus returns to Earth, the children of God are protected from Satan by God Himself. It is God who prepares places of safety for His people. And it is God who nurtures His people through His Holy Spirit during times of distress.

The children of God are nourished and provided for despite their pursuit by Satan. God has also provided for His children by giving them absolute truth to annihilate the advances of the Enemy. What is *absolute truth?* Christ Jesus himself is absolute truth!

> *Jesus said to Thomas, "I am the way, the truth, and the life: no one comes to the Father but by me."*
>
> JOHN 14:6 KJV (PARAPHRASE)

Jesus Christ is the absolute way, the absolute truth, and the absolute life because no one comes to the Father except through him. As absolute truth, Jesus holds absolute authority. It is absolute truth that slices through and annihilates the plans of the Enemy. To overcome the Enemy, we must use absolute truth. What makes this truth *absolute?* It is absolute truth because it is the *one and only* truth. Christ Jesus has absolute authority because he holds all power. Regardless of the Pretender to his throne, there is no other Sovereign but Christ Jesus and there is no real truth apart from him.

Examples of affirmations and declarations of absolute truth include:

1. Christ Jesus is my one and only life.

2. Christ Jesus is the one and only Way to salvation, healing, and restoration.

3. I have already been made a new person through the shed blood of Christ Jesus.

4. Regardless of evidence to the contrary, I am completely whole in Christ Jesus.

5. The desires of my Lord Jesus Christ are my only desires

6. My real life is hidden in God through Christ Jesus.

7. Jesus saves and heals through his absolute truth and by his power; Satan's mortal mind destroys, steals, and murders through his deceptions and lies.

Equilibrium, Equipoise, and Conflict

The spirit of rebellion has only one origin: a false sense of self. A false sense of self is due to self-absorption and self-indulgence, which manifest in us as self-pride and self-will. Although there is only one origin, the spirit of rebellion has two sources, whose trajectories regularly overlap and intersect in human beings:

One source of the spirit of rebellion is the Enemy, which term is used collectively here to refer not only to Satan but also to the fallen angels who followed him as well as to the discarnate souls of unclean spirits, demons, evil spirits, or devils[252] who are bound to him. Although the Holy Bible is never clear as to the origin of unclean spirits, demons, evil spirits, or devils, they are the souls of human beings who have become so self-absorbed and self-indulgent that they cannot progress to a higher plane of consciousness after their lives on Earth are over. Satan, fallen angels, and unclean spirits are significant evil forces that surround human beings as unseen entities existing in spiritual darkness.

---

252 "Unclean spirits," "demons," "evil spirits," and "devils" are used synonymously throughout the various translations of the Holy Bible.

Individually and collectively, these evil entities seek to implant and foster ideas within us that are displeasing to God. They seek to rob God of the praise, honor, and glory that is due Him through right-thinking and right-living. Although the noun phrase "mortal mind" is definitely descriptive of the type of consciousness that permeates these eclipsed beings, that phrase falls short in acknowledging their individual presence around, and threat to, human beings (especially those human beings who are susceptible channels and, thereby, easily influenced or even possessed by them).

In addition to the Enemy, the second source of the spirit of rebellion is the carnality that accompanies and occupies us in our own corporeality, which is the figurative "coat of skins" that we wear as a result of our fall from an *astral gelatinous*™ condition of being to a *protoplasmic* condition of being due to our *iniquity* (i.e., our *turning from God*). The Biblical noun phrase "carnal mind" is an accurate descriptor for this rebellious human spirit with which we must daily contend. It is our own carnal mind that plays upon our fallen state by way of hormones and neurotransmitters whose effects we can fall prey to and become addicted to. Such chemical messengers reinforce our addictions to pleasure and our avoidance of difficulty, pain, and toil (all three of which are required for spiritual advancement). Our carnal selves cause us to seek after our own pleasure as well as actively avoid and neglect the duties and responsibilities with which we have been entrusted by God.

When we indulge ourselves carnally through our own spirit of rebellion, we open a window to unseen evil forces that play upon and reinforce that rebellious spirit. We sometimes open that window and, when we do, we find that it is often very difficult to close. We cannot just say to ourselves: "I will indulge myself up to this point but no farther." Self-indulgence often crescendoes out of control in a downward spiral. Sometimes, we need to crash before our self-indulgence stops.

When we are rebellious, self-absorbed, and self-indulgent, we are demonstrating arrogance. And when we are arrogant, we have something in common with the Enemy. And when we have something in common with the Enemy, the Enemy is more easily able to influence, manipulate, and control us.

Fortunately for saved people, God has already forgiven them of their future sins. This is not an excuse to sin. It is an indicator of how far divine Love reaches us through the shed blood of God's only-begotten Son, Jesus Christ.

Chapter Questions

This section is intended to facilitate learning by providing relevant activities, exercises, and experiences to aid students of divine metaphysics in their quest for grasping spiritual concepts, integrating them into their own belief systems, holding them more assuredly, and making them more practical in daily life.

The following questions should be answered after reading each titled section. To answer a few of the questions, students may need to consult outside resources or external references. Students are also encouraged to answer these questions with others during group discussions.

The Essence of the Endocrine System

1. In your own words, briefly describe the essential nature of the endocrine system.

2. Name two ways in which exocrine glands differ from endocrine glands.

3. Construct a table of the major endocrine glands shown in Figure Twenty-Two and indicate whether each gland could also be considered part of another organ system. If so, give the name of that organ system. (Treat the adenohypophysis separately from the neurohypophysis and the adrenal medulla separately from the adrenal cortex.)

4. After conducting outside internet and/or library research, name and briefly discuss how chakras have been used in alternative healing practices.

5. Define *hormone, neurohormone, neuromodulator,* and *neurotransmitter.*

6. Discuss struggles (a) in which we do not battle with flesh and blood and those (b) in which we do battle with flesh and blood.

Victory over Animal Instincts and Personality Predispositions

7. Are we animals, spiritual beings with human bodies, or both?

8. Discuss ways in which people you know have conflict with their own flesh and blood. (No names please!)

9. With a close friend, confidant, or spiritual advisor/mentor, discuss ways in which you have conflict with your own flesh and blood. (No written answer is required for this assignment.)

10. List three examples of flesh and blood conflicts over which we can have victory through God's absolute truth.

Victory through Absolute Truth

11. Briefly discuss the role of Satan in our conflict with unseen evil forces.

12. (a) Who or what is absolute truth? (b) Why is this truth considered *absolute?*

Equilibrium, Equipoise, and Conflict

13. If there is only one origin for the spirit of rebellion, how can there be two sources?

14. As used in this book, what does "the Enemy" mean?

15. Discuss the strengths and weaknesses of the two noun phrases *mortal mind* and *carnal mind.* What do they convey? What do they each fail to convey? How do they overlap and intersect?

16. In what way does our carnal self keep us from doing the Will of God?

17. What is especially dangerous about arrogance?

Chapter Eleven
Divine Metaphysics of the Reproductive System

And the LORD God said: "It is not good that the man should be alone; I will make a companion for him."

GENESIS 2:18 KJV (PARAPHRASE)

Our Partitioned Identity

The most important concept that I have come to grasp during my sojourn on Earth is the signification of salvation through the shed blood of the only-begotten Son of God, Jesus Christ.

The second most important concept that I have come to grasp is that all corporeality is the visible sign of iniquity and sin. Here, (1) *iniquity* is defined as "the turning of created beings away from their Creator;" (2) *corporeality* is defined as "the shadow cast upon God's original creation from that turning;" and (3) *sin* is defined as "any action based on that turning" — which action is predicated on the false belief that iniquity is the desired and/or only reality. (This concept is fully explained in the present author's book entitled *As I See It: The Nature of Reality by God.*[253])

The third most important concept that I have come to grasp is that some seemingly divergent thoughts and ideas become convergent (i.e., intersect in meaning) when viewed through the lens of divine metaphysics. In other words, some seemingly different spiritual truths are true at the same time but only when they are seen through the framework and fabric of a spiritual, absolute, and eternal space-time. To be sure, in the framework and fabric of that space-time, we are provided with a metaphysical vantage point. This third concept may also be capsulized as follows: *Two or more seemingly incongruent perspectives, ideas, constructs, beliefs, or properties may be seen as congruent when viewed metaphysically.*

Concerning the various spiritual truths that the mother of Jesus received from Heaven, it is recorded in the Bible that "Mary kept all these things and pondered them in her heart."[254] Taking my queue from her approach to spiritual revelations, I retained in my heart the various truths that I received at different points in my life. I did this to reflect on them until they became more clearly defined as they matured in my thinking. Once I was able to articulate the concepts I grasped, I comprehended that it was time for me to write and publish them before I returned home to God. At the very beginning of my spiritual journey, I was told from Heaven that few people would share my glimpse of the truth during my lifetime. And, toward the end of my journey, I have also been told from Heaven that my written work would provide transportation to higher levels of consciousness for many of my brothers and sisters yet to come. Even though I will be in Heaven when that time comes, I still look forward to seeing it happen.

Please understand that I never would have grasped the second or third most important concepts without grasping the most important concept first. Please also understand that, concerning the third concept, although some seemingly different truths are

---

253 *As I See It: The Nature of Reality by God* by Rev. Joseph Adam Pearson, Ph.D., Christ Evangelical Bible Institute, Copyright 2015. ISBN 978-0615590615
254 Luke 2:19, King James Version

true at the same time, they are not true to the point of absurdity.

Understanding the third most important concept permits us to see that some seemingly different ideas, thoughts, trajectories, and trends can be true at the same time without compromising the level of truth ascribed to each. This is especially well-illustrated by simultaneous interpretations of the Biblical accounts of creation, Adam and Eve, and the Garden of Eden that are different but complementary. Let me explain:

In the Holy Bible, *Adam* represents original Man (pre-incarnate, unfallen man) at the same time that *Adam* represents humanity (incarnate, fallen man) at the same time that *Adam* is the name of a specific individual from whom all human beings currently on Earth are descendants:

1. As original Man, unfallen *Adam* (or *first Adam*) represents the corporate body of *astral gelatinous*™ genderless beings that God created altogether, all at once, in His complete image and perfect likeness. To be sure, these genderless *immortals* collectively possessed some of the personality traits and characteristics that we now attribute to human gender, but they were neither male nor female.

2. As incarnate and fallen man, *Adam* also collectively represents all of humanity.

3. Finally, as a specific individual, *Adam* represents the husband of Eve and father of Cain, Abel, and Seth, who all lived approximately 4,000 B.C. (i.e., six thousand years ago).

It is important to note that the Hebrew word *Adam* is not only a plural noun referring to all of humanity but also the name of a ruddy human individual made from iron-containing dust. In other words, *Adam* is a physical being with muscle and blood (i.e., "flesh and blood") whose reddish tinges are derived from the oxidized forms of iron in the protoporphyrin rings of (1) myoglobin in muscle cells and (2) hemoglobin in red blood cells.

Summarizing at this juncture, (1) the Hebrew word *Adam* is plural as well as singular; (2) the word *Adam* represents a corporate body as well as an individual; and (3) the word *Adam* represents beings in an original, pure condition as well as beings in a fallen, impure condition (*corporeality* is that impure condition). Concerning the last point, immortals became mortals at the time of the Adamic Fall and some of those mortals are now becoming immortals again through God's Plan of Salvation. (In other words, *astral gelatinous*™ beings became *protoplasmic* beings at the time of the Adamic Fall. And fallen, *protoplasmic* beings who become saved will all eventually regain an *astral gelatinous*™ somatic identity.)

Similar to the word *Adam* having multiple meanings, the phrase *Garden of Eden* not only represents Paradise, the Kingdom of God, and Heaven (all these terms are synonymous throughout the Holy Bible), the phrase *Garden of Eden* also represents an immortal state of being in the framework and fabric of a spiritual, absolute, and eternal space-time. The Garden of Eden (i.e., Paradise, the Kingdom of God, or Heaven) is an immortal state of being at the same time that it is an actual place, location, or locus in a spiritual, absolute, and eternal space-time. At times, Heaven may be an immortal state of being without a place *(for example,* while experiencing spiritual joy in the Presence of the Lord during ek'-sta-sis [G1611 in Appendix Table B]), but Heaven is never a place without an immortal state of being.

Original Man, or *first Adam,* was made in the complete image and perfect likeness of God, the one and only Creator. *First Adam* was neither a gendered male nor a gendered female. *First Adam* possessed both masculine and feminine spiritual traits and characteristics (or, at least, traits and characteristics often associated by human beings with masculinity and femininity) — just as God possesses so-called masculine and feminine traits and characteristics. In other words, all the cognitive traits and affective characteristics that human males and females possess today were uniquely and metaphysically possessed by — and combined in — *first Adam*. Although *first Adam* was both male and female, *first Adam* was neither a hermaphrodite nor an intersexual. Indeed, this original Man to whom I refer was not physical but spiritual.

When it eventually came time for God to make Eve (a complementary being designed for companionship in a dyadic and co-equal relationship with *first Adam),* God did not create her *ex nihilo*. The Genesis account clearly states that God "made" her *from* Adam. To be sure, "creating" is something different from "making." "Creating" is when God forms something from nothing. "Making" is when God takes from what already exists to form something else. To make *first Eve,* God partitioned *first Adam* into both Adam and Eve. Thus, rather than create Eve *ex nihilo,* God made Eve *de novo*.

In an earlier chapter, I referred to God cloning Eve's physical body from hematopoietic tissue in one of Adam's ribs, but the making of Eve goes much farther and deeper than that metaphysically. Because *first Eve* was made from *first Adam,* some of Eve's traits and characteristics were appropriated from *first Adam* by God to give to Eve. These traits and characteristics were not *stolen* from *first Adam*. Rather, some of Eve's traits and characteristics were *duplicated* from Adam and other traits and characteristics were *transferred* from Adam to Eve. Adam's loss was Eve's gain for the sake of the success of their companion relationship. And Eve's lack was Adam's strength also for the sake of the success of their companion relationship. Although Adam and Eve were each unique and different from one another, they still shared many of the same traits and characteristics that are unique to beings made in the complete image and perfect likeness of God. Together, *first Adam* and *first Eve* constituted a composite of God's complete image and perfect likeness.

Before God made Eve, God caused Adam to enter a suspended state of animation. This is the "deep sleep" referred to in Genesis 2:21 (KJV). During this altered state of consciousness, God caused Adam's identity to undergo a spiritual fission. Some traits and characteristics in *first Adam* were duplicated in *first Eve* and other traits and characteristics were transferred from *first Adam* to *first Eve*. Of those traits and characteristics transferred to Eve, some were transferred in a dominant state and others were transferred in a recessive, or attenuated, state. Again, this was done by God to foster complementarity between *first Adam* and *first Eve*.

It is not that Adam permanently lost any of his original traits and characteristics. It is that some of his traits and characteristics became attenuated (or recessive) in Adam at the same time that they were transferred as dominant to Eve. Conversely, there were some traits and characteristics that remained as dominant traits in Adam but were transferred to Eve in an attenuated (or recessive) state. For the sake of clarity, *dominant* and *recessive* here are not referring to biological inheritance patterns determined by genes on chromosomes. Here, *dominant* and *recessive* are being used in a metaphysical sense.

Physically as well as metaphysically, the making of *first Eve* was truly a reproductive process (i.e., a binary fission of metaphysical sorts):

> *Adam said: "This is now bone of my bones, and flesh of my flesh: she shall be called Woman* [Hebrew *Ishah*] *because she was taken out of Man* [Hebrew *Ish*]."
>
> GENESIS 2:23 KJV (PARAPHRASE)

Thus, Adam's identity was no longer whole and complete (i.e., self-sufficient) as it was before Eve was made. But neither was Eve's identity whole and complete (i.e., self-sufficient). That is why much of what remained in Adam and much of what came to be in Eve were complementary to each other. This is also true today on the corporeal level for most human beings: It illustrates why some people are well-suited for each other in a dyadic relationship.

In other words, some souls in corporeality are perfect companions for one another because: (1) what one lacks, the other possesses and provides; and (2) what the other lacks, the one possesses and provides. (Of course, for human beings, this is as true for same-sex couples as it is for opposite-sex couples.)

Immortal souls in Heaven each possess traits and characteristics that are complementary to one another. In an analogous way, so do corporeal beings possess complementary traits and characteristics but for an additional purpose:

Although reproduction by created beings does not occur in Heaven, reproduction by human beings does occur on Earth. In other words, although there are no progeny for created beings in Heaven, there are progeny for created beings on Earth.

Generally speaking, whatever exists in the world of the invisible manifests in the world of the visible — but, of course, it manifests differently. The complementary differences that exist for genderless beings in Heaven become distinguished differently for gendered beings on Earth. Unfortunately, in the world of the visible, Satan has manipulated these complementary traits and characteristics to become competitive, combative, and sometimes even corrosive for some individuals in companion relationships that were originally intended by God to be co-equal, co-dependent (but not in an addictive sense), and mutually beneficial.

What traits and characteristics, including so-called masculine and feminine traits and characteristics, each human being possesses depends on at least four things: (1) which type of human body the soul is in (male, female, or intersex); (2) what traits and characteristics each soul already possessed when it entered its assigned human body; (3) the physiology of the human body relative to its predominate hormone types, their concentration levels, and their relative proportionalities; and (4) the individual life experiences that help to shape each human being's person and personality. In other words, individual people possess: (1) some traits and characteristics (both primary and secondary) because of the genital identity of the human body that they are in; (2) some traits and characteristics that they bring with them from a pre-incarnate state; (3) some traits and characteristics that are determined and/or influenced by hormones and their concentrations and relative proportions in each person; and (4) some traits and characteristics that develop because of nurture, education, social interactions, and peer pressures.

The type of human body a soul is in can be physically male, physically female, or physically intersex. *Intersex* refers to people whose sexual identity is somewhat ambiguous at the: (1) genetic level, (2) chromosomal level, (3) biochemical and hormonal level, and/or 4) gross anatomic and visible morphological level. The phrase "sexual identity," which is used here in a physical sense, is distinct from "gender identity," which is used here in a cognitive and emotional sense. Although one's "genital identity" is generally in agreement with one's "sex" (or sexual identity), one's "genital identity" may be at variance with one's gender (or gender identity). For some people with religious biases, the use of the word *sex* to discuss male or female is distasteful; however, it need not be distasteful if they consider that farmers often "sex" their domesticated animals to see if they are either male or female to separate them. To be sure, "What *sex* is the baby?" is a perfectly legitimate question used in polite society.

At the biochemical and hormonal level, there is an overlap for sex and gender as well as for various cause and effect relationships between them. For example, one's cognitive and emotional makeup can trigger specific biochemical responses at the same time that it can be an effect of specific biochemical causes. Likewise, one's biochemical makeup can trigger specific cognitive and emotional responses at the same time that it can be an effect of specific cognitive and emotional causes.

Sexual identity and gender identity, interactions between the two, and their interactions with physical and social environments are more complex than most people can imagine because: (1) most people lack education in these areas; (2) most people hold tightly to preconceived notions about what is right and wrong concerning sexual identity and gender identity; (3) most people are less able to deal with the abstract, unseen, and invisible as opposed to the concrete, seen, and visible; and (4) most people label what is normal based on their own set of traits and characteristics or the traits and characteristics of the group with which they most closely identify.

It is the interaction of sexual identity and gender identity in a person, as well as the interactions of that person with his/her physical and social environments, that are responsible for each person's sexual and/or gender orientation(s).

Although God brings people together as companions based on their complementary traits and characteristics, and although God is not indifferent to faithfulness in human relationships, God is fundamentally indifferent to the genital, sexual, and gender identities of people in a dyadic relationship unless: (1) they are psychologically harmful to the people involved or (2) they serve a specific divine purpose.

Although "complementary differences" are not always "pleasant," it is important to point out that they are always intended to be "beneficial." *For example,* God may bring two people together where one has a predisposition to manipulate and control and the other has a predisposition to refuse to be manipulated and controlled (among many other traits and characteristics, of course). Or God may bring two people together where one is highly social and the other is extremely reserved. God knows just the right combination of personality traits and characteristics that will challenge us, refine us, and hone our individual traits and characteristics to their greatest brilliance.

Most souls in dust seek a companion because of the fission, or partitioning, of identity that occurred in *first Adam*. Consequently, each human being seeks a partner whose traits and characteristics are somewhat different albeit complementary to their own. (1) Sometimes the sought-after traits and characteristics are greatly correlated to sexual identity and gender identity, and sometimes they are not. (2) Sometimes the traits and characteristics are consciously sought, and sometimes they are unconsciously (i.e., subconsciously) sought. And (3) sometimes the sought-after traits and characteristics serve a reproductive and parenting purpose, and sometimes they do not.

Additional reasons for specific dyadic relationships are multivariate because the causes for, the effects of, the need for, and the use of differences are complex and complicated. Relative to companionship issues, the understanding of most human beings, figuratively speaking, remains somewhat medieval. And without specific education, training, and personal incentives and experiences in these areas, the understanding of most people will continue to remain primitive, backward, and even barbaric. In effect, time stands still for those who refuse to respond positively to life's various changes and the challenges those changes present.

Before I move on to the next section, it is important to clarify that *astral gelatinous*™ beings were created in God's complete image and perfect likeness as asexual and genderless beings and that the somatic identities of saved people will one day again be restored to that condition. And it is equally important to share that, while souls sojourn in dust, they are sexual and gendered beings. Unfortunately, some human beings place far too much importance on being masculine or feminine. This unhealthy imbalance even trickles down to straining out gnats and swallowing camels in the origination of masculine and feminine nouns and pronouns for various physical objects and activities in many languages throughout the world.

Concerning the events detailed in this section, the present author recognizes that many readers may have a difficult time conceptualizing which of the events occurred simultaneously and which of them occurred in succession. This relates especially to apprehending truths associated with (1) genderless, *astral gelatinous*™ somatic identities versus (2) gendered, *protoplasmic* somatic identities and (3) interrelationships between the two. To comprehend their causal relationships more fully, the reader must view events associated with the formation of gender identity and genital identity stereoscopically (in a metaphysical sense) to discern which events are synchronous and co-incident and which events are asynchronous and successive. This requires that the reader *hold the whole* while simultaneously attending to two or more seemingly independent events to see their co-incidence or sequence as related events. The reader must also comprehend that original Man was a composite of individual spiritual beings. (To find out more about immortal and mortal states of being as they relate to reproduction and sexual dimorphism in human beings, the present author recommends reading his book entitled *Intelligent Evolution*.)

The Role of DNA in the Continuity of Biological Life

All college and university textbooks of anatomy and physiology, general biology, genetics, cell biology, and molecular biology provide sufficient, detailed overviews of the components of the genetic substance known as deoxyribonucleic acid (DNA), including its nucleotides — each consisting of a phosphate group, a pentose sugar (i.e., deoxyribose), and a nitrogenous base (i.e., guanine, cytosine, thymine, or adenine) — and their cross linkages as well as repeating sequences in double helical structures. It is not the intent of the present author to duplicate that well-documented information here. Rather, it is the intent of the present author to provide a metaphysical basis for understanding the genetic continuity of all biological life not only on Earth but also on various planets throughout the physical universe.

To begin to metaphysically understand the genetic continuity of all biological life, the information provided in Footnote Fifteen of this book bears repeating here for two reasons: (1) it is highly relevant to the topic at hand; and (2) most readers skip over footnotes that are not prominently embedded within the interior text of a book (which is especially true of an e-book where notes are given as endnotes and, therefore, might never be seen, let alone read, by the e-book's readers).

Footnote Fifteen of this book states that the phrase *"astral gelatinous"*™ is coined here to describe a substance that predominantly has spiritual qualities similar to the created substance of unfallen angels, which substance may also take on physical qualities depending on the dimensionality in which it is found. *For example,* when some angels enter into the physical realm (i.e., *push* themselves into our relative time and space), they voluntarily take on human form and appear to be human even though they have not originated from a biological life form. (This is exemplified by the two angels who first visited Abraham and, later, Lot in the city of Sodom — which visitations are recorded in

Chapters Eighteen and Nineteen of the Book of Genesis.) At one time, certain angels even stepped into physicality to mate with human beings. (This interaction is recorded in Genesis 6:1-4 as having taken place between 'the sons of God' and 'the daughters of men.') The giant 'nephilim' (or 'fallen ones') are believed to have been the offspring of these unnatural sexual liaisons. (The sexual liaisons were *unnatural* because they took place between immortals and mortals.) The Holy Bible is clear that the angels who mated with human beings are now in the 'Pit' of Hades awaiting God's Final Judgment for their unholy activity. (See the Epistle of Jude, verse 6.)

It is important to note that the angels mentioned in the previous paragraph are not the only immortals who ever stepped into physicality. To be sure, there have been other angels who have entered physicality. And, in their self-imposed fall from immortality to mortality, even *first Adam* and *first Eve* were immortals who became *clothed* in *protoplasmic* corporeality.

If cytologic, histologic, and biochemical studies were done on the bodies of any angels or other immortals who enter physicality, it would be discovered that their physical bodies possess relatively normal cellular components, including relatively normal DNA, even though *astral gelatinous*™ substance has neither cellular structure nor genetic substance as we understand them. Rather, electromagnetic templates exist in *astral gelatinous*™ substance that attract the alignment of specific atoms, ions, compounds, and molecules into biochemical arrays that are typically found in association with biological life, which alignment occurs whenever an immortal being enters corporeality for whatever reason.

If extraterrestrial biological entities (EBEs) — which is to say, entities from other planets in the physical universe — were discovered and studied today, it would be natural for our scientists to conclude that all DNA contained within their cells was synthesized from the DNA of previous biological life forms and that: (1) all biological life throughout the physical universe must be ultimately traceable to a common ancestor; or (2) the origin and evolutionary development of all biological life on all host planets was accidental and/or coincidental. Although understandable, these conclusions would be misconclusions based on a physical understanding rather than a metaphysical understanding of the planetary seeding of biological life. In a metaphysical reality, it is understood that all biological life everywhere was intentionally seeded via spiritual means through the introduction of electromagnetic patterns that manifested as biological life on host planets that were specifically chosen for such introductions. Of course, the same invisible electromagnetic patterns manifested in corporeality somewhat differently on the various host planets based on each planet's physical conditions and environments.

As a side note, the present author is aware that some EBEs are interested in life on the planet Earth to learn why deception is so important to human beings: Human beings deceive not only other human beings but also themselves individually. Because human beings can so easily lie to themselves and others and readily rationalize justifications for their lies, these EBEs would like to learn if the souls of individual human beings are still capable of lying: (1) when their consciousness has dissociated from corporeality during out-of-body experiences (OBEs); and (2) when their consciousness has been permanently separated from corporeality at the time of their individual physical death. These EBEs wish to empirically determine if the condition of human corporeality itself is responsible for the deception, gullibility, and rationalization or if corruption of the soul from iniquity and sin is entirely responsible. (Because these EBEs are advanced and communicate telepathically, deception is not a possibility between or among them: Their thoughts, motives, and intents are not easily hidden from one another. This helps to explain their fascination with human deception.)

Although most authentic Christians shy away from discussions about EBEs because they think the topic will lead them to question the Adamic Fall, God's Plan of Salvation, and the Holy Bible, it is intellectually and emotionally healthy for authentic Christians to discuss such topics with an open mind.

Physical Manifestations of Metaphysical Principles

Ontogeny not only recapitulates phylogeny (loosely speaking, of course), ontogeny also recapitulates falling from an *astral gelatinous*™ condition of being to a *protoplasmic* condition of being and the partitioning of the human identity into male and female. This is exemplified in the undifferentiated reproductive system of the developing embryo at five weeks after conception and its transformation into either a male or female reproductive system during the second month after conception.

Perhaps you have heard or read that the basic human embryonic form is female. That statement is not accurate. What is accurate is that it is virtually impossible from a gross anatomic standpoint to determine the sex (i.e., genital identity) of a developing human embryo five weeks after conception even if one is using a stereomicroscope (i.e., dissecting microscope). *External and internal genitals at that early embryonic stage are neither female nor male but undifferentiated and ambiguous.*

At five weeks after conception, *external genitals* include an undifferentiated glans area that will eventually become the head of the penis in a male or the clitoris in a female. Undifferentiated labioscrotal swellings on either side of a general aperture (known as the urethral groove) will either eventually fuse on the midline to form an empty scrotum in the male or remain separate as they develop into the labia majora (i.e., the larger outer folds of the vulva) in the female. (See Figure Twenty-Three.)

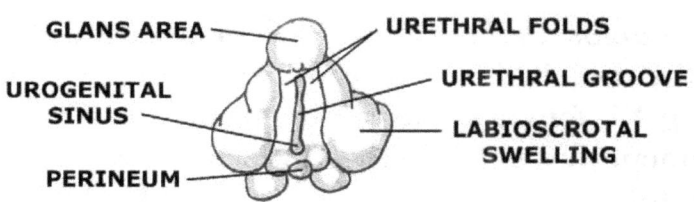
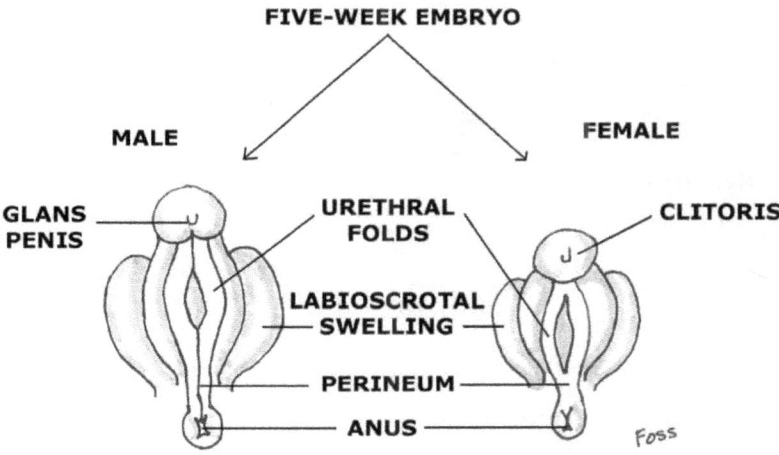

Early Development of the External Genitals
Figure Twenty-Three

At five weeks after conception, the *external genitals* of human beings are not only undifferentiated and ambiguous, they are equally capable of developing into male or female external genitals.

At five weeks after conception, *internal genitals* include undifferentiated sex glands (also known as *gonads*) that will either develop into testes in the normal male or ovaries in the normal female. In the case of an anatomic male, the testes usually make their descent into the scrotal sac from one to three months before birth. Internal genitals in the five-week-old developing XX or XY embryo also include two pairs of tubes: (1) the paramesonephric, or Müllerian, ducts and (2) the mesonephric, or Wolffian, ducts.

In the case of most developing XX males, the paramesonephric ducts degenerate and the mesonephric ducts develop into the vasa deferentia (singular *vas deferens),* also known as ducti deferentia (singular *ductus deferens*), the major sperm-carrying tubes that connect the testicles[255] to the prostatic urethra. In the case of most developing XY females, the mesonephric ducts degenerate and the paramesonephric ducts develop into the Fallopian tubes (oviducts or uterine tubes) as well as the uterus. (See Figure Twenty-Four.)

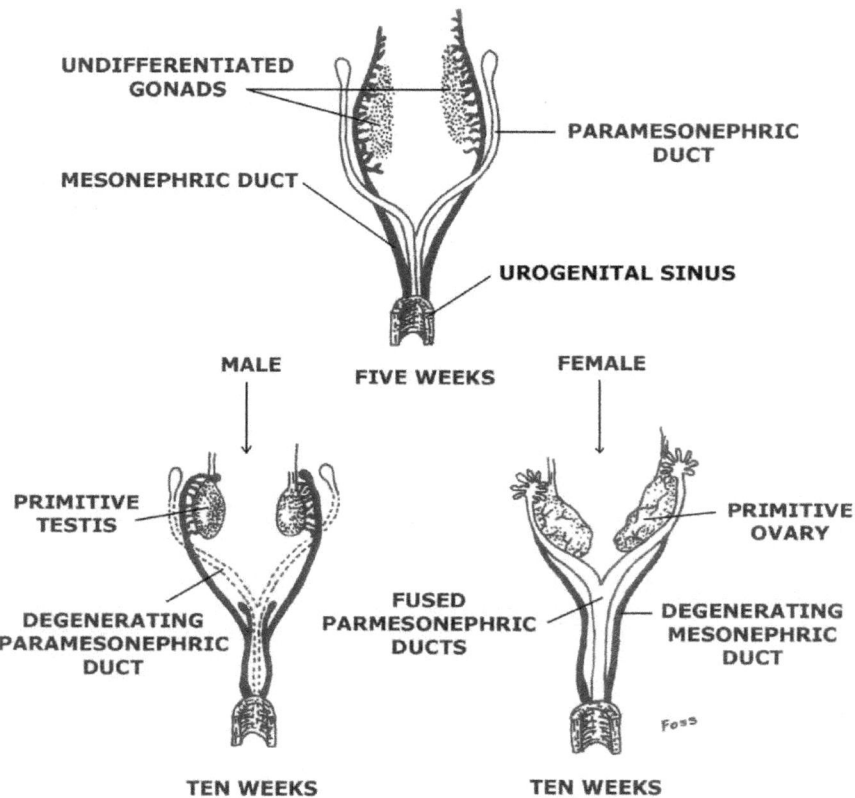

Early Development of the Internal Genitals
Figure Twenty-Four

At five weeks after conception, the *internal genitals* of human beings are not only undifferentiated and ambiguous, they are equally capable of developing into male or female internal genitals.

The external and internal changes just described are all

---

255 Although the words *testis* and *testicle* are sometimes used synonymously, the term *testicle* more specifically refers to a testis and its attached epididymis (i.e., storage sac for spermatozoa).

mediated by specific genes that trigger the release and/or inhibition of various steroidal sex hormones as well as enzymes that convert inactive hormone forms into active forms. In developing males, one of the most important regulating genes in these processes is known as the SRY gene — the so-called Sex-determining Region of the Y chromosome.[256] (See Figure Twenty-Five.)

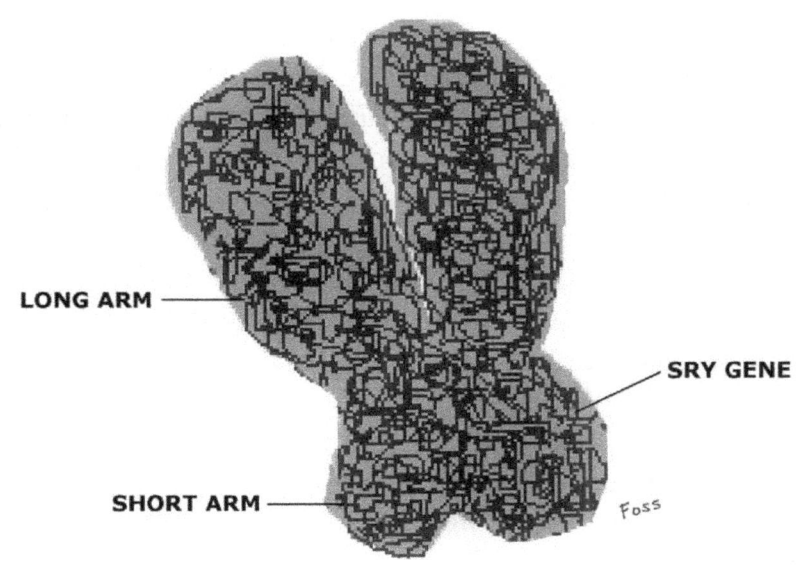

Sex-determining Region of the Y Chromosome
Figure Twenty-Five

In most developing males, the SRY gene triggers a cascade of events between the fourth and seventh weeks after conception that results in the production of testosterone by the sex glands, or gonads, as they begin to differentiate into testes. Without the production of testosterone, or its conversion into a special form

---

256 Haqq, Christopher, Chih-Yen King, Etsuji Ukiyama, Sassan Falsafi, Tania N. Haqq, Patricia K. Donahoe, and Michael A. Weiss. "Molecular Basis of Mammalian Sexual Determination: Activation of Müllerian Inhibiting Substance Gene Expression by SRY." *Science*, Volume 266, December 2, 1994, pages 1494-1500.

known as dihydrotestosterone, internal and external genitals simply would not virilize — which is to say, they would continue to remain relatively undifferentiated and ambiguous, resulting in somewhat indeterminate primary and secondary sexual characteristics.[257] *(For example,* the paramesonephric, or Müllerian, ducts might not degenerate).

Generally, the SRY gene is found on the short arm of the Y chromosome in a developing Y sperm. (By *Y sperm,* I mean a sperm that contains a Y chromosome in addition to twenty-two non-sex chromosomes, or autosomes.) However, sometimes the SRY gene translocates (fragments and moves) and ends up spliced into an X chromosome in a developing X sperm. (By *X sperm,* I mean a sperm that contains an X chromosome in addition to twenty-two non-sex chromosomes, or autosomes.)

When the SRY gene is missing from the Y chromosome of a sperm that has fertilized an egg, the resulting XY individual generally develops the anatomic form of a female. When the SRY gene has translocated and is on the X chromosome of a sperm that has fertilized an egg, the resulting XX individual generally develops the anatomic form of a male (provided succeeding events, which the SRY gene initiates, proceed as they normally would). Hence, the "intersex" category includes XY females and XX males in addition to individuals with ambiguous external genitalia and/or ambiguous internal genitalia. In other words, it is way too simplistic to define *male* and *female* based on: (1) X and Y chromosomes, (2) the presence or absence of specific external and internal genitals, (3) the kinds of sex steroids present, or (4) musculoskeletal form.

The *astral gelatinous*™ somatic identities of original Man (unfallen man, immortal man, Man, *first Adam* or original mankind) did not include reproductive organs. And the future restored somatic identities of saved souls do not include reproductive organs. There is no need for reproductive systems in

---

257 Primary sexual characteristics are those with which one is born; and secondary sexual characteristics are those that one begins to develop at the onset of puberty.

astral gelatinous™ beings. Simply stated, *astral gelatinous*™ beings do not reproduce. Christ Jesus used this analogy:

> *"For in the resurrection [when somatic identities are restored to their original state for saved souls], people neither marry, nor are given in marriage, but are as the angels of God in heaven."*
>
> MATTHEW 22:30 KJV (PARAPHRASE)

For human beings, there really is no perfect definition of *gender*. Certainly, just as one cannot define a male as someone having both X and Y chromosomes, one cannot define a male as someone having two testes. Does that person stop being a male if he has had a bilateral orchiectomy (both testes removed) because of cancer? And, just as one cannot define a female as someone having two X chromosomes, one cannot define a female as having ovaries and a uterus. Does a woman who has had a total hysterectomy stop being female? No, even from a biological standpoint, maleness or femaleness is first and foremost a state of mind.

Much of who and what we are is provided to us by our brain anatomy and physiology. Indeed, the brain is the primary organ for gender identity and sexual orientation. In nature, sex differences exist within the brain in response to varying hormone levels and their relative proportions during embryonic and fetal development. Sex hormones impinge upon the structural and functional development of the brain. *For example,* it is well known within the scientific world that a high concentration of androgens (which category of hormones includes both testosterone and dihydrotestosterone) tends to suppress the development of specific areas of the left cortex of the brain during embryonic and fetal development in males, contributing to population differences between human males and females in languaging abilities and spatial conceptualization.[258] These variations are part of the complementary differences first acquired during God's partitioning of characteristics and traits in *first Adam* and *first Eve*.

It may come as a surprise to many that even the so-called "male" and "female" hormone categories are misnomers because both males and females produce androgens and estrogens. It is the relative proportions of these two categories of hormones that differ and not the hormone categories themselves. In the adult human population, 90% of the sex steroids in males are androgens and 10% are progesterone[259] and estrogens; concomitantly, 90% of the sex steroids in females are progesterone and estrogens and 10% are androgens. (Just as "androgen" is a category of sex steroid hormones, including testosterone and dihydrotestosterone, so is "estrogen" a category of sex steroid hormones, including β-estradiol, estrone, and estriol.)

Substantial scientific investigation has been conducted to elucidate the complex differences between males and females relative to hormones and brain anatomy and physiology. Indeed, hormones not only act upon our physical development, they act on our cognitive and emotional development as well.

In summary, beginning the fourth week after conception and continuing through the seventh week of embryonic development, a cascade of hormones kicks in, causing a rather intersex-looking little embryo to begin manifestly changing from the fifth through eighth weeks into either a basic male anatomic form or a basic female anatomic form.

Not only is the appearance of external and internal genitals determined hormonally, brain anatomy and physiology are also influenced by the presence or absence of the same sex steroids and their varying levels as well as relative proportions. And because these hormones greatly impact our cognitive and emotional development in addition to our physical development, they influence the initial development of gender identity, sexual

---

258 Kimura, Doreen. "Sex Differences in the Brain." *Scientific American,* September 1992, page 124.
259 Males synthesize androgens from progesterone.

orientation, and male and female personality differences during embryonic and fetal life. This evidence leads one to conclude that how we view ourselves and how we evaluate others as potential spousal companions are at least partly biologically-predetermined through hormones. This conclusion is certainly in agreement with the latest models from developmental biology and cognitive psychology.

Although metaphysical tools for understanding the partitioning of the human self into male and female existed before *Divine Metaphysics of Human Anatomy,* few people were individually and culturally ready to receive them, accept them, or apply their full import. Today, the present author hopes more people are ready to not only receive and accept them but also incorporate them into their own worldviews.

·········

Author's Note: Escapism through sexual addiction has been (and remains) common for many human beings during *the Pre-Millennium* (i.e., the time before Christ Jesus returns for his millennial rule on Earth). One danger in this compulsive behavior comes from the possible possession of sexually-addicted human beings by demonic entities, including: (1) condemned human souls no longer in corporeality (i.e., unclean spirits); (2) fallen, demonic angels (i.e., messengers of Satan); or (3) Satan himself. When possession of the sexual addict occurs, demonic entities enter through the portal known as the Sacral Chakra (also known as the *Svadhishthana* or *Svadhisthana).* Although some resources might inform you that the Sacral Chakra is a few inches below the navel, the perineum (pictured in Figure Twenty-Three) is the more accurate anatomic location. Sexual addicts, especially those who are susceptible channels, are often willing to give up control of their Sacral Chakra to demonic beings who can then more easily pleasure themselves as well as the possessed person. (The concept of chakras was introduced to the reader in this book's discussions about the Nervous System, the Cardiovascular System, the Lymphatic System and Immunity, and the Endocrine System.)

·········

Chapter Questions

This section is intended to facilitate learning by providing relevant activities, exercises, and experiences to aid students of divine metaphysics in their quest for grasping spiritual concepts, integrating them into their own belief systems, holding them more assuredly, and making them more practical in daily life.

The following questions should be answered after reading each titled section. To answer a few of the questions, students may need to consult outside resources or external references. Students are also encouraged to answer these questions with others during group discussions.

Our Partitioned Human Self

1. How does the present author define *iniquity, corporeality,* and *sin?*

2. What does it mean to reflect on and ponder spiritual truths?

3. What are three things that the name *Adam* represents?

4. Explain the steps implied by this statement: "Immortals became mortals who are now becoming immortals again."

5. Explain the significance of this statement: "Heaven may be the state without the place, but it is never the place without the state."

6. Discuss original Man, or *first Adam,* relative to traits and characteristics associated with gender.

7. In what ways were *first Eve's* traits and characteristics appropriated from Adam?

8. Do complementary differences exist for souls in Heaven as well as for human beings on Earth? Please explain.

9. On what four things do traits and characteristics of human beings depend?

10. Compare and contrast: *genital identity, sexual identity, gender identity,* and *sexual orientation.*

The Role of DNA in the Continuity of Biological Life

11. Why should we not be surprised if extraterrestrial biological entities (EBEs) have DNA similar to our own DNA?

12. If EBEs from other planets have DNA similar to human beings on Earth, should we assume that human beings share a common ancestor with them? Please explain.

Physical Manifestations of Metaphysical Principles

13. Why is it significant that the internal and external genitals are undifferentiated and ambiguous at five weeks after conception?

14. What happens to the pair of mesonephric ducts in the developing male and in the developing female?

15. What happens to the pair of paramesonephric ducts in the developing male and in the developing female?

16. Would you expect to find Müllerian inhibiting hormone in a developing male or a developing female? Please explain.

17. Where is the SRY gene normally located, and what significance does it have for the developing embryo?

18. Give examples of primary sexual characteristics and secondary sexual characteristics.

19. (a) Are all human females XX and all human males XY? Please explain. (b) Are androgens really "male" sex hormones? Why or why not? (c) Are estrogens really "female" sex hormones? Why or why not?

20. What is an *intersex* individual?

21. Will we be gendered beings in heaven? Please explain.

22. (a) What determines genital identity? (b) What determines gender identity?

23. How are individual readiness and cultural readiness related to receiving, accepting, and applying principles of divine metaphysics to the concept of gender identity (i.e., maleness and femaleness)?

Afterword

Divine metaphysics for the third millennium of the Christian era is a way of looking at life that recognizes and acknowledges the existence of a supernatural reality and a spiritual universe in addition to the existence of a corporeal reality and a physical universe. However, divine metaphysics employs the understanding that a supernatural reality and its accompanying spiritual universe supersede any and all corporeal, physical, and material realities.

Employing divine metaphysics during the third millennium does not mean pitting it against the best practices of medicine, psychology, or other established healing arts; rather, it means seeking to complement, enhance, and work alongside those practices.

Divine metaphysics for the third millennium does not do away with relying radically on God for healing to the exclusion of all other practices. It just includes the recognition that employing such reliance varies based on time, place, condition, and situation. To be sure, we are always to trust in God completely for all healing, but divine metaphysics for the third millennium includes the understanding that God works at times not only in mysterious ways but also in different ways for different conditions in different people to address mental, emotional, physical, and spiritual healing not in just one individual but in us all collectively and corporately.

Divine metaphysics for the third millennium includes the understanding that multiple variables are involved in human conditions and, for that reason alone, men and women with God-given intelligence try to use all that God has revealed to humanity through His Goodness.

Divine metaphysics for the third millennium is completely compatible with Biblical Christianity and the millennial rule of Jesus Christ on Earth.

In their application of divine healing principles, authentic practitioners of Christian metaphysics during the third millennium always defer to the sovereignty of Jesus Christ and the supremacy of his absolute truth.

Appendix

Table A			
Strong's Number	Hebrew Word	Strong's Number	Hebrew Word
H212	אוֹפָן	H239	אָזַן
H241	אֹזֶן	H430	אֱלֹהִים
H1961	הָיָה	H2416	חַי
H3045	יָדַע	H3117	יוֹם
H3629	כִּלְיָה	H4069	מַדּוּעַ
H4093	מַדָּע	H4100	מָה
H4417	מֶלַח	H5315	נֶפֶשׁ
H5615	סְפֹרָה	H7306	רִיחַ
H7307	רוּחַ	H8050	שְׁמוּאֵל

Table B			
Strong's Number	Greek Word	Strong's Number	Greek Word
G1108	γνῶσις	G1611	ἔκστασις
G3056	λόγος	G3339	μεταμορφόω
G3510	νεφρός	G3729	ὁρμάω
G4125	πλευρά	G4151	πνεῦμα
G4436	πύθων	G5590	ψυχή

Bibliography

American Psychiatric Association. *Diagnostic and Statistical Manual of Mental Disorders DSM-IV-TR (Fourth Edition)*. Washington, D.C.: American Psychiatric Association, 2000.

Archer, G. L., Paul D. Feinberg, Douglas J. Moo, and Richard R. Reiter. *Three Views on the Rapture*. Grand Rapids: Zondervan, 1996.

Berry, George Ricker. *The Interlinear Literal Translation of the Hebrew Old Testament.* (Reprinted from the 1897 Edition). Grand Rapids: Kregel Publications, 1979.

Bull, Caroline and Michael Fenech. "Genome-Health Nutrigenomics and Nutrigenetics: Nutritional Requirements or 'Nutriomes' for Chromosomal Stability and Telomere Maintenance at the Individual Level." *Proceedings of the Nutrition Society* Volume 67, 2008: 146–156.

Bullinger, E. W. *Figures of Speech Used in the Bible*. (Reprinted from the 1898 Edition). Grand Rapids: Baker Book House, 1968.

Bullinger, E. W. *The Companion Bible (Facsimile Edition)*. Grand Rapids: Kregel Publications, 1922.

Cloud, John. "Beyond Drugs: How Alternative Treatments Can Ease Pain." *Time* Volume 177, March 7, 2011: 80-88.

Comparative Study Bible: A Parallel Bible (New International Version, New American Standard Bible, Amplified Bible, and King James Version). Grand Rapids: Zondervan Bible Publishing House, 1984.

Devitt, Michael. "Needle manipulation may hold the key to acupuncture's effects." *Acupuncture Today* Volume 03, Issue 02, February 2002: 1-4.

Eddy, Mary Baker. *Concordance to Science and Health with Key to the Scriptures.* Boston: Trustees under the Will of Mary Baker G. Eddy, 1933.

Eddy, Mary Baker. *Prose Works other than Science and Health with Key to the Scriptures.* Boston: The First Church of Christ, Scientist, 1953.

Eddy, Mary Baker. *Science and Health with Key to the Scriptures.* Boston: Christian Science Board of Directors, 1906.

Eusebius – The Church History: A New Translation with Commentary. Grand Rapids: Kregel Publications, 1999.

Fawcett, Don W. *Bloom and Fawcett: A Textbook of Histology (Twelfth Edition).* London: Hodder Arnold Publishers, 1997.

Fox, Douglas. "The Limits of Intelligence." *Scientific American* Volume 305, July 2011: 36-43.

Goldman, Lee and Andrew I. Schafer. *Goldman's Cecil Textbook of Medicine* (24th edition). Philadelphia: W. B. Saunders Company, 2011.

Gosling, J. A., P. F. Harris, J. R. Humperson, I. Whitmore, and P. L. T. Willan. *Atlas of Human Anatomy with Integrated Text.* Philadelphia: J. B. Lippincott Company, 1985.

Hall, John E. *Guyton and Hall Textbook of Medical Physiology (Twelfth Edition).* Philadelphia: W. B. Saunders Company, 2010.

Hall, Manley P. *An Encyclopedic Outline of Masonic, Hermetic, Qabbalistic, and Rosicrucian Symbolical Philosophy.* San Francisco: Crocker Company, 1928.

Haqq, Christopher, Chih-Yen King, Etsuji Ukiyama, Sassan Falsafi, Tania N. Haqq, Patricia K. Donahoe, and Michael A. Weiss. "Molecular Basis of Mammalian Sexual Determination: Activation of Müllerian Inhibiting Substance Gene Expression by SRY." *Science* Volume 266, December 2, 1994: 1494-1500.

Haushalter, Walter M. *Mrs. Eddy Purloins from Hegel.*[260] Boston: A. A. Beauchamp, 1936.

Hegel, Georg Wilhelm Friedrich. *Die Phänomenologie des Geistes (1807).* Project Gutenberg eBook, 19 June 2012 <http://www.gutenberg.org/catalog/world/readfile?fk_files=1464225>.

JPS Hebrew-English Tanakh (Second Edition). Philadelphia: The Jewish Publication Society, 2000.

Kant, Immanuel. *Prolegomena to any Future Metaphysics (translation from 1783 edition).* Indianapolis: Bobbs-Merrill (The Library of Liberal Arts), 1950.

Kant, Immanuel. *Prolegomena zu einer jeden künftigen Metaphysik die als Wissenschaft wird auftreten können (1783 edition).* Leipzig: L. Heimann Verlag (Erich Koschny), 1876.

Layman's Parallel Bible: King James Version, Modern Language Bible, Living Bible, and Revised Standard Version. Grand Rapids: Zondervan Bible Publishers, 1973.

Leonhardt, Helmut. *Innere Organe.* Stuttgart: Georg Thieme Verlag, 1991.

Maier, Paul. L. *Eusebius – The Church History: A New Translation with Commentary.* Grand Rapids: Kregel Publications, 1999.

McMinn, R. M. H. and R. T. Hutchings. *Color Atlas of Human Anatomy (Second Edition).* Chicago: Year Book Medical Publishers, Inc., 1988.

Nelson, David L. and Michael M. Cox. *Lehninger Principles of Biochemistry.* New York: W. H. Freeman, Fifth Edition, 2008.

New King James Version Holy Bible. Nashville: Thomas Nelson, 2006.

---

[260] The inclusion of Haushalter's book in this bibliography should not be construed as an endorsement; its major premise is contrived and supported by specious arguments.

Odell, Catherine M. *Faustina: The Apostle of Divine Mercy.* Huntington: Our Sunday Visitor Publishing Division, 1998.

Pearson, Joseph Adam. *As I See It: The Nature of Reality by God.* Dayton: Christ Evangelical Bible Institute, 2015.

Pearson, Joseph Adam. *Intelligent Evolution.* Dayton: Christ Evangelical Bible Institute, 2021.

Piel, Jonathan (editor). "Mind and Brain: Special Issue." *Scientific American* Volume 267, Number 3, September 1992: 1-159.

Platzer, Werner. *Bewegungsapparat.* Stuttgart: Georg Thieme Verlag, 1991.

Park, Alice. "Healing the Hurt: Finding New Ways to Treat Pain." *Time* Volume 177: 64-71.

Ponce', Charles. *Kabbalah.* Wheaton: The Theosophical Publishing House (Quest Books), 1978.

Romer, Alfred Sherwood. *Vertebrate Body (Fourth Revised Edition).* Philadelphia: W. B. Saunders, 1970.

Sharot, Tali. "The Optimism Bias." *Time* Volume 23, June 6, 2011: 40-46.

Strong, James. *Strong's Exhaustive Concordance of the Bible.* Nashville: Crusade Bible Publishers, Inc., 1890.

Suddath, Claire. "Living with Pain: What Happens When You Can't Make It Go Away?" *Time* Volume 177, March 7, 2011: 72-79.

Tortora, Gerard J. and Sandra Reynolds Grabowski. *Principles of Anatomy and Physiology (Seventh Edition).*[261] New York: HarperCollins College Publishers, 1993.

---

[261] Joseph Adam Pearson is listed in the Preface, page xxiii, of *Principles of Anatomy and Physiology* by Tortora and Grabowski as a "Seventh Edition Reviewer." The present author's responsibilities as a paid reviewer included carefully reading the entire manuscript that eventually became the 1,000-page textbook, reviewing it for scientific accuracy, and submitting written comments with recommendations for change directly to the editorial staff of the publisher.

Tortora, Gerard J. and Bryan H. Derrickson. *Principles of Anatomy and Physiology (Thirteenth Edition)*. New York: HarperCollins College Publishers, 2011. [See also Tortora, Gerard J. and Sandra Reynolds Grabowski in this Bibliography]

Walvoord, John F. and Roy B. Zuck (editors). *The Bible Knowledge Commentary: An Exposition of the Scriptures by Dallas Seminary Faculty [New Testament Edition]*. Elgin: David C. Cook, 1983.

Walvoord, John F. and Roy B. Zuck (editors). *The Bible Knowledge Commentary: An Exposition of the Scriptures by Dallas Seminary Faculty [Old Testament Edition]*. Colorado Springs: Cook Communications Ministries, 2000.

Vine, William E., Merrill F. Unger, and William White. *Vine's Complete Expository Dictionary of Old and New Testament Words*. Nashville: Thomas Nelson, Inc., 1985.

Webster, Noah. *Noah Webster's First Edition of An American Dictionary of the English Language (Facsimile Edition)*. Anaheim: Foundation for American Christian Education, 1967.

Wyngaarden, James B. and Lloyd H. Smith, Jr. *Cecil Textbook of Medicine* (17th edition). Philadelphia: W. B. Saunders Company, 1982. [See also *Goldman, Lee* in this Bibliography]

Zondervan Parallel New Testament in Greek and English. Grand Rapids: Zondervan Bible Publishers, 1975.

Books by the Author

As I See It: The Nature of Reality by God by Rev. Joseph Adam Pearson, Ph.D., Christ Evangelical Bible Institute, Copyright 2015. ISBN 978-0615590615.

Classroom Version of As I See It: The Nature of Reality by God by Rev. Joseph Adam Pearson, Ph.D., Christ Evangelical Bible Institute, Copyright 2021. ISBN-13: 978-1734294705.

God, Our Universal Self: A Primer for Future Christian Metaphysics by Rev. Joseph Adam Pearson, Ph.D., Christ Evangelical Bible Institute, Copyright 2020. ISBN 978-0985772857.

Divine Metaphysics of Human Anatomy by Rev. Joseph Adam Pearson, Ph.D., Christ Evangelical Bible Institute, Copyright 2022. ISBN 978-0985772819.

Hello from 3050 AD! by Rev. Joseph Adam Pearson, Ph.D., Christ Evangelical Bible Institute, Copyright 2021. ISBN 978-0996222402.

Christianity and Homosexuality Reconciled: New Thinking for a New Millennium! by Rev. Joseph Adam Pearson, Ph.D., Christ Evangelical Bible Institute, Copyright 2021. ISBN 978-0985772888.

The Koran (al-Qur'an): Testimony of Antichrist by Rev. Joseph Adam Pearson, Ph.D., Christ Evangelical Bible Institute, Copyright 2020. ISBN 978-0985772833.

Telugu Version of Quran: Testimony of Antichrist by Rev. Joseph Adam Pearson, Ph.D., Christ Evangelical Bible Institute, Copyright 2020. ISBN 978-0996222457.

Urdu Version of Quran: Testimony of Antichrist by Rev. Joseph Adam Pearson, Ph.D., Christ Evangelical Bible Institute, Copyright 2021. ISBN 978-0996222440.

Revelation of Antichrist by Rev. Joseph Adam Pearson, Ph.D., Christ Evangelical Bible Institute, Copyright 2021. ISBN 9780996222488.

Intelligent Evolution by Rev. Joseph Adam Pearson, Ph.D., Christ Evangelical Bible Institute, Copyright 2021. ISBN 978-0996222426.

The Biology of Psychism from a Christian Perspective by Rev. Joseph Adam Pearson, Ph.D., Christ Evangelical Bible Institute, Copyright 2020. ISBN 978-0996222464.
http://www.christevangelicalbibleinstitute.com/Psychism.pdf

The Threeness of God by Rev. Joseph Adam Pearson, Ph.D., Christ Evangelical Bible Institute, Copyright 2021. ISBN 978-1734294729.
http://www.christevangelicalbibleinstitute.com/English3.pdf

*The author may be contacted
at
drjpearson@aol.com
and
drjosephadampearson@gmail.com*

*Visit the author's legacy websites
at
www.christevangelicalbibleinstitute.com
and
www.dr-joseph-adam-pearson.com*